Financial Regulation in the European Union After the Crisis

T0270897

In the wake of the financial crisis, new regulatory measures were introduced which, along with changes in monetary and macroeconomic policy, have transformed the global financial structure. However, this new financial structure displays various fragilities. A new shadow banking system has grown both inside and outside the traditional banks and the divergence between core and periphery countries' banks has increased further due to both the new regulations and the European Central Bank's very peculiar interventions.

Following Minsky's approach, this volume explores the interplay between monetary policy, regulation and institutions in the aftermath of the great financial crisis. Minsky's insights are used to interpret the recent regulatory changes and consider how they have affected the evolution of banks and financial markets. The unfortunate conclusion is that the changes in financial regulation introduced in various jurisdictions and inspired by the work of the Basel Committee have not succeeded in thwarting the instability of the economic system. Instead, the mix of policies implemented so far has brought about increased fragility in the financial system. Minsky's work on financial stability offers alternative solutions that policy-makers need to consider to resolve these issues.

Financial Regulation in the European Union After the Crisis is an important volume for those who study political economy, banking and monetary economics.

Domenica Tropeano is Associate Professor at the Department of Economics and Law. University of Macerata, Italy.

Routledge Critical Studies in Finance and Stability

Edited by Jan Toporowski

School of Oriental and African Studies, University of London, UK.

The 2007–8 Banking Crash has induced a major and wide-ranging discussion on the subject of financial (in)stability and a need to revaluate theory and policy. The response of policy-makers to the crisis has been to refocus fiscal and monetary policy on financial stabilisation and reconstruction. However, this has been done with only vague ideas of bank recapitalisation and 'Keynesian' reflation aroused by the exigencies of the crisis, rather than the application of any systematic theory or theories of financial instability.

Routledge Critical Studies in Finance and Stability covers a range of issues in the area of finance including instability, systemic failure, financial macroeconomics in the vein of Hyman P. Minsky, Ben Bernanke and Mark Gertler, central bank operations, financial regulation, developing countries and financial crises, new portfolio theory and New International Monetary and Financial Architecture.

For a full list of titles in this series, please visit www.routledge.com/series/RCSFS

Financial Regulation in the European Union After the Crisis

A Minskian Approach

Domenica Tropeano

LONDON AND NEW YORK

First published 2018 by Routledge

2 Park Square, Milton Park, Abingdon, Oxfordshire OX14 4RN

52 Vanderbilt Avenue, New York, NY 10017

Routledge is an imprint of the Taylor & Francis Group, an informa business

First issued in paperback 2019

British Library Cataloguing-in-Publication Data
A catalogue record for this book is available from the British Library

Library of Congress Cataloging-in-Publication Data
Names: Tropeano, Domenica, author.
Title: Financial regulation in the European Union after the crisis : a
Minskian approach / Domenica Tropeano.
Description: 1 Edition. | New York : Routledge, 2018. | Includes index.
Identifiers: LCCN 2017032015 | ISBN 9781138668478 (hardback) |
ISBN 9781315618609 (ebook)
Subjects: LCSH: Financial services industry–State supervision–European
Union countries. | Banks and banking–State supervision–European Union
countries. | Monetary policy–European Union countries.
Classification: LCC HG186.A2 T76 2018 | DDC 332.1094–dc23
LC record available at https://lccn.loc.gov/2017032015

ISBN: 978-1-138-66847-8 (hbk)
ISBN: 978-0-367-87830-6 (pbk)

Typeset in Times New Roman
by Cenveo Publisher Services

Contents

Figures and tables

Figures

Tables

Abbreviations

ABS	Asset Backed Securities
AFME	Association for Financial Markets in Europe
ASF	Available Stable Assets
BCBS	Basel Committee on Banking Supervision
BIS	Bank for International Settlements
BRRD	Bank Recovery and Resolution Directive
CBR	Correspondent Banking Relationship
CCP	Central Counterparty Risk
CCR	Counterparty Risk Exposure
CDO	Collateralized Debt Obligation
CDS	Credit Default Swap
CEM	Current Exposure Method
CLOs	Collateralized Loans Obligation
CoCos	Contingent Convertibles
CRR	Capital Requirements Regulation
CVA	Credit Valuation Adjustment
EBA	European Banking Authority
ECB	European Central Bank
EDIS	European Deposit Insurance Scheme
ELA	Emergency Liquidity Assistance
EMIR	European Market Infrastructure Regulation
ESMA	European Securities and Markets Authority
ETF	Exchange-Traded Funds
FASB	Financial Accounting Standards Board
FDIC	Federal Deposit Insurance Corporation
FSB	Financial Stability Board
FSLIC	Federal Savings and Loan Insurance Corporation
GAAPS	General Accepted Accounting Principles
GDP	Gross Domestic Product
GFC	Global Financial Crisis
G-SIB	Global Systemically Important Banks
HQLA	High Quality Liquid Assets
IAS	International Accounting Standard

IASB	International Accounting Standards Board
ICMA	International Capital Markets Association
IFRS	International Financial Reporting Standards
IIF	Institute for International Finance
IRB	Internal Ratings Based
IRI	Institute for Industrial Reconstruction
IRS	Interest Rate Swaps
ISDA	International Swaps and Derivatives Association
LCR	Liquidity Coverage Ratio
LR	Leverage Ratio
LTRO	Long-Term Refinancing Operation
MBS	Mortgage Backed Security
MREL	Minimum Required Eligible Liabilities
NSFR	Net Stable Funding Ratio
OTC	Over The Counter
PFE	Potential Future Exposure
PPIP	Public–Private Initiative Programme
PSE	Public Sector Entity
RC	Replacement Cost
RMBS	Residential Mortgage-Backed Securities
RSF	Required Stable Funding
SA–CCR	Standardized Approach–Central Counterparty Risk
SEC	Security and Exchange Commission
SFTs	Securities Financing Transactions
SM	Standardized Method
SMEs	Small and Medium Enterprises
SRF	Single Resolution Fund
SPV	Special Purpose Vehicle
SRM	Single Resolution Mechanism
VAR	Value At Risk

Part 1

Changes in financial regulation in the European Union

A critical analysis

1 Minsky on the institutional development of the economy

Introduction

In this chapter, Minsky's reflections on the task of economic policy in the phase of capitalism he was living in are used to sketch some guidelines on the goals and means of financial regulation. In the rest of the book, these insights will be applied to the details of the changes in financial regulation already enacted in the European Union or that will be implemented in the future.

In the first section, regulation policy is introduced in the framework of the interaction between endogenous dynamics of the economic system and institutions and interventions. Regulation uses institutions such as laws and contracts to intervene in the otherwise unstable dynamics of the economic system. The aim is to avoid inflations, deflations and all rapid changes in prices that hinder the achievement of the goals of development that are pursued. Although these goals are not always clearly stated, in the last works Minsky wrote clearly that the growth objective should be replaced by those of full employment and an equitable distribution of income. The financial system should contribute to that. A more narrow interpretation may entail a smooth working of the payments system and the ability to finance the type of enterprises that should lead to the previously stated objectives.

The assumption is that the financial system left to itself will produce instability through financial innovation and the pursuit of its own gain by any participant in the market. The issue of financial innovation in the present context is discussed by comparing some contemporary insights of economists and sociologists with Minsky's views.

In the third section, the more specific problem of thwarting systems in an era of money-manager capitalism are discussed and the validity of the central bank as the main pillar of the stabilization policy is put into enquiry. Minsky's ideas in the 1990s, shortly before his death and a decade before the great financial crisis, are reconstructed from fragments and published notes. In this period and since then, the possibility of cumulative processes in prices and of markets that send signals that exceed computational possibilities are even more pronounced, although the link of these processes with investment in real capital is much weaker. The new cumulative processes arise and feed themselves distinctly in the financial sphere, are the reflection of a new type of capitalism of a predatory nature and threaten the very survival of the economic system in its last evolution. In this context, the central bank can no longer act as a barrier to financial crises that are forecast as being very likely. This inability of the central bank to act as a part of the thwarting system is linked to the insufficient protection offered by the deposit insurance by the state that must be backed by a central bank liquidity line. On the role played by the central bank that was an essential part of the pre-money-manager capitalism phase thwarting devices, Minsky's last writings express scepticism. This scepticism contrasts with the current widespread persuasion that the central bank, through its unconventional policies, is the only thwarting system left. In this chapter, the consensus view of the post-crisis, post-great recession will be challenged, starting with Minsky's own ideas from the 1990s.

Finally, the need for new institutions that reject the indiscriminate inclusion of private goals as the guiding principles of financial regulation is stressed. As long as these goals remain embedded in the current legislation, any change dispels only powerful illusions. If this is not changed, the central bank will be not able to contribute to the goals of full employment and an equitable distribution of income.

The system's endogeneous dynamics versus institutions and interventions

This section aims at presenting Minsky's institutional analysis of the development of the economy and how financial regulation fits in it. It begins with an illustration of Minsky's starting points in the analysis of the economic system that were developed in his later works from the 1990s, where the awareness of the institutional dimension of the economic activity was more explicit (Sinapi, 2011; Minsky, 1996; Minsky and Whalen, 1996).

In particular, the unfolding of business cycles and long waves is presented as the interaction between, on one hand, the system's endogeneous dynamics, and on the other hand, the impact institutions and interventions. Those institutions and interventions have the task of constraining the outcomes of capitalist market processes, thus selecting only the viable or acceptable outcomes.

> In this paper we argue that the current state of economic theory as well as the performance of capitalist economies in recent years support the view that the path through time of a capitalist economy is best described as the result of the interaction between the system's endogenous dynamics, which if unconstrained would lead to complex paths that include periods of apparent growth, business cycles and economic instability, and the impact of institutions and interventions which, if apt, constrain the outcomes of capitalist market processes to viable or acceptable outcomes. We call these institutions and interventions 'thwarting systems'.
>
> (Minsky, 2008)

Institutions and interventions should constrain market processes to viable or acceptable outcomes. The outcomes that are judged viable or acceptable depend on the social goals that policy interventions aim to achieve. In theory, there could be thwarting processes that do not satisfy these goals and therefore should not be considered viable or acceptable. So it follows that not all thwarting processes are alike. There can be many of them, their properties change across times and geographical areas, and they must be guided by some explicit policy goals.

Market economies, rather than being bound to reach an equilibrium position by themselves, are prone to generate instability that must be prevented by intervening and changing the initial conditions. According to Ferri and Minsky: 'We postulate that institutions and interventions thwart the instability breeding dynamics that are natural to market economies by interrupting the endogenous process and starting the economy again with non-market determined values as "initial conditions"' (1991, p. 4). This intervention to constrain market outcomes is needed more in periods in which financial innovation flourishes. The essence of financial innovation is a very myopic process whereby each agent exploits minor changes in legislation and usages to increase its own gain, thus often causing damage to society as a whole. The process by which hedge units become speculative and Ponzi ones with the passing of time belongs to that framework. Instability is the result of this process:

> Once the domain of what economists must explain is broadened to include such economic activities as resource creation, finance, innovation, market power and the creation and modification of institutions, then the Adam Smith proposition that each agent promotes '... an end which was no part of his intention ...' need include among the ends promoted not only the effective working of markets, economic progress and growth but also instability. Agents each intending '... only his own gain ...' contribute to market relations that make a breakdown of the economy, such as occurred over the years 1929–33, endogenous phenomena.
>
> (Ferri and Minsky, 1991, p. 10)

The theory of competitive equilibrium ignored too many elements belonging to the real world and in particular the modalities of financing the economy and their unfolding in time. Equilibrium theory ignores time and uncertainty. When these elements are introduced, it is necessary to get a semblance of stability introducing thwarting systems. These thwarting systems, rather than being specific policies like the traditional monetary and fiscal policy of macroeconomic models, are combinations of elements that change the institutional structure. For this reason, financial regulation has an important role to play. Ferri and Minsky (1991) explicitly name institutions, customs and policy interventions:

> Technical change, innovations, capital assets, institutional behavior, and ever evolving financing relations are aspects of the economy that were ignored when the theorem that competitive equilibrium exists and is an optimum was

derived. When these ignored elements are taken into account the theory needs to link yesterday, today and tomorrow. The models become complex, the problems even more difficult to deal with, and the policy conclusions less straightforward.

(p. 11)

The quotation above reminds us of the recent interpretation of the crisis according to a complexity inspired paradigm (Mirowski, 2010, 2013). In particular, the stress by Ferri and Minsky on innovation and technological change that conjures to make unusable the neoclassical paradigm and requires human intervention in the form of a thwarting system has echoes again in Mirowski's works (Mirowski, 2010, 2013). In his words, markets express a tendency to undermine themselves under a regime of laissez-faire. The same theme of market signals that exceed computational capabilities rather than leading to allocation or stabilization efficiency can be found in Ferri and Minsky (1991):

> If the pursuit of individual gains or well being in the market leads the system to rush off into inflation, deflation, or rapid oscillations, which throw off signals that exceed computational capabilities, then the economy will from time to time be moving rapidly away from any reasonably defined notion of 'allocation' or 'stabilization efficiency'.

(p. 21)

The malfunctioning of markets may become so pronounced that they reach a point where they are unable to perform any calculation of rational prices and quantities (Mirowski, 2013, p. 390). At that point, a human intervention is needed to restart the system. This human intervention is also seen by Mirowski as a circuit breaker and could be compared to a thwarting system in Ferri and Minsky's world.

Mirowski (2013), in a different way from Ferri and Minsky, does not assign to economic policy a meaningful role either in the prevention of the collapse or in the recovery process. The solution, after some human intervention has avoided the apocalypse, is a simplification of the markets. This simplification is depicted as a spontaneous evolution that follows the rescuing human intervention. Ferri and Minsky (1991) argue instead that economic policy can play a role in avoiding the natural instability of market economies even before cumulative processes lead to the system's collapse. Circuit breakers do not intervene when the system has collapsed, but they may be able to change its dynamics before this happens.

> In a world where the internal dynamics imply instability, a semblance of stability can be achieved or sustained by introducing conventions, constraints and interventions into the environment. The conventions imply that variables take on values other than those which market forces would have generated: the

constraints, and interventions impose new initial conditions or affect parameters so that individual and market behavior change.

(Ferri and Minsky, 2001, pp. 20–1)

Other institutionalist economists agree that, if the economy is a complex adaptive system, then economic policy must act to steer it towards some trajectories out of the many possible evolutions that may spontaneously occur (Elsner, 2017). This seems also the idea expressed by Ferri and Minsky (2001):

> The study of complex systems is incomplete without the examination of specific thwarting systems. The theory tells us what we have to look for: we have to look for customs, institutions, or policy interventions that make observed values of variables different from what would have been if each economic agent pursued 'only his own gain'.

(p. 13)

In this regard, financial regulation matters as it can be thought of as a thwarting system in itself. It is part of the institutions and policy interventions that may make the observed values of the variables different from what would have been if each economic agent pursued its own gain. This definition fits perfectly in the modern financial world, in which financial innovation results exactly from each financial agent pursuing its own (be it small or large) gain.

Financial innovation as bricolage

The idea that each individual, by pursuing their own gain, may give rise to heavy fluctuations in prices rather than maximising collective welfare and that this applies especially to the finance sector where innovation is continuous, may also be found in some recent sociological studies on finance.

According to Engelen *et al.* (2010), finance may proceed almost randomly by adding new innovation, while each actor pursues its own little increase in gain without a big central planning agency. The interaction of continuous innovation with agents and groups ready to exploit them to ensure a higher gain for themselves is sufficient to create big problems at the macroeconomic level. The innovations may well be reactions to policy moves rather than autonomous inventions.

Erturk *et al.* (2013) and Engelen *et al.* (2010) reject the rationality of innovation as the result of the improvements in finance theory and claim that financial innovation is just the result of bricolage activity which lasts only some years; it has no long period dimension. This short, but not too short, time span is called *conjuncture*.

Bricolage in each new conjuncture creates fragile, complex circuits between heterogeneous acts and instruments. Individuals temporarily align themselves along current prices and flow of funds. However, these arrangements can be easily disrupted and replaced by different actors, instruments and chains in the next conjuncture after a transition period. Each agent in the chain acts to increase its own profits without being able to see the whole picture. Innovation is not the outcome of a rational plan in so far as various agents and entities simply take what is given in a particular lapse of time and arrange these bricks in order to create something that increases their own gain. In this respect, rational calculation is not at the base of innovation, although in implementing the use of new products, those calculations may be used.

> Financial innovation may involve calculative rationality and algebraic formula in valuing derivatives, but this is limited to calculation at a particular node or link in a complex structure of cash flow obligations between a heterogeneous group of financial actors and institutions that constantly look for the next big thing generating high yield. Financial innovation is bricolage that involves improvisation, creation of structures out of events and what comes to hand readily and what is available conjuncturally.
>
> (Erturk *et al.*, 2013, p. 345)

Erturk *et al.* (2013) show that the very complex financial instrument, called jazz CDO, was not based on some scientific project, but was just the evolution through time of simpler products. The passage from simpler CDO to more complex ones depended on the decision by ISDA to change the definition of CDS in 2005. After that decision, a CDS could be created by referencing simply to ABS. Before that decision was taken, in order to offer a CDS, having as reference assets ABS, cash ABS had to be selected and the supply of CDS was limited by the supply of those ABS. While the issue of CDO before this decision was limited by existing asset-backed securities, which in turn were originated by loans, after that decision the CDO could simply be backed by a combination of assets including bonds, CDS, ABS, CDO and loans (Erturk *et al.* 2013, p. 347). This allowed an expansion in the market and was useful to all the institutions involved to gain fees in the various stages of the process. In this way, the size of securities issued and sold could be bigger than that of securitized assets. With the introduction of this new type of CDS, the opaqueness in the system increases as the portfolio is constantly traded, so it is difficult to know what is behind any particular CDS. In this structure, fragility accumulates in the system as the number of interconnections increases.

The similarity with Minsky's institutional thought is that each agent pursuing his own gain contributes to market relations that make a breakdown in the economy, such as occurred over the years 1929–33, endogenous phenomenon (Ferri and Minsky, 1991). This is exactly what happened in 2007–8.

The same is true for the other example of chain given by Engelen *et al.* (2010). In the last quarter of 2008, Deutsche Bank announced a big loss in its proprietary trading of €2 billion. The loss was due to the unravelling of a very simple transaction: the purchase through borrowing of corporate bonds hedged by CDS. After the crisis in the US erupted, the cost of CDS increased over the yield on bonds, making the deal unprofitable and the credit crunch made it impossible to borrow to buy bonds. The decision to retreat from the position by selling the bonds caused a fall in their prices and heavy losses.

Another recent example is the rise in food and other commodities prices following the pension funds investment in commodities, as well as the increase in pension funds investment in hedge funds. The rationale may be totally legitimate to ensure workers a better pension, but if each pension fund pursued this aim, in the end aggregate workers' conditions would worsen.

This view of finance applies particularly well to the last stage of capitalism that Minsky called 'money manager capitalism' (Whalen, 2001; Sinapi, 2011). Money manager capitalism, translated into the vocabulary of the sociological school, is the *frame* within which the various conjunctures, based on innovation as bricolage activity, emerge. The analogy works as the frame has a longer time dimension than both conjuncture and bricolage.

The thwarting systems do not last forever. For example, the lender of last resort intervention by the central bank and deposit insurance jointly with deficit spending by the state worked as stabilizing devices in the period after the Second World War. However, in money manager capitalism, conditions have changed and the efficacy of these circuit breakers is not warranted (Sinapi, 2013).

It should be pointed out that the interplay between endogenous dynamics and conventions, customs and policy interventions changes in time, too. In the period starting with the breakdown of the Bretton Woods system at the beginning of the 1970s, conventions and customs changed under the influence of supranational forces. In the finance sector, international organizations like the Basel Committee on Banking Supervision, international accounting standards organizations (IASB and FASB), treaties on free trade in which finance had a part too, all these institutions changed the inherited conventions in a way that destabilized the system.

Although often talking in the name of free markets and free competition, the rules that were suggested and then adopted by the states really privileged some specific groups organized at the international level and thus, in the neoclassical sense, they distorted free competition. In this respect, as Mirowski (2014) has observed, neoliberalism and the neoclassical school of economic thought do not coincide. So, the groups representing neoliberal ideas used the state to change regulations to a direction that was actually destabilizing for economies as a whole, although they contributed to the profits of the wealthy ones.[1] Once again, in the frame of neoliberal rules and conventions, bricolage activity gave rise to different conjunctures.

After the great financial crisis, the rules were redesigned by the same groups and adopted with different nuances by the various states, while the central bank was trusted for many years after the inception of the crisis as the circuit breaker with its new policies of dealer of last resort and buyer of financial assets in large quantities. An interpretation along the lines put forward by Ferri and Minsky (2001) would point at the different patterns of change to the conventions relative to those of the institutions and interventions.

The conventions ruling before the crisis erupted did not change and are still embedded in the principles of international financial regulation that have come out of the coordinated global effort to redesign the system. The institutions and interventions have changed in so far as the central bank has changed its intervention tools and policy, temporarily caring more about financial stability than inflation. The central banks, through their ordinary and extraordinary interventions reset the system by allowing the prices of financial assets to assume values that were much higher than those that would have been determined by the markets. So, they changed the initial conditions. In this respect, they fulfilled literally Ferri and Minsky's requirement for a thwarting system.

The unintended consequence of this intervention was that new conjunctures due to renewed bricolage activities flourished, of which the commodities prices cycle is just an example. The discussion on the new role played by the central bank and its contribution to stability is still open. In some countries such as the US, the new regime of heavy intervention by the central bank, with a moderate increase in spending by the state, hindered depression and deflation, although it allowed fluctuations in financial prices. In other areas such as the EU, depression and deflation have not been avoided, at least for some of the countries included in it.

In the next section, Minsky's own ideas on the evolution of money manager capitalism, the return of big financial crises and the response that would likely dismantle instability are summarized.

Minsky on money manager capitalism, finance and thwarting systems

In this last period of capitalism that Minsky called 'money manager capitalism' (Minsky, [1986] 2008) the traditional thwarting mechanisms that were able to stop the incoherence and avoid the disaster no longer worked well. In particular, the evolution of finance in the frame of the stage of capitalism called money manager was posing higher threats to state intervention, and the central bank was not adequately prepared to deal with the new problems that would probably develop. This last stage of capitalism was not only characterized by money managers, but also by globalization and deregulation (see Sinapi, 2013). All these changes taken in their interaction weakened the ability of the state to act as a thwarting agent. In the 1990s, Minsky believed, however, that the state cannot be replaced in its main task and that the central bank alone would not be able to cope with the inevitable wave of bank failures that would occur in the future. He had doubts that the mix of big state and big bank interventions could avoid a crisis at that time and also in the future. He spoke explicitly of the repeated bailout of banks as necessary. The reasons for that position are the transformation of the big state, and of the structure of both financial and non-financial enterprises. Behind all these transformations was globalization and what is now called financialization. This causes the impossibility or unwillingness by the state to maintain high profits. The impossibility and unwillingness to spend more to relieve unemployment due also to a fall in fiscal revenue was the result of both globalization and bad performances by firms (see Minsky, 1993, 1994).

On the finance side, the return of painful crises was seen as a sign of the change in the economy. In order to contrast these crises, the main burden would fall on the state, which was, according to Minsky, the final guarantor of deposits and also had to deal with the insolvency of financial firms (Minsky, [1986] 2008; Kregel, 2013).

The central banks should intervene, of course, to mitigate liquidity problems and manage uncertainty, but in the 1990s, their role at that particular stage of capitalism was not so central. In the 1980s instead, Minsky had warned that increased deregulation was accompanied by a greater intervention by the central bank rather than the opposite: 'It is a mistake to equate deregulation with a shift to the market determination of outcomes. Instead, constraint by regulation has been supplanted with protection by refinancing' (Minsky, 2008, p. 16).

The idea that deregulation had been made possible by the accommodation policy of the central bank is also shared by de Cecco (1999), who wrote that the central bank of the United States rather than being a lender of last resort had become a 'lender of first resort'. de Cecco (1999) argued that the interventions by the central bank in the US rather than being an emergency tool had become a continuous normal support that banks expected to always be available.

In Minsky ([1986] 2008, 1993), there are also warnings that internationalization and deregulation may constrain the role of the lender of last resort of the Federal Reserve, and that at the global level there is no international lender of last resort. The rising globalized finance world based on the dollar would risk not having a lender of last resort if institutional arrangements were not changed (Gray and Gray, 1994; Felix, 1994).

Minsky argued in the 1990s that the central bank alone would not be able to deal with the future crises: 'The central bank is not fit to deal with solvency problems at banks. For that, a government investment bank or a government liquidator is needed.'

A government investment bank, however, would be a better solution because it would allow continuing the activity of the bank. He goes on to ask whether a permanent government investment bank like the Reconstruction Finance Corporation would be needed in the future. A government deficit rather than a central bank is the main stabilizing factor.

Minsky is sceptical on the deposit insurance design legislation that had emerged from the world crisis of 1929. The deposit insurance had been a stabilizing device for a very long time from the 1930s to the 1990s, but as the financial structure and usages among institutions changed, its stabilizing powers were seriously weakened. One of the new usages that had spread among financial institutions was the recourse to the securitization of loans.

Minsky thought that derivatives and securitization increase layering and lower liquidity because under conditions of stress they require the sale of assets, thus starting a debt deflation process. By reviewing securitization, Minsky (1986) describes precisely how it may require the creator of the paper (or the trust organization) to liquidate the assets when the value of the collateral sinks below a certain threshold or is downgraded. The same idea is more clearly expressed in the note on securitization, originally from 1986 and republished later in 2008, with a Preface and Foreword by Wray (Minsky, 2008) discussing the trustee's duties:

> ... (the trustee) and is empowered to end the trust, sell out the corpus, and transmit proceeds to security holders according to the hierarchy of rights *if the securities rating falls below some agreed level.* [In many cases, the paper creator agrees to take the securities back onto its own balance sheet if they cannot be sold at a guaranteed price or if the rating falls below the agreed level.]
>
> (Minsky, 2008, p. 5 [emphasis added])

The sentence within the square brackets has been written by Wray. During the last crisis in the US, what happened is exactly what is written in that sentence. The banks that were the paper creators took the securities back on their balance sheets, because the structured investment vehicles that held them and were their off balance sheet arms were no longer able to finance them.

Securitization in itself as well as the normal behaviour of money managers is a danger for the system's stability because of the consequences that the rating and downgrading of securities pose:

> A need by holders of securities who are committed to protect the market value of their assets (such as mutual or money market funds, or trustees for pension funds) may mean that a rise in interest rates will lead to a need by holders to make position by selling position, which can lead to a drastic fall in the price of the securities.
>
> (Minsky, 2008, p. 3)

Minsky was well aware of the likely buying of rating by the banks that were the creators of the paper and of the consequences of downgrading by the rating agencies.[2]

Beyond that, he makes another important and neglected observation: the legal structure of trusts may cause the state to spend much more than in the past for deposit insurance. This is a prescient intuition that anticipated most of the events now displayed before us. What he failed to anticipate is that the very depositors would be legally deprived of their claims to the bank in order to save prior claimants and to relieve the states from the burden of providing an increasing amount of insurance (bail-in). That notwithstanding, it is a great insight to see how the clauses of private contracts in finance may constrain the state in pursuing its stabilization tasks and may disrupt one of the most salient features of the thwarting system operating in the pre-money manager capitalism era. This point has not yet received the attention it deserves, either in the scholarly literature on Minsky or in the heterodox literature on financial regulation after the crisis. The message is that the design of financial contracts according to the goals of private groups may weaken the lender of last resort.

> Suppose the creator of paper is a protected banking organization. The creation of securities establishes a claim on the organization's assets that stands prior to the depositor's claim. But the depositor's claim is still guaranteed by the insurance fund (FDIC or FSLIC). Hence the lender of last resort is now exposed to greater risk.

(Minsky, 1986, p. 27)

Although this observation is related to the process of securitization and to the creator banks that may be in charge if the paper created were to fall in value, the same applies to all other assets that are created by banks and that have the characteristics of depending for their remuneration on the return from paper rather than from income flows or the disposition of assets. If the value of the underlying paper falls and no remuneration is available for the securities, their value will fall as well; the same point raised by Minsky in the sentence quoted above could be made for the effects of derivatives losses in a bank balance sheet. Those losses indeed, because of the safe harbour clauses and bankruptcy remote status included in the contracts, will not fall on their issuers but on normal depositors, and this could put in jeopardy the institution of deposit insurance. So, the point raised by Minsky is more important now than at the time when it was made because of the rate of growth of this type of assets in the balance sheets of depository institutions.

To resolve the problem, Minsky proposed that the insurance should be replaced by the assumption of a contingent liability by the state as a guarantee for all deposits. As Kregel (2014) writes, the alternative to the state assuming contingent liabilities would be to create a permanent government investment bank along the lines of the Reconstruction Finance Corporation. This is because, according to the legislation, the Federal Reserve could not take an equity position in an insolvent bank.[3] Kregel (2014) adds that this is exactly what the Federal Reserve and the Treasury were compelled to do during the 2007–8 crisis. Minsky, however, did not recommend a change in the legislation to allow the central bank to do that; rather, it was for the state to assume directly the contingent liability or to change the structure of the financial system by separating the payments system from the financing system (see Kregel, 2010, 2012, 2014).

One very old proposal was that of separating totally deposits from loans – that is, to have on one hand a narrow bank that accepts deposits and holds government bonds on the side of assets, and on the other hand a bank that lends to the public but holds riskier bonds and shares as assets. Under this peculiar arrangement, deposits would be protected by the oscillations in the value of assets and the deposit insurance would not be needed. Lending, however, would be constrained by the available savings and credit could not foster the development of the economy in a Schumpeterian fashion: 'The most important implication of this proposal, as Minsky seems to have admitted, would be that in such a segregated, dual system there would be neither a deposit-credit multiplier, nor leverage, nor private creation of liquidity' (Kregel, 2014, p. 231).

To Kregel, this scenario would not be compatible with a capitalistic economy.[4] If such a radical solution is excluded, then the only way to make the system survive the changes in regulation and usages is to increase the stabilizing properties by changing the rules again. Minsky was not really keen on repealing the Glass–Steagall Act, but was neither convinced that preserving it was essential. He pointed out that the Glass–Steagall was just one of the several policy interventions that were made after the 1929 financial crisis and these included securities and exchange legislation, housing and agriculture financing institutions, rural electrification financing authorities, a government investment bank (Reconstruction Finance Corporation) and a revised Federal Reserve System (Minsky, 1995, p. 16). He wrote clearly: 'I believe that the repeal of the Glass–Steagall Act, in itself, would neither benefit nor harm the economy of the United States to any significant extent' (Minsky, 1995, p. 7). He adds, however, that in case such repeal would occur, great attention should be devoted to preserving the protection of liabilities of banks and non-bank financial institutions as well. Presumably in this sentence Minsky was referring to the liabilities of money market mutual funds that are considered as a very close substitute to bank deposits in the opinion of the public:

> The importance of the repeal would thus depend upon the scope permitted to institutions chartered as commercial banks or bank holding companies and the extent to which liabilities of bank and non bank financial institutions will be protected by government agencies or the Federal Reserve.
>
> (Minsky, 1995, pp. 7–8)

In the same essay, he stresses that the separation that is important in an era of money manager capitalism is not that between commercial and investment banking, but rather between investment banking and the managing of mutual funds and pension funds. He concludes that the repeal would not change in a meaningful way the capital development of the economy and that in this regard it was more important to look at the evolution of mutual and pension funds. He insisted that even after the repeal, if it were enacted, the liabilities of banks would be protected in order to avoid instability in finance and a depression that would follow.

> Given the evolution of institutions over the past decades I would like to suggest that those institutions which manage money and are in a fiduciary relation with households be separated from institutions whose primary focus is on trading and investing for the benefit of the owners' of the firm's capital and their staff whose compensation is based upon performance.
>
> (Minsky, 1995, p. 20)

It is worth stressing that Minsky's opinions on the effects of the repeal are based on the financial structure of the United States in the 1990s, so they cannot be easily extended to any financial structure in any country. There, the banks had retained their role as a provider of safe assets, deposits insured by government agencies and ultimately by the full faith and credit of the United States. Yet they did not have instead a special position in financing investment. This reflects the evolution of the financial structure in the United States. In this situation, Minsky warned that separated banks would not perform better than universal ones, provided that deposits were kept safe and the payments system smooth. This reasoning would not apply to the European Union now because in many countries banks are still the main providers of loans to firms.The important point is that even in the case of repeal and return to a universal banking system, the deposits should be protected. This is relevant for the discussion of the state of the European banking systems under the new regulation after the great financial crisis.

Conclusions

In this chapter, the latest part of Minsky's thought on the development of the economy has been explained. In particular, the interaction between endogenous dynamics on one hand and institutions and interventions on the other plays an important part in the explanation of wide oscillations and sometimes even of abrupt crises. Such a system is supposed not to work smoothly without thwarting systems. The thwarting systems that were able to stop the instability during the post-Second World War era are not supposed to do so in the money manager capitalism phase.

So far, this work is concerned that financial regulation could be included among the institutions that may contribute in their interaction with the endogenous dynamics to shape the evolution of the economic system. It is highlighted that Minsky did not express any preference on the type of structural regime that should be imposed on the financial system. In his discussion on the possible repeal of the Glass–Steagall Act, he did not express a preference for any of the two regimes in themselves. He underlined that the success of the regime that had started with the introduction of the Glass–Steagall Act was due to a series of concomitant measures rather than just to the separation of the different types of banking. Among those measures, deposit insurance was particularly relevant.

Minsky warned, however, that the evolution of usages in the financial markets could make ineffective the thwarting systems already in place like deposit insurance. The main message was that the design of financial contracts according to the goals of private groups might weaken the lender of last resort.

The thwarting systems should work to hinder or to constrain financial innovations according to some goals that are shared by society. The prevailing attitude of the central bank and supervisory authorities both in the 1980s and 1990s and nowadays is instead to passively accept them without worrying about the consequences.

Notes

1   This is what Mirowski writes:

> While neoliberal think tanks are busy riling up the groundlings with debt clocks and boogeyman statistics of ratios of government expenditure to GDP, neoliberal politicians organize to extravagantly increase incarceration and policing of those whom they deem unfit for the marketplace; expand both state and corporate power to exercise surveillance and manipulation of subject populations while dismantling judicial recourse to resist such encroachments; wildly introduce new property rights (like intellectual property) to cement into place their extensions of market valuations to situations where they were absent; strengthen international sanctions such as the Trans Pacific Partnership and the Transatlantic Trade and Investment Partnership to circumvent and neutralize national social legislation they dislike; bail out and subsidize private banking systems at the cost of many multiples of existing national income; define corporations as legal persons in order to facilitate the buying of elections; and so on.
>
> (Mirowski, 2014, pp. 10–11)

2   For an analysis of the process of empowerment of rating agencies by the legislation in the United States, see White (2010).
3   This is explicitly stated in Minsky (1994).
4   However, the financial system in Italy before the liberalization in the 1990s was not very different from the one described in Minsky (1994). The big difference was that instead of a truly narrow bank, there were a certain number of public banks that had on the liabilities side deposits and on the assets side short-term loans to businesses and households. There was credit creation by banks, then, although limited to certain uses. The long-term loans for investment were granted instead by special institutions that had as liabilities medium- and long-term certificates of deposits and bonds issued on the market. However, there was no holding company structure, but many types of specialized financial institutions not linked in a single company. Some of them were public but some were also private.

References

de Cecco, M. (1999) The lender of first resort, *Economic Notes*, 28(1): 1–14.

Elsner, W. (2017) Policy and state in complexity economics, in N. Karagiannis and J. King (eds) *Handbook of Government Intervention* (forthcoming). Available at: www.researchgate.net/publication/315625332_Policy_and_State_in_Complexity_Economics_Chapter_submitted_for_the_Handbook_of_Government_Intervention_ed_by_N_Karagiannis_and_JE_King_forthcoming_2017_EE (accessed March 2017).

Engelen, E., Erturk, I., Froud, J., Leaver, A. and Williams, K. (2010) Reconceptualizing financial innovation: Frame, conjuncture and bricolage, *Economy and Society*, 39(1): 33–63.

Erturk, I., Froud, J., Johal, S., Leaver, A. and Williams, K. (2013) (How) do devices matter in finance?, *Journal of Cultural Economy*, 6(3): 336–52.

Felix, D. (1994) Debt crisis adjustment in Latin America: Have the hardships been necessary? in G. Dymski and R. Pollin (eds) *New Perspectives on Monetary Macroeconomics*. Ann Arbor, MI: University of Michigan Press, pp. 169–97.

Ferri, P. and Minsky, H.P. (1991) Market processes and thwarting systems, Economics Working Paper Archive wp_64. Levy Economics Institute, New York. Published as Market processes and thwarting systems, *Structural Change and Economic Dynamics*, Elsevier, 3(1): 79–91.

Gray, H.P. and Gray, J.M. (1994) Minskian fragility in the international financial system, in R. Pollin and G. Dymski (eds) *New Perspectives on Monetary Macroeconomics*. Ann Arbor, MI: University of Michigan Press, pp. 143–67.

Kregel, J. (2010) No going back: Why we cannot restore Glass–Seagall's segregation of banking and finance. Levy Economics Institute, New York. Public Policy Brief, 107. Available at: www.levyinstitute.org/publications/no-going-back-why-we-cannot-restore-glass-steagalls-segregation-of-banking-and-finance

Kregel, J. (2012) Using Minsky to simplify financial regulation. Levy Economics Institute and Ford Foundation, New York.

Kregel, J. (2013) Lessons from the Cypriot deposit haircut for EU deposit insurance schemes. Levy Economics Institute, New York. Policy Note 4.

Kregel, J. (2014) Minsky and dynamic macroprudential regulation, *PSL Quarterly Review*, 67(269): 217–38.

Minsky, H.P. (1986) Global consequences of financial deregulation, Archive: Paper 378. Available at: http://digitalcommons.bard.edu/hm_archive/378 (accessed August 2016).

Minsky, H.P. (1993) Financial integration and national economic policy. Available at: http://digitalcommons.bard.edu/hm_archive (accessed July 2016).

Minsky, H.P. (1994) The financial instability hypothesis and current common problems of rich capitalist economies. Fausto Vicarelli Lecture at the University of Macerata.

Minsky, H.P. (1995) Would repeal of Glass–Steagall Act benefit the US economy? New York: Archive Levy Economics Institute of Bard College. Available at: http://digital-commons.bard.edu/hm_archive (accessed February 2017).

Minsky, H.P. (1996) Uncertainty and the institutional structure of capitalist economies, Economics Working Paper Archive wp_155. Levy Economics Institute, New York.

Minsky, H. (2008) Securitization, Preface and Afterword by L. Randall Wray, Levy Economics Institute Policy, No. 2. Archive, Levy Economics Institute of Bard College, New York. Available at: http://digitalcommons.bard.edu/hm_archive (accessed February 2017).

Minsky, H.P. ([1986] 2008) *Stabilizing an Unstable Economy*. New York: McGraw-Hill.

Minsky, H.P. and Whalen, C.J. (1996) Economic insecurity and the institutional prerequisites for successful capitalism, Economics Working Paper Archive wp 165. Levy Economics Institute, New York.

Mirowski, P. (2010) Inherent vice: Minsky, Markomata, and the tendency of markets to undermine themselves, *Journal of Institutional Economics*, 6(4): 415–43.

Mirowski, P. (2013) Market complexity and the nature of crises in financial markets, in L. Taylor, A. Rezai and T. Michl (eds) *Social Fairness and Economics*. London and New York: Routledge: 374–93.

Mirowski, P. (2014) The political movement that dared not speak its own name: The neoliberal thought collective under erasure, Working Paper No. 23. New York: Institute for New Economic Thinking.

Sinapi, C. (2011) Institutional prerequisites of financial fragility within Minsky's financial instability hypothesis: A proposal in terms of 'institutional fragility'. Levy Economics Institute, New York, Working Papers Series (0674): 1–34.

Sinapi, C. (2013) The role of financialization in financial instability: A post-Keynesian institutionalist perspective. *Limes*, 9: 207–32.

Whalen, C.J. (2001) Integrating Schumpeter and Keynes: Hyman Minsky's Theory of Capitalist Development, *Journal of Economic Issues*, XXXV(4): 805–23.

White, L.J. (2010) The credit rating agencies, *Journal of Economic Perspectives*, 24(2): 211–26.

2 Minsky on central banking and the current debate

Introduction

In this chapter it will be argued that, although there has been a revival of Minsky's ideas in the post-crisis environment, not enough attention has been devoted to the issue of thwarting systems in a regime of money manager capitalism. This consideration includes also the proposals for changes in financial regulation and the discussion on the future of central banking.

The proposals for changes in financial regulation discuss mainly the design of financial systems and the type of prudential regulation that should be introduced with the bulk of discussions concerning capital regulation versus other types of prudential regulations. Capital requirements that are risk based and rigorously risk weighted are often contrasted with other types of prudential regulations aimed at improving liquidity or financial stability, even systemic stability, although the word systemic is often a misnomer.

In particular, a proposal literally taken from Minsky is that of avoiding excessive leverage by constraining the distribution of dividends by banks and then the rate of growth of their capital. It will be argued that lowering the leverage in that way will not deliver a financial structure that promotes the capital development of the economy and does not hinder the emergence of cumulative processes in financial assets prices and their consequences on the distribution of income and wealth.

Another proposal, apparently unconnected to the previous theme of financial regulation but indirectly and deeply linked to it, is the one to extend the extraordinary measures enacted by central banks during the crisis to normal life. This would mean that the central bank should be committed at any time to support dealers in the markets of new financial assets that innovation continuously creates and so sustain their prices. In a way, this would fulfil the requirement for a thwarting system to establish prices that are different from what the market would have spontaneously generated and would also resemble Minsky's idea of rigging the markets. Unfortunately, that rigging would be used to favour the already powerful and rich minority whose interests are reflected in usages and norms. Thus, the capital development that would emerge from this policy would be one in which inequality would be considered as a positive and desirable outcome.

Recent proposals of change in financial regulation inspired by Minsky

A proposal to constrain the growth rate of banks' assets

Minsky made a proposal in the 1980s to limit the expansion of banks' assets (see Tonveronachi, 2013; Kregel, 2014). He argued that banks maximize profit by trying to increase the volume of assets for any given return on assets, thus increasing return on equity. Tonveronachi (2013), inspired by Minsky's idea, has updated it and proposed a radical change in banks' regulation in the European Union. Minsky had proposed to use the dividends pay-out ratio to affect the rate of growth of the banking firm. The maximum rate of a bank's growth would depend on the return on assets, net of the pay-out ratio of dividends to shareholders divided by the minimum capital requirements. In order to constrain the growth rate of assets, a mandatory dividend pay-out ratio would act counter-cyclically to prohibit a high retention when the return on assets was high and to impose a lower one when it was low. Tonveronachi (2013) proposes targeting the rate of growth of gross domestic product in order to avoid uniform capital regulations hindering economic growth in countries with a low return on assets. In this way, capital regulations could not be uniform for all countries in the European Union, but should be tailored to national conditions, macroeconomic conditions such as output growth and inflation, and microeconomic ones as the profitability of local banks. Minimum capital requirements should be changed to ensure that the desired rate of output growth is reached, so the desired output growth rate and the return on banks' assets should determine the minimum capital requirements. He argues that in countries in which the return on assets is very low, high minimum capital requirements would hinder economic growth being achieved.

This proposal does not grant the decreased leverage of banks to be accompanied by a lending activity that fosters the capital development of the economy. We recall that for Minsky, capital development did not mean just growth of output, but a development that warranted some shared goals as, for example, full employment and an equitable distribution of income and wealth (Whalen, 2001; Kregel, 2012, p. 5). For example, after the crisis the major banks have decreased leverage and built-up capital, but the composition of their assets has changed, too, with an increased share of securities most of them linked to derivatives rather than to loans to business or households.

In the current environment, in order to stop the asset multiplication by banks and other financial institutions, it would be wise to put some brakes on the financial circuits that make such an expansion in balance sheets possible. This would require a distinction among financial institutions as to their functions in the economy. Liquidity-creating institutions should enjoy reserves by the central banks at favourable conditions, while other institutions would be limited in their use of financing techniques on the money markets.

Referring to the US experience, Kregel (2012) proposes various ways of constraining the creation of fictitious liquidity by both banks and non-banks that would require neither the reintroduction of the Glass–Steagall Act nor the implementation of the Dodd–Frank Act. It would be sufficient to abolish the provisions of the Gramm–Leach–Bliley Act that aimed at levelling the playing field between banks and non-bank financial institutions. To that aim, Kregel sketches several small changes to the existing US legislation that could be implemented quite rapidly without requiring a large overhaul. For example, given the apparent scarcity of safe assets and the money pools' preference for dollar short-term insured assets, a solution would be to extend deposit insurance to large deposits, thus removing the upper limit. Another useful measure in restoring proper banking would be to regulate money market funds and prohibit them from offering a constant net asset value to their customers, which they perceive as identical to a bank deposit. Other measures regard the repo market and the possibility of rehypothecating collateral. On the side of loans it would be useful to reintroduce sound underwriting practices rather than relying on external ratings by private agencies. Actually, some of the measures that Kregel advocated are being realized in the United States. The reform of the triparty repo market (Federal Reserve Bank of New York, 2010; Dudley, 2013) and that of the money market mutual funds (Financial Stability Oversight Council, 2012; Dudley, 2013) have been carried out while rehypothecation in the US was already limited.

In the European Union, similar measures to those introduced in the US with the Gramm–Leach–Bliley Act have been introduced in the national regulations by the reception of European directives. In the EU, there was no strong competition between banks' and non-banks' financial institutions, and thus the aim of the new legislation was simply to realize the single market and to deregulate the financial markets. The same orientation is still alive and has shaped its post-crisis regulatory activity. For example, no measures to reform the repo market and securities lending have been enacted and the introduction of a new common legislation on the resolution of banks (Single Resolution Mechanism – SRM), which is valid for the majority of banks in the EU, puts uninsured depositors lower in the hierarchy with respect to repo creditors and securities lenders.

Criticism of that proposal as a unique solution to the problem of financial instability

An explanation of the criticism of the proposal described in the last section is now offered. It is argued that just putting a cap on banks' assets is not sufficient to thwart instability. In particular, the proposal had been advanced by Minsky in the 1980s, while the financial structure and the ways of increasing leverage have changed in the last twenty years. Some structures of financing have prevailed over others, particularly in the shadow banking system. So, the original objective set by Minsky of decreasing leverage holds but must be pursued with means adequate to the change in the structure of financing.

Using Minsky to simplify financial regulation is a very challenging task and must start from his analysis of instability and leverage linked to the stage of the economy's development in which the regulation must be implemented.[1] A changing economy may change the way that leverage develops, too. Minsky (1986) argued that the tendency to increase leverage as a means to increase the return on equity by bank managers could contribute to an upward tendency in the price of bonds, common stocks and real assets, including capital assets and investment. This upward tendency would be cumulative because of an endogenous feedback mechanism.

> The investment process depends upon the flexibility banking gives to the financial system. But bankers and other money market operators, being profit-minded, are always seeking new ways to turn a dollar. It is necessary for the financial system to be responsive to changing business demands but if financial innovation and aggressive seeking of borrowers outpaces the demand for funds for investment financing, excess funds will be available to finance demand for existing bonds, common stock and capital assets. This leads to a rise in the price of capital assets relative to the supply price of investment output. This, as has been explained, increases investment activity and thus profit – leading to a further rise in the price of capital assets and long-lived financial instruments. The behavior of financial markets, then, can trigger a boom from seemingly stable expansions.

(Minsky, [1986] 2008, p. 278)

The feedback mechanism concerns the interaction of financial and real markets in a context in which credit supply is endogenous. The result may be a non-linear behaviour of the real and financial variables with instability or limit cycles. The actual evolution of the variables would depend on the value of parameters and on institutional characteristics (Taylor, 1994). Taylor stresses that this type of instability is not just a static instability, but a dynamic structural one like the one that is measured by engineers wanting to know whether a bridge is stable.[2]

The link between stock market prices and cycles in investment, however powerful they might have been in the period until the 1980s, does not survive the money manager phase of capitalism. Higher stock prices do not induce an increase in the production of capital goods but rather attempt to incorporate new firms through the process of mergers and acquisitions financed by debt. The realization of profits becomes delinked from the sale of goods and helped by financial management techniques, including taxation, investment in offshore centres, delocalization. New cumulative processes have arisen that start from the rise in the price of assets that are linked by contractual clauses like derivatives to the underlying assets. These may spill over to the incomes of workers and producers through many different channels like saving, consumption, retirement income. Investment, just as Minsky believed, has become a speculative activity but one that is totally detached from the production of physical capital goods and thus from their prices. Cumulative processes in the price of financial assets do not cause rising investment and profits, but rather carry forward new management strategies that aim at profiting without investing or at least investing in the purchase of machinery and other real assets. This includes strategies to increase profit through property rights enhancements and participation in financial activity directly or the selling of titles that refer to the attributes of assets like risk rather than employing labour or building new factories. Another way to increase profits would be to rely on the redefinition of the main business by splitting it over a range of different corporations located in different jurisdictions in order to hide profits and avoid taxation.[3]

The feedback mechanism arising from cumulative increases and decreases in financial assets prices, however, is still an important feature of the present stage of capitalism and is reinforced by the financing practices that are used to take positions in assets based on secured lending (through collateral) between private financial institutions. According to Minsky, those practices decrease liquidity as they may require the fire selling of assets and lead to debt deflation (Minsky, 1982a, 1982b).[4] While investment is no more the main transmission mechanism from money supply to oscillation in price of financial assets, excessive credit expansion fuels the increase in the price of new financial assets that have underlying financial assets as references. The price of derivatives and of the underlying assets increases jointly, often reinforcing each other, or falls abruptly in the same fashion. The excessive credit creation causes a greater demand for these new products due to financial innovation, while the greater demand and higher price is an incentive to develop new ones. The price of derivatives and that of the underlying assets, rather than being equalized by arbitrage in efficient markets at a level that corresponds to fundamentals, often runs in the same direction in ascending or descending phases (Mirowski, 2010; Tropeano, 2016). This process seems detached from the development of the real economy except for the abnormal expansion of the weight of the financial sector's wages and profits with respect to other branches of the economy and the social costs that the losses in these instruments localized in banks' balance sheets cause through the insurance guaranteed by the state. In the post great financial crisis period, the central banks themselves have contributed with their programmes of asset purchase that have lasted for many years after the inception of the crisis to the upward phase in their prices (see, for example, the commodities bubble).

Sometimes the regulation itself may be behind the feedback as is now happening in the Netherlands. In that country, given the very low interest rates set by the European Central Bank (ECB), pensioners and insured people were asked to post higher contributions, which in turn increased the demand for domestic government bonds that are the main financial security in which pension funds invest and interest rate swaps, which they have to buy to protect themselves from interest rate changes. The excess demand by pension funds and insurance companies for domestic government bonds made their prices rise and their interest rates fall. Lower interest rates on government bonds reduced pension funds' returns again and caused another increase in pension fund contributions. The whole story could repeat itself. This may have macroeconomic repercussions if future pensioners increase saving and decrease consumption in order to pay for the higher contributions (Dirks *et al.*, 2014).

The central bank as a dealer of last resort or as a guide to the financial system?

Minsky's theory of central banking: the central bank as a guide to the financial system

In the last section we argued that simply putting a cap on banks' assets would not be sufficient to thwart instability. An explicit commitment by the central bank to guide[4] the evolution of financial usages and practices would be necessary.

> If the disrupting effects of banking are to be constrained, the authorities must drop their blinders and accept the need to guide and control the evolution of financial usages and practices. In a world of businessmen and financial intermediaries who aggressively seek profit, innovators will always outpace regulators; the authorities cannot prevent changes in the structure of portfolios from occurring. *What they can do is keep the asset-equity ratio of banks within bounds by setting equity-absorption ratios for various types of assets.* If the authorities constrain banks and are aware of the activities of fringe banks and other financial institutions, they are in a better position to attenuate the disruptive expansive tendencies of our economy.
>
> (Minsky, [1986] 2008, p. 281, emphasis added)

Setting equity-absorption ratio for various types of assets may remind the notion of risk-weighted capital requirements. This way of differentiating the equity requirements with respect to the assets has been pursued in the second edition of the Basel agreement rules and has been changed again after the crisis to reflect the changed perceived riskiness of assets. The idea of risk in the Basel agreement is that of a calculable entity. Therefore, equity absorption ratios in Basel II and III do depend on risk weights.

Yet Minsky did not think of calculable risk but meant to fix equity absorption ratios in relation to development goals rather than to some risk measure. Loans may be very risky, but if to foster development in a specific sector or favouring a section of borrowers are policy goals, the equity absorption for those specific loans should be lower than for other assets. Development finance is based on multiple interest rates as well as exchange rates and preferential loans conditions. Those tools have been put aside or prohibited by financial liberalizations carried out almost in any country. A credit allocation policy directed at social goals could be reintroduced and would allow to rig markets (Pollin and Dymski, 1994, pp. 387–90).

Another idea by Minsky is that the central bank should use the discount window rather than open market operations in the conduct of monetary policy. He recalled that in the first phase of the Federal Reserve System, the central bank was discounting banks' assets:

> The original Federal Reserve Act based the reserves of member banks on bank rediscounting of eligible paper at the discount window of the district

Federal Reserve Banks. Rediscounting was not just a lender of last resort activity reserved for a crisis, it was the mechanism by which part of the normal reserve base of banks was brought into being. By being the channel through which the demand for reserves by banks led to the creation of reserves, the discount window made the ability of banks to lend responsive to the needs of trade. In the original bank Reserve Act bank reserves were endogenously determined.

(Minsky, 1994b, p. 7)

Minsky adds that by using the rediscounting and by the oversight the central bank could facilitate the capital development of the economy. Thus, central banks could influence the portfolio choices of banks by their preferences on the assets to be discounted (Minsky, [1986] 2008, p. 282).

Money, according to Minsky, was not lent by banks but created by them in the act of lending. In this idea, he was following his master Schumpeter. Banks lend when they buy a note that they have previously accepted. The fundamental banking activity is accepting (Minsky, [1986] 2008; Wray, 2015). In the same way as banks accept debts by their customers based on the valuation of their borrowers' reliability, so the central banks should discount only those assets that they choose to and should address the banking community towards certain behaviour.

The central bank, therefore, stands in a banker relation to ordinary banks and other financial institutions. By providing a guaranteed line of credit to protected institutions, the central bank has the banker's right to set standards for borrowing. Thus central banks and depository insurance organizations set standards for assets, liabilities, equity and reserves of their potential borrowing clients. Prudential regulation represents an extension of normal business practice.

(Minsky, [1986] 2008, p. 15)

Here the stress is on standards for assets, liabilities, equity and reserves. Those standards for assets, liabilities and reserves have been replaced in the regulatory practice by credit ratings assigned by private agencies and/or by insurance bought on the market and acknowledged by regulatory authorities. Both the central bank in relation to banks and the banks in relation to each other rely on external ratings and statistical scores for judging solvency and use derivatives to cover risks, including counterparty risk, in the illusion that the markets for derivatives are always able to price properly the risk. Failure to do so would call for state intervention to absorb the losses incurred by banks in their balance sheets. Minsky has warned that the 'Financial game has taken the form in which complex combinations of positions are taken in order presumably to protect against income or capital values losses but which can lead to greatly amplified losses if market developments are "wrong"' (Minsky, 1994a, p. 3). In the current state, regulation sanctions the fact that the standards for assets, liabilities, equity and reserves are established in the markets by private organizations that are portrayed as developing soft law rules. This is accepted as normal in so far as the markets are trusted to deliver the optimal outcomes. In the EU, dealing with these topics would require an agenda, which is exactly the opposite of the one that is now being pursued with the aim of a Capital Markets Union.

Although leverage is not the only problem, the way in which leverage increases may depend on the structure of the financial markets and on the rules that govern them. Then, the mechanisms that contribute to leverage building should be disactivated. Fom this viewpoint, just putting a cap on the expansion of banks' assets in general or on the rate of growth of particular banks would not be sufficient as it would not change the quality of the balance sheets. Without a change in usages and institutions, no thwarting system can be built.

The institutional mechanisms that nurture leverage in the European Union are derivatives requirements by capital regulation, repo markets law that transfer the property of the repoed asset to the lender, rehypothecation and securities lending, and resolution procedures for banks that subordinate uninsured deposits to other assets in the hierarchy of claims. The state does not guarantee all deposits, but guarantees that many other assets are privileged with respect to them in the resolution procedure (bail-in).

As some scholars have noticed, banks now use government bonds for balance sheet expansion (Gabor and Vestergaard, 2016: 18).They add that the legal right to reuse collateral is critical because it allows financial institutions to issue repo liabilities against the same government bond and to finance less liquid, but higher yielding assets.

While in the United States some of the measures proposed by Kregel (2012) are being implemented, in the EU in order to pursue the goal of capital market union the inverse path has been chosen. In the European Union, the extraordinary monetary policy of the central bank has become de facto the only thwarting mechanism. The outcomes that has produced, however, may not be considered viable or acceptable if the goals to be pursued are full employment and an equitable distribution of income. The unconventional monetary policy by the ECB has not reduced inequality either among states or within them, and has not reduced unemployment.

The central bank as a dealer of last resort for ever?

After the global financial crisis (GFC) of 2007, the stabilizing forces of the combination of big state and big bank seem to have become even more diminished. Although fiscal expansions were implemented in many countries immediately after the crisis, the longest continued expansion has been in the central banks – ten years after the GFC – which are considered the most relevant policy makers. This continued and extraordinary intervention has produced many attempts to explain their new role (BIS, 2014; Goodhart, 2016; Mehrling, 2014). They have been praised as though they were the new circuit breakers and speculation about their future conduct has flourished.

According to some scholars, the central bank's main task after the great financial crisis was to ensure international liquidity (Mehrling, 2014). The central bank set a limit on the prices of the risks attached to the assets – interest rate risk, exchange rate risk, credit risk – by supporting the prices of derivatives that deal with those risks. In doing so, it stabilized the international monetary system based on the dollar and provided international liquidity. Mehrling's ideas on the role of the central bank (Mehrling, 2014) can be reconciled with the view on derivatives by Bryan and Rafferty (2006). They argue that derivatives are the new money as they work as universal equivalents and allow the transformation of value through time and space. In their view, the central bank should ensure international financial liquidity and stability.

This view contrasts with the lack of trust in the central bank as a stabilizing force in the money manager phase of capitalism that Minsky expressed on many occasions. Although in his earlier works (Minsky, 1982a, b) he had often written that the central bank is able to stabilize the value of any asset it wishes, in the 1990s Minsky does not envisage as a solution to the likely return of big financial crises the stabilization of an intrinsic crisis-prone collateral system based on margin calls, upon which derivatives are based, by the central bank. One may guess that he would rather share the opinion of those (for example, Sissoko, 2014) who think that this help to the collateral-based system would further destabilize the financial system based on unsecured debt, such as traditional lending activity. In the same way, one can speculate that he would not approve the intervention carried out in the US, and particularly in Europe, after the crisis as a means to contrast depression and debt deflation. Similarly, one can have doubts that he would approve the main principles and details of the financial reforms enacted.

In his last works in the 1990s, Minsky did not trust the central bank as the institution capable of thwarting instability, given the evolution of the financial system that had taken place until then. Minsky's thoughts on the future seen from 1994 were quite pessimistic. He foresaw a 'financial catastrophe' and the 'periodic need to bail out financial institutions' (Minsky, 1994a).

Minsky did not hint anywhere in his later writings at the development of new financial instruments as a solution to the financial instability problems in the new historical circumstances. To put it simply, he did not imagine derivatives as a part of the solution to the problem (Mehrling, 2011), neither did he believe that the central banks could stabilize the system by putting a floor to the prices of derivatives or buying them directly. In the current context, providing global liquidity through derivatives support would be in contrast with providing other goods that were more important in his scale of value – equality and full employment – which would perpetuate and further increase inequality. It would certainly maintain in value all financial investment around the world by ensuring their equivalence across time and space (Bryan and Rafferty, 2006). It would thus serve well the globalization of trade and finance. From the economic policy perspective, however, it could be questioned whether this is a public good. The central bank, by pursuing that goal, would work to maintain the constant value of the wealth of those who belong to the 0.01 per cent in the wealth distribution scale, and who presumably have accumulated their wealth by committing fraud and/or eluding taxes.

The essential point is that if the bank were to act in this way, it would not guide the evolution of usages and financing practices but just accommodate them. The issue is paramount nowadays in so far as new usages and financing practices developed by private financial institutions contribute to the multiplication of assets almost automatically. The demand for financial assets that trade the attribute of a commodity rather than the commodity itself multiplies the size of the universal claims and liabilities among entities, while their practice of protecting themselves by hedging in the same or similar assets is a driver behind the expansion of the market and the issuers' profits. Central banks, through their regulatory arm, the Basel Committee on Banking Supervision, acknowledged this practice and introduced it into the regulation toolkit. If central banks were to put floors to the price of derivatives, it would encourage a type of development characterized by large oscillations in prices, which are incompatible with full employment and an equitable distribution of income. Such action would put a floor to those prices but it would not put an upward limit. The floor would be fixed, but the ceiling could be lifted higher and higher. The people who would benefit from that lifting would be the already very rich individuals.

If the idea of the bank as a guiding institution is to be preserved and the concept of guiding is central in the institutionalist interpretation of Minsky, then this thwarting system may not be apt. The word guiding recurs frequently in Minsky's writings on the role of the central bank. In the article first published in 1957 (see Minsky, 1982a) on the central bank and changes in the money market he argues that the central bank cannot avoid guiding the evolution of the money markets. This usage of the word may be taken from the American institutionalist J. Commons. Sinapi (2011) traces back the idea of institution by Minsky to Commons's definition of institution. Institutions, according to Commons, are collective actions that guide (or control) individual actions. In turn, these collective actions can be distinguished in informal institutions like customs or norms and formal institutions like the government and the central bank (Sinapi, 2011, p. 9). So, a central bank that guides cannot by definition approve whatever new financial product the market creates by supporting its price, which is the contemporary form in which discounting happens.[5] In the latter case, the central bank would not control individual actions but would be controlled by them.

In the current environment, for example, the central bank may affect certain markets by making the securities issued eligible as collateral for its financing or by designating them as high liquid assets. In this regard, the choice of the regulators to include mortgage-backed securities among the high liquid assets appears as a support to the building industry, which has already expanded excessively and prospered thanks to high prices for real estate. The expansion of that branch was one of the causes of the global financial crisis.

In the case of the European central bank, the issue is more complicated because the principle upon which its action rests is stated in the treaties signed by the

European states to join the European Union. The main aim of these treaties is to develop the common market and ensure that free competition conditions prevail in this unified common market. This means giving up the intention of controlling the markets, but creating the conditions to enhance market principles. So, according to the treaties, the European Central Bank should not act to guide the markets but rather be guided by them.

Which regulatory changes should be pursued in order to enhance stability and avoid cumulative processes?

The main message of Minsky's work is that thwarting systems must act as circuit breakers that avoid cumulative processes and feedback effects. The main point is to avoid excessive layering and interconnectedness. Decreasing leverage in itself is a good policy, but if decreasing leverage increases interconnectedess and the danger of feedback effects, then this policy will not work as a circuit breaker. Some measures that have been proposed – for example, the use of the leverage ratio rather than risk-weighted capital requirements, or the use of the leverage ratio to affect the rate of growth of output in a particular country – may be an improvement on current practice but the devil is in the detail.

The most important message by Minsky is that the central bank should guide the evolution of usages and practices and the banks should do proper underwriting. In the current context, the national central banks, however powerful they may be, act within the frame of rules that are agreed at the international level by supranational organizations jointly with governments. The G-20, the Financial Stability Board and the Basel Committee on Banking Supervision have been behind the package called Basel III.

Institutions are also creating accounting rules and contracts written by international organizations – mainly international financial firms, which are not concerned with any society's values but only with the profits of their members. Such contracts as noticed by Minsky with respect to securitization may increase the burden of deposit insurance for the states, as many claims are cleared before any other claimants, including depositors, are satisfied. The inclusion in the regulation of such contracts is the first step to avert the scale of values in favour of international private financial interests and against small countries, weaker groups and ordinary citizens. This means that regulation is not serving any capital development goal, but rather it is used to maximize profits by multinational financial corporations.

Big jurisdictions such the US or the EU are using international private organizations as partners to carry out difficult tasks. For example, the US government used the International Swaps and Derivatives Association (ISDA) to value derivatives sitting in the balance sheets of banks within the Public–Private Initiative Programme (PPIP) afer the 2008 crisis. The EU and the ECB before the 2012 restructuring of Greek debt converted the ECB holdings of Greek state bonds into new bonds with different identification numbers. The ISDA determination committee for Europe established that this exercise did not amount to a subordination of the remaining creditors and so derivatives were not triggered for that reason (Biggins and Scott, 2013, p. 23).

International private institutions that use soft law power to address problems within the financial system related to accounting, definitions, property law, bankruptcy, and so on may qualify for destabilizing systems as all they do is to increase cyclicality and feedback effects, although they increase the gains of the groups they represent. In this respect, the explicit and implicit acknowledgement by the states of their external technical authority amounts to making regulation based on it (accounting rules, definition of financial instruments, trading rules and contracts) a feedback-producing rather than a thwarting system. The problem with the post-crisis regulatory reform is that those rules in the background either have not been changed or they have been but always following the suggestions of the same interest groups. For example, using the leverage ratio rather than risk-weighted capital requirements now is fashionable among heterodox economists (Tonveronachi, 2013; Avgouleas, 2015), but few studies have looked at how exactly the leverage ratio is defined. This could be considered nonsense as the leverage ratio is simply the ratio of equity capital to total assets. However, total assets may be defined in many different ways. For example, the leverage ratio that has been included in the Basel III package and then adopted by the European Commission has a definition of total assets that makes them risk-weighted again. These details matter.

Another example is whether the new regulation threatens the existence of banking as it is usually conceived. The bank, which creates credit and whose liabilities are insured deposits, may be the next casualty of the new regulation. The existence of such an institution should not be considered obvious and warranted for ever. A bank that has both deposits and loans on its balance sheet is the result of an historical evolution that took several centuries but could easily disappear and be relegated to an historical accident. Although innovation in finance is pervasive, is it really worth destroying it? If the answer is yes, what would replace it? Are online deposits only banks and online peer-to-peer lenders a sensible replacement? How stable would such a financial system be? Although in theory no financial reform dares to challenge this institution, in practice the evolution of legislation in some jurisdictions jointly with macroeconomic conditions and fiscal rules may make banks reluctant to lend and their deposits become increasingly less safe or perceived as less safe than they have been up to now. This applies in particular to the European Union.

In the following chapters, we will examine in detail the new regulation that has been implemented or will soon be implemented in the European Union looking at the characteristics of this legislation that may make it a circuit breaker in the sense that Minsky gave to this expression. Beyond the single measures, which may have a higher or lower rate of approval, what matters is the type of financial structure they wish to promote and whether this is compatible with the avoidance of depression and deflation, or in any case of wild movements in prices that exceed computational capabilities. So what matters is the relation among many different and sometimes minuscule changes in financial regulation in many fields.

These details are often neglected by economists of whatsoever orientation, while interest groups professing to be pro *laissez-faire* are very eager to exploit them (Mirowski, 2014). An effort will be made to connect the dots and evaluate the whole picture beyond the single measures.

Conclusions

In this chapter, an interpretation of Minsky's approach to the role that financial regulation should play has been attempted, and his observations have been updated to take into account the evolution of the financial structure that has occurred since his death.

While the high leverage of banks is surely a problem for financial stability, it does not automatically cause a financial crisis if other conditions related to the structure of the economy are not satisfied. These conditions are the degree of interconnectedness and the percentage of Ponzi agents over the total and the share of assets whose prices are stabilized by the central bank. In the current shape of capitalism, an expansion in investment is not a prerequisite for the boom expansion that precedes the financial crisis. What remains, however, is a cumulative process in the price of financial securities that cannot be stopped by the central bank without itself starting a crisis. This occurred before the last big financial crisis, while successive interventions by the central banks since then have constantly maintained high valuations of financial assets whatever their nature. While this guarantees a floor and hinders new crises from arising, it does not lead to any societal shared goals. So, the most simple regulatory change that has happened and, according to some scholars should continue in the future, is simply that central banks should continue with their extraordinary policies as the new normal. This would not have been shared by Minsky according to the reconstruction given here.

Another proposal focuses on restraining leverage either by increasing capital or decreasing the rate of the growth of assets. This proposal, however, does not change the usages and practices in the financial markets that the central bank should guide.

In the next part of the book, the changes in the financial regulation in the European Union will be critically examined and it will be shown that, beyond the content of the many new metrics introduced, the main aim is simply to maintain unchanged those same usages and practices, and to reinforce their continous operation. In turn, this means validating the accounting rules, property and bankruptcy law changes that are embedded in the contracts that are behind the new securities that are issued. This type of regulation therefore cannot be a thwarting system.

Notes

1   For analysis of the importance of Minsky's thoughts on the stages of the development of the economy, see Whalen (2001).

2　Taylor (1994) offers a few models that could provide examples of such dynamic instabilities, although the main difference between these models and Minsky's own narrative in the passage quoted above is that the money market is not thought to be the market in which the demand and supply of money and credit are brought to equality by changes in interest rates. Minsky's endogenous money view is missing in Taylor's (1994) analytical models.

3　For all aspects of the financialization process, see Lapavitsas (2009) and Bryan and Rafferty (2006, 2014).

4　The risk of fire sales in repo markets is also discussed in current research (Begalle *et al.*, 2013).

5　Mehrling *et al.* (2013) are right in stressing the similarity between the modern money markets and the 19th-century money markets in which the central bank, the Bank of England, discounted bills but the institutional and legal characteristics of the bills eligible for discounts were very different from today's financial products (see Sissoko, 2014; Tropeano, 2015).

References

Avgouleas, E. (2015) Bank leverage ratios and financial stability: A micro- and macropru-dential perspective. Levy Institute of Bard College, New York, Working Paper No. 849. Available at: https://ssrn.com/abstract=2682675 or http://dx.doi.org/10.2139/ssrn.2682675

Bank of International Settlements (BIS) (2014) Re-thinking the lender of last resort. BIS Papers No. 79, Basel. Available at: www.bis.org (accessed 17 February 2017).

Begalle, B., Martin, A., McAndrews, J. and McLaughlin, S. (2013) The risk of fire sales in the tri-party repo market. Federal Reserve Board of New York, Staff Report No. 616. Available at: www.newyorkfed.org/research/staff_reports/sr616.html (accessed 31 March 2017).

Biggins, J. and Scott, C. (2013) Private governance, public implications and the tightrope of regulatory reform: The ISDA Credit Derivatives Determinations Committees, Osgoode CLPE Research Paper No. 57/2013. Available at: https://ssrn.com/abstract=2360278 or http://dx.doi.org/10.2139/ssrn.2360278

Bryan, D. and Rafferty, M. (2006) *Capitalism with Derivatives*. London: Palgrave Macmillan.

Bryan, D. and Rafferty, M. (2014) Financial derivatives as social policy beyond crisis, *Sociology* 48(5): 887–903.

Dirks, M., de Vries, C. and van der Lecq, F. (2014) Macroprudential policy: The neglected sectors, in D. Schoenmaker (ed.) *Macro-prudentialism*. London: CEPR Press, pp. 73–85. Available at: http://voxeu.org/sites/default/files/file/macroprudentialism_VoxEU_0.pdf

Dudley, W. (2013) Fixing wholesale funding to build a more stable financial system. Speech. Available at: www.newyorkfed.org/newsevents/speeches/2013/dud130201.html (accessed 31 March 2017).

Federal Reserve Bank of New York (2010) Tri-party repo infrastructure reform, White Paper, 17 May. Available at: www.newyorkfed.org/banking/nyfrb_triparty_whitepaper.pdf

Financial Stability Oversight Council (2012) Proposed recommendations regarding money market mutual fund reform (November). Available at: www.treasury.gov/initiatives/fsoc/Documents/Proposed%20Recommendations%20Regarding%20Money%20Market%20Mutual%20Fund%20Reform%20-%20November%2013,%202012.pdf

Gabor, D. and Vestergaard, J. (2016) Towards a theory of shadow money, INET Working Paper. Available at: www.ineteconomics.org/research/research-papers/towards-a-theory-of-shadow-money

Goodhart, C. (2016) Central bank evolution: Lessons learnt from the subprime crisis. In M.D. Bordo, Ø. Eitrheim, M. Flandreau and J.F. Qvigstad (eds) *Central Banks at a Crossroads: What Can We Learn from History? Studies in Macroeconomic History.* Cambridge: Cambridge University Press.

Kregel, J. (2012) Using Minsky to simplify financial regulation. Levy Economics Institute and Ford Foundation, New York.

Kregel, J. (2014) Minsky and dynamic macroprudential regulation. *PSL Quarterly Review*, 67(269): 217–38.

Lapavitsas, C. (2009) Financialised capitalism: Crisis and financial expropriation. *Historical Materialism*, 17(2):114–48.

Mehrling, P. (2011) *The New Lombard Street*. Princeton, NJ: Princeton University Press.

Mehrling, P. (2014) Re-imagining central banking. BIS Paper No. 79.

Mehrling, P., Poznar, Z., Sweeney, J. and Neilsson, D.J. (2013) Bagehot was a shadow banker: Shadow banking, central banking, and the future of global finance. Available at: https://ssrn.com/abstract=2232016 or http://dx.doi.org/10.2139/ssrn.2232016

Minsky, H.P. (1986) Global consequences of financial deregulation. Hyman P. Minsky Archive: Paper 378. Available at: http://digitalcommons.bard.edu/hm_archive/378 (accessed August 2016).

Minsky, H.P. (1994a) The financial instability hypothesis and current common problems of rich capitalist economies. Fausto Vicarelli Lecture. Macerata: University of Macerata.

Minsky, H.P. (1994b) Financial instability and the decline (?) of banking: Public policy implications. Hyman P. Minsky Archive. New York: Levy Economics Institute of Bard College. Available at: http://digitalcommons.bard.edu/hm_archive (accessed July 2016).

Minsky, H.P. ([1986] 2008) *Stabilizing an Unstable Economy*. New York: McGraw Hill.

Minsky H. (1982a) Central banking and money market changes. In H. Minsky, *Can it Happen Again?* New York: M.E. Sharpe, pp. 162–78.

Minsky, H. (1982b) The new uses of monetary powers. In H. Minsky, *Can it Happen Again?* New York: M.E. Sharpe, pp. 179–91.

Mirowski, P. (2010) Inherent vice: Minsky, Markomata, and the tendency of markets to undermine themselves. *Journal of Institutional Economics*, 6(04): 415–43.

Mirowski, P. (2014) The political movement that dared not speak its own name: The neoliberal thought collective under erasure, Working Paper No. 23, Institute for New Economic Thinking.

Pollin, R. and Dymski, G. (1994) The costs and benefits of financial instability: Big government capitalism and the Minsky paradox. In R. Pollin and G. Dymski (eds) *New Perspectives on Monetary Macroeconomics*. Ann Arbor, MI: University of Michigan Press, pp. 369–401.

Sinapi, C. (2011) Institutional prerequisites of financial fragility within Minsky's financial instability hypothesis: A proposal in terms of 'Institutional Fragility'. Levy Economics Institute, New York, Working Papers Series (0674): 1–34.

Sissoko, C. (2014) Shadow banking: Why modern money markets are less stable than 19th c. money markets but shouldn't be stabilized by a 'dealer of last resort'. USC Law Legal Studies Paper No. 14–21. Available at: http://ssrn.com/abstract=2392098 or http://dx.doi.org/10.2139/ssrn.2392098 (accessed September 2016).

Taylor, L. (1994) Financial fragility: Is an etiology at hand? In G. Dymski and R. Pollin (eds) *New Perspectives on Monetary Macroeconomics*. Ann Arbor, MI: University of Michigan Press, pp. 21–50.

Tonveronachi, M. (2013) De-globalising bank regulation, *PSL Quarterly Review*, 66(267): 371–85.

Tropeano, D. (2015) Lender of last resort, in S. Rossi and L.-P. Rochon (eds) *The Encyclopedia of Central Banking*. Cheltenham, UK and Northhampton, MA: Edward Elgar, pp. 294–6.

Tropeano, D. (2016) Hedging, arbitrage, and the financialization of commodities market, *International Journal of Political Economy*, 45(3): 241–56.

Whalen, C.J. (2001) Integrating Schumpeter and Keynes: Hyman Minsky's theory of capitalist development, *Journal of Economic Issues*, XXXV(4): 805–23.

Wray, R.L. (2015) Minsky on banking: Early work on endogenous money and the prudent banker. Levy Economics Institute of Bard College, New York. Available at: www.levy-institute.org (accessed December 2016).

3   Main changes in regulation after the crisis

Introduction

In this chapter the main changes in capital requirements under the Basel III revision are discussed. It is argued that the risk-weighted capital requirements are still the main tool of banking regulation in the European Union legislation, although with amended risk weights. This contrasts with the changes in regulations implemented in other jurisdictions. In particular, the regulation that introduced the major changes to the existing capital requirements apparatus insists on the concept of proportionality that must be applied at any level, not only of risk-weighted capital but also in devising standards and other rules for the implementation. At any level, authorities must ensure that the proportionality between capital and risk is exactly respected. Despite this obsession with proportionality, it is argued that the new risk weights are just as likely to be gamed as the old ones through the process of risk optimization and through the use of internally based models. The possibility of gaming are still higher given the importance that the legislation attaches to the use of complex models that fit in well with complex assets structures. This is an explicit invitation to capital elusion and has been warmly received. While encouraging capital elusion by big banks, this type of new risk-weighted regulation increases the costs for small banks that do not have the resources to build sophisticated models to elude it. The main complementary measure to risk-weighted capital requirements is the leverage ratio that has been welcomed as a new and more effective measure because it is not subject to the same gaming process as the former. Unfortunately, it will be shown that this is an unwarranted illusion.

The revised capital requirements: just a change in the weights?

The revision of the Basel II framework for capital requirements after the big financial crisis has been characterized in the European Union by the intention of reinforcing the proportionality approach – that is, to assign to any conceivable risk in the portfolios of banks an adequate valuation and a coefficient that exactly measures the riskiness. This approach is different from that pursued by other jurisdictions after the crisis. In the US, for example, the stress has been on leverage ratio in a modular way that differentiates banks according to their function size and governance structure (see Masera, 2013). In the UK, leverage ratio has been introduced and also structural measures of separation among different types of business activity have been envisaged.

The stress on proportionality is a distinguishing feature of EU legislation and this is clearly stated in Regulation No. 575/2013. To ensure that solvency is necessary to require capital according to the degree of risk of assets both on and off balance sheets:

> It is essential to take account of the diversity of institutions in the Union by providing alternative approaches to the calculation of capital requirements for credit risk incorporating different levels of risk-sensitivity and requiring different degrees of sophistication. Use of external ratings and institutions' own estimates of individual credit risk parameters represents a significant enhancement in the risk-sensitivity and prudential soundness of the credit risk rules. *Institutions should be encouraged to move towards the more risk-sensitive approaches. In producing the estimates needed to apply the approaches to credit risk of this Regulation, institutions should enhance their credit risk measurement and management processes to make available methods for determining regulatory own funds requirements that reflect the nature, scale, and complexity of individual institutions' processes. In this regard, the processing of data in connection with the incurring and management of exposures to customers should be considered to include the development and validation of credit risk management and measurement systems.* That serves not only to fulfil the legitimate interests of institutions but also the purpose of this Regulation, to use better methods for risk measurement and management and also use them for regulatory own funds purposes. *Notwithstanding this, the more risk-sensitive approaches require considerable expertise and resources as well as data of high quality and sufficient volume.* Institutions should therefore comply with high standards before applying those approaches for regulatory own funds purposes ... [emphasis added]
>
> (Regulation 575/2013/EU, Recital 42)

The objective clearly stated is to use more complex methods to measure risks as they are likely to deliver better results. The more complex the better, according to this view. It is also clear that the use of these more complex methods will require resources and expertise, but this is not an inconvenience. The potential disadvantage of smaller or poorer institutions in using these methods is not a worry for the regulators. Complexity of methods is not only required, but it is explicitly encouraged.

> Member States should ensure that the requirements laid down in this Regulation apply in a manner proportionate to the nature, scale and complexity of the risks associated with an institution's business model and activities. *The Commission should ensure that delegated and implementing acts, regulatory technical standards and implementing technical standards are consistent*

with the principle of proportionality, so as to guarantee that this Regulation is applied in a proportionate manner. EBA should therefore ensure that all regulatory and implementing technical standards are drafted in such a way that they are consistent with and uphold the principle of proportionality. [emphasis added]

(Regulation 575/2013/EU, Recital 46)

The only difference apart from the weightings attached to different assets with respect to the main Basel II construction is in adding another source of risk: the risk of bankruptcy of a counterparty in an over-the-counter transaction. To deal with this risk, a new tool called credit valuation adjustment has been added:

Institutions should hold additional own funds due to credit valuation adjustment risk arising from OTC derivatives. Institutions should also apply a higher asset value correlation in the calculation of the own fund requirements for counterparty credit risk exposures arising from OTC derivatives and securities-financing transactions to certain financial institutions. *Institutions should also be required to considerably improve measurement and management of counterparty credit risk by better addressing wrong-way risk, highly leveraged counterparties and collateral, accompanied by the corresponding enhancements in the areas of back-testing and stress testing.* [emphasis added]

(Regulation 575/2013/EU, Recital 83)

In order to address this counterparty risk, however, derivatives are allowed as risk mitigating devices. This has encouraged the expansion of their markets and the creation of new securities from existing ones through financial innovation (see Chapters 6 and 7).

After explaining that the main aim of the legislation is to refine the weightings of risks and the addition of a new risk, it is explained that other supplementary measures will be enacted but that these measures should be used only as a back-stop to the proportionality structure and with a timing that will postpone their full adoption to 1 January 2018. At this point, the text introduces the notion of leverage risk, adding the adjectives 'excessive' and 'unsustainable' (Regulation 575/2013/EU, Recital 91). Although it may be excessive and unsustainable, the measures proposed to deal with it are quite small.

The G-20 meeting of September 2009 is quoted as the source of the international agreement to implement a leverage ratio. The leverage ratio is described as a new regulatory and supervisory tool for the EU. There is a long implementation time, during which the details of its definition must be approved, while its introduction will be an additional feature that can be applied on individual institutions at the discretion of supervisory authorities:

In December 2010, the BCBS published guidelines defining the methodology for calculating the leverage ratio. Those rules provide for an observation period that will run from 1 January 2013 until 1 January 2017 during which the leverage ratio, its components and its behaviour relative to the risk-based requirement will be monitored. Based on the results of the observation period the BCBS intends to make any final adjustments to the definition and calibration of the leverage ratio in the first half of 2017, with a view to migrating to a binding requirement on 1 January 2018 based on appropriate review and calibration. The BCBS guidelines also provide for disclosure of the leverage ratio and its components starting from 1 January 2015.

(Regulation 575/2013/EU, Recital 93)

The hierarchy of tools is clearly stated. First are capital requirements that are proportional to risk and this proportionality must be enhanced by the provision of better and more data, and the use of more sophisticated risk-management techniques. Then, a supplementary and new measure may be applied that does not rest on proportionality but is simply a complement to the first.

The difference, with respect to Minsky's thought, is that the excessive expansion of banks' balance sheets in relation to macroeconomic activity is not considered as a problem in itself, which conflicts with the aim to foster the capital development of the economy, but only something that can be cured by introducing more capital. The only danger is that the solvency of banks may be endangered because capital is too scarce, which may unfortunately happen because the proportions between the capital and the risk are wrong. Another of Minsky's ideas that the expansion of banks' balance sheets to unprecedented high values may strain deposit insurance provided by the states and require very strong interventions is not shared by the new regulation proposals or is considered only to exclude future interventions by the states by introducing the means by which the banks can save themselves however big they are. This may happen by introducing a further layer of capitals to be raised by systemic financial institutions, by converting bail-outs to bail-ins, by changing the same definition of capital that includes not only newly issued shares and retained profits but also hybrid financial tools that are sold as bonds but may be converted to capital when this is necessary. Thus, the excessive expansion of the financial sector and the excessive layering that follows are not problems in this line of thought. A bank or financial system may be as big and as interconnected as possible, provided that enough capital has been raised to absorb occasional losses. The bulk of regulatory measures, especially in the EU, while in other jurisdictions other structural measures have been considered and enacted, is focused on asking for more capital, although with different features from traditional capital. Financial innovation considers the definition of capital, too.

In addition, there is complete faith that the risk can be exactly measured and calculated if data are sufficient and managed in the proper way. The invitation for banks is to develop better data-collection and data-management strategies, but not to change their business models. The risk is usually the individual risk of each single exposure calculated by using familiar statistical tools like the probability of default, loss given default, exposure at default and correlations parameters.

Moreover, while the parameters for the exposures to various risks are pre-calculated by the regulators in the standardized approach in the internal risk-based one, they have to be calculated by the same banks that are regulated. The models, however, require supervisors' approval. The 2013 regulation quoted above seems to encourage internal risk-based model building because it would better address the complexities of modern bank enterprises.

Furthermore, the picture is complicated by the ongoing revision of the International Accounting Standards Board (IASB), which should take effect from 1 January 2018. The new accounting standards would make the freedom left to internal rating models greater by allowing new innovative reporting standards that take into account the hedging practices by banks. The IASB claims that the accounting prescriptions should be aligned with the banks' hedging practices by introducing not only single items hedging, but also portfolio hedging and the hedging of whole balance sheets (called macro-hedging). Each bank would thus build its own model that reflects its risk-management tools and methods in order to calculate its capital requirements. These new hedging methods, even if not yet approved, have already affected the way in which some of the metrics of the new regulation are calculated. For example, to calculate the leverage ratio for the EU, which is still in a preparatory phase, it has to be recognized that in the definition of exposure at default (a proxy for total assets), new hedging possibilities should be allowed. In fact, in the regulation there is a long and detailed discussion regarding which hedging sets may be used in order to calculate the exposure at default deriving from derivatives and off-balance sheet items.

At the time of writing, as many research studies have found that the variation of risk-weighted assets in relation to total assets is high, even for banks with similar business models and size (Basel Committee on Banking Supervision, 2013, 2016; Le Leslé and Avramova, 2012; Mariathasan and Merrouche, 2014, Behn *et al.*, 2016), the regulators are going to change this again, requiring input and output floors to be introduced in order to ensure that the amount of capital required under the Internal Ratings Based (IRB) model does not fall below the one that would have resulted under the Standardized Approach. A similar measure was adopted in the US some years ago. The so-called Collins Amendment of the Dodd–Frank Act (Section 171) prevents US banks from using the IRB model approach (which in the US is called the Advanced Approach) from having minimum capital requirements below the general risk-based capital requirements. The debate now is between the US that approves this proposed change by the Basel Committee on Banking Supervision (BCBS) and the EU that strongly opposes it.

How the revision in capital requirements works in practice

The mix of measures adopted in their practical implementation, although formally directed at introducing penalizing weights for the trading book and increased capital requirements for derivatives, ends up damaging commercial banking with respect to investment or other types of business models. The reason can be simply explained by reporting what McKinsey was advising to its banking customers as early as 2010.

According to the simulations made in Härle *et al.* (2010), the major cost of the implementation of the Basel III framework for banks goes to retail banking, over-the-counter derivatives and other off balance sheets items such credit lines to corporates and financial institutions. The more penalized according to this scheme will be banks that have a major trading book and have also more off balance sheets assets.

This impression, however, is misleading. The reasons are explained in the advice the report gives to banks on how to minimize the costs of the new regulation. Some techniques can be used to maintain the same return on equity after complying with the new regulation by changing the composition of portfolios. In the report, it is suggested how to avoid increased costs in the trading book by introducing credit risk models and central counterparties, in particular credit valuation adjustment and internal counterparty risk models, and greater use of central counterparties. The latter move is more likely to reduce risk-weighted assets, but it is necessary to weigh the balance between less capital costs and reduced margins (due to the cost of central clearing). On the last point, one has to observe that the original Basel III draft recommended a capital weighting of 1.250 for funds deposited at the clearing house by members – the banks that want to use their facilities. The clearing house should avoid the sudden stresses in the market caused by the failure of one link in a long collateral chain. In order not to create an institution that is too big to fail, the clearing house must have firewalls so that members' default funds can be used in case of problems. The Basel Committee, however, decided in a Final Rule issued in 2014 to lower the risk weight from 1.250 per cent to 0.20 per cent (Leising, 2014; BCBS, 2014a) for the clearing member bank's risk-sensitive capital requirement for its default fund contribution (KCMi).[1] Given this change, the cost of new rules on derivatives will likely fall.

The basic tool, however, to lower costs is to optimize market risk models. Given the introduction of stressed value at risk, banks should identify the core drivers for market risk in their portfolio and hedge them to reduce stressed-VAR exposure. Härle *et al.* (2010) add that the same hedging operation can be performed at different levels in the aggregate for a subportfolio and even for individual positions. Given the new regulation and the macroprudential part of it that consists of stressing the measured risk with respect to some changes in parameters, the problem becomes how to neutralize the cost of eventual changes in parameters that are stressed to reduce capital expenses. This does not require shrinking the size of securities in portfolio, but only developing an appropriate hedging strategy by inventing some hedge between the assets. Of course, the supervision should oversee that all the hedging strategies proposed should be consistent with the proposed rules, but since these rules are becoming more and more complex, their compliance is open to many interpretations and negotiations.

The new measures are more penalizing for simple commercial banks that do not have enough resources to perform risk optimization strategies by setting up internal-based risk models. Moreover, the weights on retail banking and other off-balance sheet liquidity and credit lines that include traditional tools to finance commercial credit and foreign trade have been increased. It is clear that the Basel Committee's intention was to avoid a repeat of big banks lending to special purpose vehicles in order to avoid capital requirements, something that was very common before the financial crisis (see Citigroup as an example). Yet the same rules hold also for much more mundane liquidity and credit provisions, such as bill discounting and factoring that are used to finance business enterprises. A small commercial bank then has to increase the resources devoted to compliance with regulation and has presumably to increase the cost charged for very simple anticipations on receivables by firms. This is just an example of how measures considered beneficial for some banks may not be ideal for others.

The strict calculation of risks according to the exposure leads to a ratio of risk-weighted assets to total assets, which is very asymmetric in the EU. The core countries' banks have a ratio of risk-weighted assets to total assets much lower than the peripheral countries' banks. Consequently, the former have to contribute less capital than the latter. The difference may be due both to the composition of portfolios and to the adoption of an internal risk-based model instead of the standardized approach. Peripheral countries banks' have a business model based on loans, while northern and core countries banks' portfolios have more securities. Further, the use of internal-based models is more widespread in the northern and core countries banks than in the southern ones.[2]

Ferri and Rotondi (2016) conclude that Italian banks need more capital because they do not use internal models in calculating credit risk. They regress the variable credit risk exposure, defined as the ratio of risk-weighted assets to exposure at default for loans on various independent variables, among which is the internal model, and find that the use of internal models causes a decrease in the credit risk exposure. Italian banks are penalized because they do not use internal models to the same extent as French and German banks. Another study by Cannata *et al.* (2012) that uses Italian supervisory data produces a different conclusion. They find that the main determinant for capital expenses is not whether banks use the internal model or the standardized approach, but rather their business model. Banks that have mainly loans to corporate and small and medium enterprises (SMEs) as assets have higher capital needs than banks that have securities and interbank loans as assets. They conclude that the difference in capital needs does not depend on the model, standardized versus internal, but on the portfolio composition.

Now after some years of costly passage to the new regulatory framework the fragility of the new rules are emerging and new changes are being proposed by the Basel Committee to overcome the shortcomings of the new risk weights and the diffusion of risk-weighted optimization strategies (BCBS, 2013, 2016). However, the main changes proposed by the Basel Committee (the package is vulgarly denominated Basel IV) concern only higher minimum default weightings for the banking book in the calculation of capital requirements. All European countries are strongly arguing against their application and at the moment the deal has not yet been concluded. Germany even threatened to withdraw unilaterally from the agreement. As of February 2017, no agreement has been reached after two meetings on the issue and the question remains on the agenda.

Other macroprudential measures

Beyond the risk-weighted capital requirements, the Basel Committee has introduced new measures that show concern not only about the evaluation of the risk added by any incremental new exposure but also about the total risk, which, presumably, is not the sum of the risks of the single exposures. These measures include a leverage ratio, which is vulgarly described as the ratio of capital Tier 1 and 2 to total assets, although in reality total assets are weighted here, too, and the weightings are important for translating off-balance sheet items into credit equivalent. It also introduced a countercyclical capital buffer and a supplementary capital charge for systemic important institutions. For the latter it is allowed to issue as a form of capital new bonds that are convertible into capital when capital falls below a certain threshold.

Furthermore, as a macroprudential measure the Basel Committee has introduced the carrying out of stress tests by the supervisory authorities that should control the resiliency of the financial institutions to various imagined stress situations and ask for corrective measures in case they do not pass the tests. These practices should prevent the stress situations by urging capital injections before the difficulties occur. So, behind all these new tools and practices, the notion of systemic risk is explicitly mentioned, and it seems that systemic risk as a risk that is other than the sum of individual risk exposures is acknowledged. If we examine each of these measures one by one, however, it is clear that they do not decrease the risk arising from interconnectedness and debt deflation tendencies, but rather increase it through various channels.

The leverage ratio should be more important to mitigate financial fragility as recognized by Minsky, who was keen to propose measures that decrease leverage by banks and thus the danger of crises and potential state intervention. On one hand, the leverage ratio proposed is very low – only 3 per cent – in relation to total assets. On the other hand, the way to calculate it is highly discretionary for banks that have securities and derivatives as assets. The credit conversion factors can be lowered by carefully constructed models. All that is needed are data and mathematical applications. So, in the end the leverage ratio can be gamed in the same way that risk-weighted capital requirements were. The more likely this is, the deeper will be the changes proposed in reporting and hedging possibilities.

Other measures, such as the capital surcharge for systemic important financial institutions, are burdened with potential systemic risk implications due to the introduction of new financial tools that should count as Tier 2 capital. Thus, these measures rather than thwarting the natural instability of the system could cause wild price fluctuations linked to debt deflation processes. Paradoxically, measures designed to relieve the burden of the state during financial crises would aggravate it.

The stress tests and other special interventions are indeed based on the same microprudential apparatus in which apparently systemic risk does not exist and the macroeconomic scenario in which they are embedded consists of a model in which finance does not exist and equilibrium is always reached by default. The consequences of changes in aggregate demand on output and thus on balance-sheet relations default rates and interest rates payments are not included in the models used for the stress test exercises.

The leverage ratio

The definition of leverage ratio and how to calculate it

According to many practitioners and academics, the leverage ratio is a simpler tool than risk-based capital requirements because the denominator of the ratio is supposed to be total assets rather than a fraction of it, which depends on the weights assigned and on the portfolio composition. It would be very simple to calculate it just by dividing a measure of capital (Tier 1 in the EU application) by total assets, which, one might guess, are based on information publicly available in the accounts.

The leverage ratio would thus be easier to calculate and more difficult to be gamed than normal risk-weighted capital requirements. Unfortunately, it is not so. While the definition of capital that stays on the numerator depends on the legislation, the number to be entered into the denominator is not easily available information that can be obtained just by browsing the accounts. Even the expression 'total assets' has no unanimous meaning, as it can point to assets in the accounting definition (according to the International Financial Reporting Standards (IFRS) or General Accepted Accounting Principles (GAAPS)), or to assets in the taxing definition, or in the prudential definition. For example, in the EU, assets that have been temporarily sold in a repurchase agreement and have become legally owned by the buyer (lender) are not part of the accounting assets of the buyer, but are still recorded in the accounting assets of the seller (borrower).

The definition of leverage in the Capital Requirements Regulation, 2013 is as follows:

> 'leverage' means the relative size of an institution's assets, off-balance sheet obligations and contingent obligations to pay or to deliver or to provide collateral, including obligations from received funding, made commitments, derivatives or repurchase agreements, but excluding obligations which can only be enforced during the liquidation of an institution, compared to that institution's own funds;

(Regulation 575/2013/EU, Article 93)

The leverage ratio in the EU legislation has a complicated story (see EBA, 2016a). The calculation of the leverage ratio defined in Article 429 of the CRR was amended in a Delegated Act 15 (European Commission, 2015) of the Commission to incorporate revisions published by the BCBS in January 2014 (BCBS, 2014a). The amendment followed a report (EBA, 2014) that highlighted the differences in the interpretations of Article 429 of Regulation (EU) No. 575/2013 for the calculation of the leverage ratio and proposed to align the leverage ratio to BCBS (2014b). In turn, the leverage ratio calculation that had been proposed in BCBS (2013) had been changed after consultations with the industry. The EU definition of leverage ratio takes into account some additional technical specificities due to the wider scope of the application of EU regulations. While the Basel standards are designed for large, internationally active institutions, the EU framework applies to all credit institutions at both consolidated and individual level, as well as to certain types of investment firms.

The numerator should be capital defined as common equity Tier 1. The denominator must be carefully calculated by adding to balance sheets assets off-balance sheets items that must be multiplied by a parameter that depends on supervisory discretion. Besides that, derivatives and securities financing assets may be subject to netting and thus decrease their weight in the calculation with regard to deposits and loans that by definition cannot be netted out. So, the leverage ratio rather than being a simple tool is weighted, too, and the way its calculation must be performed has been at the centre of a discussion between the representatives of the industry, the Basel Commission and European Banking Authority. The main difference between the risk-weighted and the non-risk-weighted ratio is that the former should not allow netting. However, this basic principle stated in BCBS (2013) has been challenged with success by representatives of the industry.

Netting is allowed to calculate the exposures to derivatives where an eligible bilateral netting contract is available. According to BCBS (2014b, p. 19), to calculate the leverage ratio derivatives exposure must consist of the replacement value plus the potential future exposure. For a single derivative exposure not covered by an eligible bilateral netting contract, the amount to be included in the exposure measure is determined as follows:

exposure measure = replacement cost (RC) + add-on

where
RC = the replacement cost of the contract (obtained by marking to market), where the contract has a positive value.
add-on = an amount for PFE over the remaining life of the contract calculated by applying an add-on factor to the notional principal amount of the derivative.

The add-on factors are established by the regulators according to the maturity and the perceived riskiness of the product – for example, add-ons on credit default swaps are higher than on other products. When there is a bilateral eligible netting contract, then both the replacement cost and the potential future exposure have to be calculated on a net basis. In the calculation of prospective future value, banks have to use in the standardized approach add-on values provided by regulators on different items' notional volumes that reflect the historical volatilities in the value of the tool; thus, again, the ergodic principle is used that the future will be like the past. For example, since the credit default swap (CDS) has proved particularly problematic in the global financial crisis (GFC), then the add-on factor for them will be higher than for other derivatives. This means that regulators are always fighting the last crisis. This may well validate the forecast as the expansion of certain segments of the derivatives universe may also benefit from low past volatilities values and thus lower regulatory add-ons.

If the bank opts for an internal risk-based model, then the methodologies for calculating the prospective future exposures are more refined. The latter may be calculated by using the traditional value-at-risk methodology, where all possible future outcomes are considered and an average is calculated as well as a variance. Under this approach, it is assumed that future values of variables are calculable, although with a margin of error. Alternatively, it is possible to use historical past data and calculate averages out of them.

Even if these discussed statistical measures for prospective future exposure (PFE) were reliable, then the problem arises on how the risk calculation is framed. For example, for a long maturity interest rate swap linked to short-term interest rates, it would have not been reasonable to assume negative values for interest rates. Now that negative values for interest rates are a reality, this means that losses on the side of fixed-rate payers in the swap are much higher than those expected using either historical data or VAR models. This is just an example of how estimates based on past values can be wrong in a world in which everything changes very rapidly and in which ergodic principles do not apply.

Netting is now allowed for securities financing transactions, too, after a long process of defining and modifying the rules. It is not allowed to net accounting exposures of Securities Financing Transactions (SFTs), but it is allowed to net accounting cash payables and receivables arising out of them. The treatment for SFTs in Basel III consists of the following two components:

a)   A measure of the accounting (cash) payables and (cash) receivables. Banks may net accounting payables and receivables for transactions between the same counterparties if certain supervisory netting criteria are met. These criteria are based on both IFRS and US GAAP netting rules to ensure international comparability:

- transactions have the same explicit final settlement date;
- the right to set off the amount owed to the counterparty with the amount owed by the counterparty is legally enforceable both currently in the normal course of business and under the following circumstances: (i) default; (ii) insolvency; and (iii) bankruptcy; and

- the counterparties intend to settle net, settle simultaneously, or the transactions are subject to a settlement mechanism that results in the functional equivalent of net settlement, that is, the cash flows of the transactions are equivalent, in effect, to a single net amount on the settlement date.

b) A measure of counterparty credit risk representing any over-collateralisation (the total fair value of securities and cash lent to a counterparty less the total fair value of cash and securities received from the same counterparty, floored at zero.

(EBA, 2014, pp. 15–16)

This was the exposure method in Basel III after the revision BCBS (2014b). The reason why the no-netting approach was removed is that many commentators warned against the risk of a falling liquidity in the repo market and the possibility of returning to unsecured and therefore riskier transactions. The Basel Committee in its revised version of the rule (BCBS, 2014b) accepted the objections and allowed netting for payables and receivables linked to securities financing transactions (EBA, 2014, pp. 16–17). Among securities financing transactions, the repo market is the most important.

While both derivatives and securities financing transactions (mainly repurchase agreements) can be netted, off-balance sheets items cannot be netted out, but they must be entered into the exposure at default at the denominator of the ratio by using conversion factors, which are actually weights. The higher the conversion factor, the higher will be the contribution to the exposure at default and the lower the leverage ratio, so banks will also have to optimize these weights to get the return on equity they wish to reach. Off-balance sheets items may be credit lines granted to non-bank financial institutions, as is usual in the securitization of loans, or simply trade financing both domestic and foreign. The weights on these items have been increased in the risk-weighted capital requirements to avoid credit granting to special-purpose vehicles that were used to securitize loans and that during the crisis transferred the losses to their lenders.

The increase in conversion factors both for risk-weighted capital requirements and for the leverage ratio seems to have favoured the expansion of the realm of securitizations rather than having reduced it. This may have contributed to the crisis of correspondent banking that is unfolding (World Bank-RD, 2015). Correspondent banking is very important for trade credit. In World Bank (2015), a survey has been conducted among international banks, local banks and banking authorities throughout the world on the types of products for which the demise of correspondent banking has caused more problems. For local/regional banks, the decline in foreign CBRs (Correspondent Banking Relationship) of financial institutions affected their ability to access three products/services: cheque clearing, clearing and settlement services, and trade finance (letters of credit). More generally, however, after the great financial crisis, new realms for securitizations have been opened. Among them, trade receivables, health insurance-related expenses, fee payments and utilities bills have been opened to securitizations. All these claims now back asset-backed securities (Bryan and Rafferty, 2014; Assonime – CEPR, 2015).

The conversion factors for trade credit in the EU leverage ratio are still being discussed. The principle that governs them is that the credit extensions that are unconditionally cancellable have a low (10–20 per cent) conversion factor while those that are not so retain a full 100 per cent conversion factor. As EBA (2016a) admits, it is difficult to define what is unconditionally cancellable and what is not, so there is some room here too for regulatory arbitrage. Thus, it can be inferred that there is enough space for risk optimization within the leverage ratio, too. This space will become wider as the accounting rules and both the standardized and the internal-based model of calculating derivatives and securities financing exposures are again being changed in order to become more risk-sensitive.

The rules contained in BCBS (2014b) are being revised to take into account the change in the way to calculate derivatives exposure from the current exposure method of Basel II, which is also called mark-to-the-market method, to the SA–CCR (Standardized Approach–Central Counterparty Risk). At present, the Basel III leverage ratio framework uses the Current Exposure Method (CEM) to measure the replacement cost (RC) and the potential future exposure (PFE) for derivative transactions, with certain leverage ratio-specific modifications to limit the recognition of collateral. This approach captures the exposure arising from the underlying of the derivative contract and counterparty credit risk (CCR) exposure. However, when the Basel III leverage ratio framework was published in January 2014, the Committee noted that it would consider replacing the Basel III leverage ratio framework's use of the CEM with an alternative approach adopted under the risk-based framework. In March 2014, the Committee published the standardized approach for measuring counterparty credit risk exposures to specify the measurement of derivative exposures for risk-based capital purposes in replacement of both the CEM and the Standardized Method (SM).

The new framework for replacing current exposure method is based on the notion of hedging set. This will be used also for the standardized approach not only for the internal method, so in order to calculate both replacement cost and potential future exposures the bank has to build hedging sets with some characteristics. Hedging is possible within the same asset class and the same maturity totally. Instead, it is allowed only partially across assets and maturities.

The calculation is very technical and complicated, but the more complicated the more useful it will be for risk management officials of big institutions. By summing up data, it is possible to construct many possible hedging sets in order to minimize regulatory costs. As Jonsson and Ronnlund (2014) argue, the exposure at default will be lower with the new approach than with the older one; in fact, CEM allows recognition of netting benefits up to 60 per cent, whereas the SA–CCR, due to its incorporated delta, can recognize full netting benefits in the add-on within the hedging sets. They conclude that a change from CEM to SA–CCR could result in lower minimum capital requirements in general for mid-sized and large institutions that have netting sets large enough to benefit from the increased netting. Instead, for small institutions or institutions with fewer trades per counterparty, on the other hand, the effect might be the opposite. They find further that the portfolio composition is more important under SA–CCR than under CEM. Therefore, banks could try to optimize their portfolios with respect to exposure at default to a higher extent under SA–CCR than under CEM. If the same method with some modifications is applied to the higher leverage ratio, this will allow banks with big derivatives and securities financing books to calculate a lower exposure at default and therefore a higher leverage ratio. The key to this minimization of the weight of derivatives is simply the familiar process of netting and hedging. Derivatives with the same counterparty with opposite values are allowed to be netted out if contracts including safe harbours and early termination rights in case of defaults are valid. This means that since most derivatives are traded among the biggest banks and financial institutions, they are jointly benefiting from their own reciprocal involvement in the business. Moreover, the amount to be included in the ratio would further be lowered if in their internal models the banks can use hedging possibilities. Since hedging is supposed to reduce the risk, then any derivative that is used to hedge another risk entailed in an asset on the balance sheets must be considered in the joint relation. That is the risk of the derivative and that of the asset that is supposed to hedge cancel each other. Banks can therefore use hedging portfolios to drastically lower the supposed risk of derivatives holding. This again eases enormously the capital requirement (both risk-weighted and leverage ratio) of big banks dealing in complex products as they have within themselves a myriad possibilities of constructing portfolios that would comply with the regulation. The regulation implicitly assumes that hedging always works.

Too much hope in this new tool?

In this perspective it is difficult to hope that the leverage ratio will constrain the leverage of big banks. Avgouleas (2015) argues that an unweighted leverage ratio is simple to apply and monitor, and eliminates regulatory arbitrage, the bank's ability to engage in risk-weighted optimization. As we have seen, given the way in which the ratio has to be calculated, room for risk optimization is plenty and growing with the scheduled application of the new accounting standards in the future.

Moreover, given the level of the ratio, 3 per cent is not binding for the majority of banks in the EU (see EBA, 2016a). An increase in the proposed ratio higher than 3 per cent could create problems even to the smaller or commercial banks. Research by EBA (2016a) shows that currently commercial banks and smaller banks would not be constrained by a 3 per cent leverage ratio, while some investment banks with a high share of low-risk assets (low risk, according to Basel criteria and approved internal models) would. The same would not hold for higher levels of leverage ratio — for example, 4–5 per cent to 6–8 per cent. If leverage ratio levels higher than 4 per cent were applied, supposing that the adjustment was carried out by exposure reduction only (called extreme adjust-ment scenario, in contrast to a moderate adjustment scenario where the ratio is reached by both raising capital, 50 per cent, and cutting exposure for the remain-ing 50 per cent), loans portfolios to SME and other non-financial corporations loans could be cut, too (EBA, 2016a, p. 197). The legislation so enacted, particu-larly with the introduction of new accounting and reporting methods and with the replacement of the CEM with the SA–CRR, will encourage too-big-to-fail banks to become even bigger and to continue trading among themselves, as they can, through netting, relieve the capital they need.

A wiser way of enacting the ratio could have been considered. The leverage ratio could have been modelled according to the size of the banks as it has been made in the US:

> Specific attention is drawn here to the one-size-fits-all issue. In view of the (i) much higher relevance in Europe of banking finance, compared to markets, and (ii) the very high relevance of small and medium enterprises (SMEs) and of small banks credit flows to this vital sector of the EU economy,[8] it might have been expected that banks of modest size should have been given preferential treatment in Europe.[9] Somewhat paradoxi-cally, this is not the case.
>
> (Masera, 2013, p. 396)

The EU did not apply the modular approach pursued in the US because this would have been in contrast to the free competition principle according to which every bank should not have a preferential treatment over any other. This is also the reason for the initial adoption of the Basel Committee rules at the EU level for all banks, although they had been designed only for internationally active banks. Masera (2013) argues that the strict application of the Basel rules to all EU banks will distort competition in favour of the too-big-to-fail banks rather than create a common playing-field.

Some learning from the Swiss application of the rule would have been useful, too. The Swiss regulatory authority that introduced the leverage ratio in 2008 excluded the whole domestic loan book from the denominator of the ratio concerned about the impact of the ratio on loans during a depression (Avgouleas, 2015, p. 33). This exclusion was then removed in 2013. The Swiss leverage ratio has been applied only to the two largest banks, Credit Suisse and UBS, and it was designed in order to be always binding for banks (Kellermann and Schlag, 2013).

To sum up, the leverage ratio that will be applied in the European Union is different in many aspects from that applied in the US and Switzerland. The differ-ences seem to worsen its impact and to leave more room for risk-weighted opti-mization. In the EU, the leverage ratio has been planned to be applied later than in other jurisdictions (US, UK, Switzerland) as it will apply only as of 1 January 2018. This has allowed most banks to continue their business as usual. It is the same for all banks irrespective of size and business model. It has been consciously planned in order not to be binding.

Total loss-absorbing capacity in the EU

Another capital measure that has been proposed at the international level by the Financial Stability Board is the issue of a special type of capital that should be converted into equity automatically if a resolution procedure starts or even before it is implemented as a precautionary measure. This would consist of a total loss-absorbing capacity that would require minimum required eligible liabilities, own funds and liquidity by financial institutions. The modalities of the minimum required eligible liabilities (MREL) in the EU are still being discussed (see EBA, 2016b). It is not clear which type of securities will be part of the cushion of bail-in-able ones and what stays at the denominator, whether total liabilities and own funds as recommended by the Financial Stability Board (FSB) or other factors. EBA (2016b) proposes putting at the denominator the risk-weighted assets so that both capital requirements and MREL are calculated, having the same entity at the denominator. Needless to say, in that case the risk-weighting optimization will affect also the MREL and total loss-absorbing capacity, too. In the following, we will discuss the main features of the MREL project as proposed by the FSB without entering into the details of the EU implementation as they are still in a phase of definition. The basic idea is that instead of equity and retained earnings, banks should be allowed to issue new bonds that could be convertible into capital in case of shortfalls.

Another way of avoiding systemic consequences is to introduce new financial instruments that are supposed to cover bankruptcy risk. These are not credit default swaps but rather convertible bonds that must be issued by too-big-to-fail banks in order to cover prospective losses during a resolution procedure. These bonds amount to another supplementary type of capital called Tier 2 capital. Tier 2 capital is not common equity, but bonds that can be converted into equity. These bonds, however, cannot be bought by other financial institutions because this would increase counterparty risk. They are sold, therefore, to other entities, hopefully not retail customers, but pension funds and insurance companies. This, of course, increases the interconnectedness because it means that in case of the failure of a bank, not only its shareholders, bondholders and unsecured depositors will be asked to contribute, but also pensioners and insured people. These new tools again increase the already wide menu of financial innovations. The impact of the new rules on pension funds and insurance companies is that they will flood their balances with derivatives that are mandatory to cover risks and probably new CoCo bonds, and actively participate on the lender's side in the thriving repo market while rehypothecating collateral to enhance returns. This means that in a crisis scenario, the contagion would touch all the institutions in the market rather than just banks:

> Bail-in securities may make sense for an idiosyncratic bank failure—like the 1995 collapse of Baring Brothers, which was the result of a single rogue trader. But they do not make sense in the more common and intractable case where many banks get into trouble at roughly the same time as the assets they

own go bad. On such occasions these securities, which may also have encouraged excessive lending, either will inappropriately shift the burden of bank resolution on to ordinary pensioners or, if held by others, will bring forward and spread a crisis. Either way they will probably end up costing taxpayers no less and maybe more. In this regard, fool's gold is an apt description.

(Persaud, 2014, p. 2)

The new regulation will probably require G-SIB (Global Systemically Important Banks) to hold capital ratio in the range of 20–25 per cent, but they may issue these new bonds instead of equity or using retained earnings. They have already started doing so in advance and have issued €150 million of these bonds. A share of 80 per cent of the bonds has been issued by European banks. These bonds automatically become capital if minimum capital requirements fall below a certain trigger level that is specified in the contract. This is a way of encouraging assets expansion by allowing new forms of automatic recapitalization or anticipated recapitalizations. As Persaud (2014) observes, the long-term holders of the new instruments, given their long maturity, should be long-term investors and the securities issued by banks, in fact, have maturities of 5–10 years. He adds that, before the financial crisis, if banks had a total loss absorbing capacity of 25 per cent of risk-weighted assets in so-called bail-in securities, they would more likely have had more assets in their books rather than less. The situation would not improve, however, if the bail-in securities were sold to short-term investors. Most of these short-term investors, like hedge funds, want to exploit short-term gains but are ready to sell assets very quickly if losses are expected. They would, if a crisis were approaching, dump them on the market, causing a heavy fall in price, a downgrading by rating agencies and another fall in price. The possibility that a downgrade by rating agencies could start a forced sale of assets, a decline in their prices and a full-blown crisis had already been envisaged by Minsky while dealing with the effects of securitization on the financial structure (see Minsky, 2008).

In the end, Persaud (2014) warns, 'bail-in securities will bring forward and spread a crisis, not snuff it out'. The issue of these new securities will increase financial fragility not only because of interconnectedness but because the assets that are held in portfolio will be highly dependent on the cycle. These measures will not constrain leverage by big banks but may even increase it. The leverage ratio in the way in which it will be calculated is not able to stop leverage. It will simply increase the burden for traditional banking systems whose main task is lending to non-financial companies. The question is worrying because the main issuers of this new tool, though not yet introduced in the legislation, are European banks which have a higher leverage than US banks. The events that followed in October 2016 the announcement of a US$14 millions fine by the US to the Deutsche Bank seem to confirm Persaud's fears. The price of contingent convertibles (CoCos) issued by Deutsche Bank fell in the expectations either of a missed coupon payments and/or of a trigger of the conversion. Of course, the market for these CoCos was very limited in size and Deutsche Bank was ready to be supported by liquidity provision by the European Central Bank in case of need.

However, if the market were as big as the proposed increase in total loss-absorbing capacity would imply, the consequences would have been worse. The possibility of issuing this new type of bond would thus allow European banks to maintain or increase existing leverage, and would make the financial system even more fragile by increasing the share of risky assets in the portfolio of other financial institutions.

Decreasing leverage would instead require acting on the main lever, repo transactions and rehypothecation that feed leverage. Rehypothecation is limited in the US but not in the EU, and repo markets are shrinking there because of the new rules on triparty repo that have been introduced and because of the Fed borrowing through repo from non-bank financial institutions like money market mutual funds that drain liquidity from the market. So, important actors in the market like banks intermediating in the triparty repo and money market mutual funds lending through repo have withdrawn from it. In the European Union, banks – and particularly big ones – are still very active and none of the rules enacted so far or those scheduled to be implemented in the future will impact on it. Repo are usually netted so their weight in the leverage ratio is negligible and the possibility of repoing an asset is equated to the asset being liquid in the definition of highly liquid assets while their financing need as an asset in the net stable funding ratios is low. The issue of CoCo bonds for regulatory reasons would nurture a feedback loop in prices of securities and increase interconnectedness. Feedback loops in prices do not thwart the instability of the system but enhance it, according to Minsky.

In order to construct the hedging sets that minimize capital requirements, big banks may use everything from clients' assets under custodia, to securities lending, to received collateral in repo transaction that has not been rehypothecated. The combinatorial possibilities are infinite. The data-processing and information-technology resources are essential to that task. The bigger and the more interconnected banks are, the more likely they are to save regulatory capital. The ability to move assets between parent company and affiliates, or between the client's portfolio and proprietary ones may help in building false hedging sets. Regulators should dig very deeply in all the presented data, arguably a great number, to find proof of fraud. There is anecdotal evidence that banks transform losses to gains by manipulating the accounts and by changing the internal-based model that they use (Haldane, 2014; US Senate, 2013).[3] The amount of data to be collected and processed is so big that fraud has a low probability of being proved and pursued. The London Whale scandal received attention because of the big losses that this strategy caused, otherwise the strategy would have probably been continued.

Conclusions

In this chapter, the main shortcomings of the revised capital weights have been highlighted. While the single weights may be higher for some selected assets that have performed badly in the period before the financial crisis, the possibility of hedging and constructing internal-based models of risk favours the big institutions, which are the ones whose business model is the farthest from traditional lending. On the contrary, small banks are disadvantaged because they do not have the funds to hire the staff and build the models that would allow them to save capital.

The leverage ratio, the new measure that should complement risk-weighted capital requirements, suffers from many problems of implementation. It has been designed, like any other measure in the Basel III version of the new regulation, to be applied to all banks irrespective of their size and business model. However, as it has been shown, while the measure can be easily accomplished by the big banks, given its very low threshold value and the possibility of netting and hedging that has been allowed for certain assets, it may pose problems in future for small banks. The leverage ratios that have been implemented in the United States and Switzerland are more focused on constraining big banks' expansion. In the US, the leverage ratio, like any other measure, is modelled according to the size of the bank; in Switzerland, it applies only to the two biggest banks and for a period loans have been totally excluded from the assets in the denominator of the ratio.

Notes

1   The text of BCBS (2014a, p. 207) is:

> First, calculate the hypothetical capital requirement of the CCP due to its counterparty credit risk exposures to all of its clearing members and their clients. This is calculated using the formula for KCCP:

$$K_{CCP} = \sum_{CM\ i} EAD_i \cdot RW \cdot capital\ ratio$$

> *RW is a risk weight of 20 per cent.* Capital ratio means 8 per cent. *EADi* is the exposure amount of the CCP to CM 'i', including both the CM's own transactions and client transactions guaranteed by the CM, and all values of collateral held by the CCP (including the CM's prefunded default fund contribution) against these transactions, relating to the valuation at the end of the regulatory reporting date before the margin called on the final margin call of that day is exchanged. The sum is over all clearing member accounts. [emphasis added]

2   For an estimate on the role of internal-based risk models on credit risk exposure for Italian banks in relation to other countries, see Ferri and Rotondi (2016).
3   The more recent case is the scandal concerning Morgan Chase derivatives losses in its London division:

> In December 2011, JPMorgan Chase instructed the CIO to reduce its Risk Weighted Assets (RWA) to enable the bank, as a whole, to reduce its regulatory capital requirements. In response, in January 2012, rather than dispose of the high risk assets in the SCP (Synthetic Credit Portfolio) – the most typical way to reduce RWA – the CIO launched a trading strategy that called for purchasing additional long credit derivatives to offset its short derivative positions and lower the CIO's RWA that way.
> (United States Senate, 2013, p. 3)

Actually, what the CIO did was hedging its hedges, which was dismantling the original hedge but was useful to save capital and lower risk-weighted assets. In order to achieve that result, the CIO changed the internal model VAR.

References

Assonime – CEPR (2015) Restarting European long-term investment finance. A Green Paper discussion document.

Avgouleas, E. (2015) Bank leverage ratios and financial stability: A micro- and macroprudential perspective. Levy Economics Institute of Bard College, New York, Working Paper No. 849.

Basel Committee on Banking Supervision (BCBS) (2013) Regulatory consistency assessment programme: Analysis of risk-weighted assets for credit risk in the banking book.

BCBS (2014a) Capital requirements for bank exposures to central counterparties. Available at: www.bis.org/publ/bcbs282.pdf (accessed 28 February 2017).

BCBS (2014b) Basel III leverage ratio framework and disclosure requirements.

BCBS (2016) Reducing variation in credit risk-weighted assets – constraints on the use of internal model approaches. Consultative document.

Behn, M., Haselmann, R. and Vig, V. (2016) The limits of model-based regulation, European Central Bank Working Paper No. 1928.

Bryan, D. and Rafferty, M. (2014) Financial derivatives as social policy beyond crisis, *Sociology*, 48(5): 887–903.

Cannata, F., Casellina, S. and Guidi, G. (2012) Inside the labyrinth of Basel risk-weighted assets: How not to get lost. Bank of Italy Occasional Paper No. 132.

European Banking Authority (EBA) (2014) Report on impact of differences in leverage ratio definitions.

EBA (2016a) EBA report on the leverage ratio requirements under article 511 of the CRR. EBA-Op-2016-13.

EBA (2016b) Interim report on MREL. Report on implementation and design of the MREL framework. EBA-Op-2016-12,|19 July.

European Commission (2015) Commission delegated regulation (EU) 2015/62 of 10 October 2014 amending regulation (EU) no. 575/2013 of the European Parliament and of the Council with regard to the leverage ratio, *Official Journal of the European Union*, 17 January.

Ferri, G. and Rotondi, Z. (2016) Misure del rischio di credito nel finanziamento delle imprese e incidenza dei prestiti in default: Un'analisi comparata per le banche Europee. Mofir Working Paper No. 122.

Haldane, A. (2014) Constraining discretion in bank regulation. In C. Goodhart, D. Gabor, J. Vestergaard and I. Erturk (eds) *Central Banking at a Crossroads: Europe and Beyond*. London and New York: Anthem Press, pp. 15–32.

Härle, P., Lüders, E., Pepanides, T., Pfetsch, S. and Poppensieker, T. (2010) Basel III and European Banking: Its impact, how banks might respond and the challenges of implementation, McKinsey Working Paper on Risk, No. 26.

Jonsson, S. and Ronnlund, B. (2014) The new standardized approach for measuring counterparty credit risk. Master's thesis project, Royal Institute of Technology, Stockholm.

Kellermann, K. and Schlag, C.-H. (2013) Occupy risk weighting: How the minimum leverage ratio dominates capital requirements—A Swiss example, *Journal of Financial Regulation and Compliance*, 21: 353.

Le Leslé, V. and Avramova, S. (2012) Revisiting risk-weighted assets: Why do RWAs differ across countries and what can be done about it? IMF WP 12/90.

Leising, M. (2014) Derivatives rules softened in victory for banks, 10 April. Available at: www.bloomberg.com/news/2014-04-10/derivatives-rules-softened-in-victory-for-banks.html (accessed 5 November 2016).

Mariathasan, M. and Merrouche, O. (2014) The manipulation of Basel risk-weights, *Journal of Financial Intermediation*, 23(3): 300–21.

Masera, R. (2013) US Basel III Final Rule on banks' capital requirements: A different-size-fits-all approach. *PSL Quarterly Review*, 66(267): 387–402.

Minsky, H. (2008) Securitization, The Levy Economics Institute of Bard College Policy Note 2008/2.

Persaud, A. (2014) Why bail-in securities are fool's gold. Peterson Institute for International Economics, Policy Brief Number PB14–23.

Regulation (EU) No. 575/2013 of the European Parliament and of the Council of 26 June 2013 on prudential requirements for credit institutions and investment firms and amending Regulation (EU) No. 648/2012. Text with EEA relevance. *Official Journal of the European Union*, 176: 1–337, 27 June.

United States Senate (2013) Permanent Subcommittee on Investigations Committee on Homeland Security and Governmental Affairs. JPMorgan Chase: Whale trades: A case history of derivatives risks and abuses. Majority and Minority Staff Report.

World Bank Group and International Bank for Reconstruction and Development (2015) Withdrawal from correspondent banking: where, why, and what to do about it. Report by the Finance and Markets Global Practice of the World Bank Group. Available at: http://documents.worldbank.org/curated/en/2015/11/25481335/withdraw-correspondent-Banking (accessed January 2017).

4 Liquidity coverage and net stable funding ratios

Introduction

In this chapter two additional metrics of the new regulation will be described. Their methods of calculations will be examined in detail.

These two metrics are inspired by the events that have displayed themselves during the great financial crisis – that of markets becoming suddenly illiquid and of the disappearance of short-term finance for banks and other financial institutions. The problems that emerged during the crisis are thought to be dealt with by the imposition of a share of high liquid assets over total assets and of a required stable funding for assets as well. Although the word systemic is sometimes employed in official sources to describe some of the measures, their calculation and implementation are based on the microeconomic calculation of a liquidity risk and of a funding risk, against which some liquidity or funding reserve must be held. This in turn totally ignores the problems with interconnections in the market. Still worse, in order to calculate the extent of the liquidity and funding risk that an institution is subject to, the whole apparatus of weights, already used in the definition of capital requirements, is used again in order to respect even in that case the sacred principle of proportionality. The weights as always depend on external circumstances, subjective valuations and a lot of arbitrariness. The whole exercise, as some representatives of the industry have highlighted, rests on a contradiction, which is to try to increase liquidity and long-term funding by allowing at the same time those practices embedded in the legislation that undermine it.

The liquidity coverage ratio

According to the new legislation, the liquidity coverage ratio (LCR) is defined as the ratio of the stock of high-quality liquid assets over the total net cash outflows over the next 30 calendar days, which must be greater or equal to 100 per cent. During a period of stress, however, banks may have a lower value for the ratio. The ratio serves only as a prime line of defence against a possible liquidity crisis.

In the following paragraphs it will be explained in detail how to calculate the numerator and the denominator of the ratio.

How to calculate the numerator of the ratio

The numerator of the Liquidity Coverage Ratio is the 'stock of HQLA'. Under the standard, banks must hold a stock of *unencumbered* High Quality Liquid Assets (HQLA) to cover the total net cash outflows (as defined below) over a 30-day period under the prescribed stress scenario. In order to qualify as HQLA, assets should be liquid in markets during a time of stress and, ideally, be central bank eligible. The following sets out the characteristics that such assets should generally possess and the operational requirements that they should satisfy.

Definition of liquid assets is arbitrary as any asset can be liquid or illiquid, and depends on market conditions and the behaviour of the central bank. Moreover, as Keynes remarked, liquidity cannot hold for all units. If anyone tried to sell its assets, it would not succeed. Liquidity cannot apply to the whole market, but only to some operators in it.

The rationale of introducing such a measure is clearly explained by the Basel Committee:

> During the early 'liquidity phase' of the financial crisis that began in 2007, many banks – despite adequate capital levels – still experienced difficulties because they did not manage their liquidity in a prudent manner. The crisis drove home the importance of liquidity to the proper functioning of financial markets and the banking sector. Prior to the crisis, asset markets were buoyant and funding was readily available at low cost. The rapid reversal in market conditions illustrated how quickly liquidity can evaporate, and that illiquidity can last for an extended period of time. The banking system came under severe stress, which necessitated central bank action to support both the functioning of money markets and, in some cases, individual institutions.

(BCBS, 2013(2))

The report acknowledges that the main problem was liquidity, but the lack of liquidity is due to bad management by banks. Liquidity is related to the behaviour of individual institutions rather than to market characteristics, so banks have been compelled through new rules to care about liquidity by holding an amount of high liquid assets in relation to the outflows foreseen in the next 30 days.

The legislation is very long and detailed as it contains a list of the assets that must be considered liquid, as well as a detailed prescription of how the net outflows must be calculated (though part of these prescriptions may be changed by national regulators).

Assets are considered to be HQLA if they can be easily and immediately converted into cash at little or no loss of value. The liquidity of an asset depends on the underlying stress scenario, the volume to be monetized and the timeframe considered.

(BCBS, 2013, p. 24)

Although the liquidity is defined as the possibility of being converted into cash under a stress scenario, another definition appears in the following paragraphs (BCBS, 2013): to be used in a repo transaction to obtain cash. So being accepted as repo is equivalent to being liquid under a stress scenario.

It is noteworthy that repo is equivalent to being sold and receiving cash or a deposit as settlement. Yet, according to the repo contract agreements, selling an asset requires the promise to repurchase it at the termination date of the contract and, given that most of the contracts have very short maturity – between one night and one month (ICMA, 2017, p. 19) – this means that selling it requires immediate or quick repurchase. This is easy in normal times, but it is not in stress times. When the counterparty does not repurchase the security, the lender having received the security and having become the legal owner, can sell it on the market, but its price will depend on the conditions of the market. If everyone tries to sell it, there will be big oscillations in price. If the lender has already rehypothecated the asset, then it will have to unwind another contract and its counterparty will be compelled to do it too, thus starting a chain of selling.

The characteristics of liquid assets are so listed: low risk, easy and with certain valuation, low correlation with risk assets, listed on developed and recognized exchange, active and sizeable market (either sale or repo), low bid-ask spreads, high trading volumes, diversity of market participants, robust market infrastructure in place, low volatility of prices and spreads, and flight to quality.

As outlined by these characteristics, the test of whether liquid assets are of 'high quality' is that, by way of sale or repo, their liquidity-generating capacity is assumed to remain intact even in periods of severe idiosyncratic and market stress. Lower quality assets typically fail to meet that test.

(BCBS, 2013, p. 25)

High Quality Liquid Assets should be central bank eligible. HQLA comprise Level 1 and Level 2. Level 1 can be included without any cap and without haircut, while Level 2 assets, both A and B, can be included up to a certain cap and with a haircut foreseen in detail. A 15 per cent haircut is applied to the following Level 2A assets:

a) Marketable securities representing claims on or guaranteed by sovereigns, central banks, PSEs or multilateral development banks that satisfy all of the following conditions:[17]

- assigned a 20% risk weight under the Basel II Standardized Approach for credit risk;
- traded in large, deep and active repo or cash markets characterized by a low level of concentration;
- have a proven record as a reliable source of liquidity in the markets (repo or sale) even during stressed market conditions (i.e. maximum decline of price not exceeding 10% or increase in haircut not exceeding 10 percentage points over a 30-day period during a relevant period of significant liquidity stress); and
- not an obligation of a financial institution or any of its affiliated entities.

b) Corporate debt securities (including commercial paper) and covered bonds that satisfy all of the following conditions:

- in the case of corporate debt securities: not issued by a financial institution or any of its affiliated entities;
- in the case of covered bonds: not issued by the bank itself or any of its affiliated entities; either (i) have a long-term credit rating from a recognized external credit assessment institution (ECAI) of at least AA– or in the absence of a long term rating, a short-term rating equivalent in quality to the long-term rating; or (ii) do not have a credit assessment by a recognized ECAI but are internally rated as having a probability of default (PD) corresponding to a credit rating of at least AA–;
- traded in large, deep and active repo or cash markets characterized by a low level of concentration; and
- have a proven record as a reliable source of liquidity in the markets (repo or sale) even during stressed market conditions: i.e. maximum decline of price or increase in haircut over a 30-day period during a relevant period of significant liquidity stress not exceeding 10%.

(BCBS, 2013, p. 52)

A larger haircut is applied to the current market value of each Level 2B asset held in the stock of HQLA. For example, residential mortgage-backed securities, under certain conditions, may be included, subject to a 25 per cent haircut:

54. A larger haircut is applied to the current market value of each Level 2B asset held in the stock of HQLA. Level 2B assets are limited to the following:

(a) Residential mortgage backed securities (RMBS) that satisfy all of the following conditions may be included in Level 2B, subject to a 25% haircut:

- not issued by, and the underlying assets have not been originated by the bank itself or any of its affiliated entities;

- have a long-term credit rating from a recognized ECAI of AA or higher, or in the absence of a long-term rating, a short-term rating equivalent in quality to the long-term rating;
- traded in large, deep and active repo or cash markets characterized by a low level of concentration;
- have a proven record as a reliable source of liquidity in the markets (repo or sale) even during stressed market conditions, i.e. a maximum decline of price not exceeding 20% or increase in haircut over a 30-day period not exceeding 20 percentage points during a relevant period of significant liquidity stress;
- the underlying asset pool is restricted to residential mortgages and cannot contain structured products;
- the underlying mortgages are 'full recourse' loans (i.e. in the case of foreclosure the mortgage owner remains liable for any shortfall in sales proceeds from the property) and have a maximum loan-to-value ratio (LTV) of 80% on average at issuance; and
- the securitizations are subject to 'risk retention' regulations which require issuers to retain an interest in the assets they securitize.

(BCBS, 2013, p. 54)

Corporate debt securities may be included, also subject to a 50 per cent haircut if they are not issued by financial institutions, have a credit rating between A+ and BBB– or are internally rated in the same range, are traded in liquid markets and have a good record of liquidity even under stressed market conditions. Even common stocks can be included in HQLA if they are not issued by financial institutions, are traded in the stock exchanges, have a proven record of liquidity if their price has not fallen by more than 40 per cent or their haircut increased by the same percentage points in a period of 30 days during a liquidity episode.

It is foreseeable that, contrary to the spirit of the regulation, those assets that are recognized as liquid because of the rating or of the characteristics that are numerated in the catches of the norms will be also the most required. Their markets therefore will become distorted as the demand side may be bigger than the supply side. The power of rating agencies will increase as they will be able with their rating to determine the liquidity of the assets and their demand. Some corporate bonds and some government bonds will trade at a premium with respect to others. If a shortage of a particular bond or security occurs, there will be a rush to demand them, thus contributing to volatility and big oscillations in prices. In turn, the rise in prices will make their demand increase because of the regulation imposed on pension funds and insurance companies. The rate of discount to calculate future liabilities of pension funds is 'the market redemption yields on government or other high-quality bonds' (Woods, 2017, p. 158). So pension funds and insurance companies subject to fair value accounting regulation will be obliged to buy those high-quality assets exactly when their price is rising and their yield is falling, as the fall in yield will increase the amount of assets to be bought to guarantee the same expected return.

If the financial institutions reshuffle their portfolios in order to be compliant with the ratio, they will sell other assets that are not considered high-quality liquid ones according to the regulation to buy those that indeed have these characteristics. This means that the other residual assets will fall in value and their yield will increase in parallel unless a buyer of last resort for them intervenes, as is now the case with the European Central Bank purchases. That situation, however, will not last forever.

The European Central Bank (ECB) now buys the government bonds of all Eurozone countries according to the capital key in the capital of the same ECB, so the pressure on the lower rated bonds with respect to the highly rated ones is not visible. But once the programme has been completed, and if the new proposal of the reform of capital requirements for sovereign exposures[1] is approved, then the rush towards high-quality assets will mean a dumping of lower quality ones and the spread between stronger and weaker countries' governments bonds will re-emerge. Pension funds' and insurance companies' obligation to adjust their asset structure to the future expected liabilities, in which the yield of the high-quality bonds is the discount factor, will automatically create an excess demand for them that will make their prices rise again. This has already happened in the Netherlands (Dirks *et al.*, 2014). It could be called a bonds market inflation, to paraphrase the capital market inflation definition by Toporowski (1999).

The LCR depends also on the way the denominator is calculated, as will be shown in the next paragraph.

How to calculate the denominator of the ratio

In order to calculate the net cash outflows, one has to assign a runoff rate to liabilities. The runoff rate is 100% for committed credit lines to other financial institutions, as well as to other legal entities as special purpose vehicles. Trade finance has a low runoff rate of 5 per cent.

Inflows are conservatively considered if they stem from reverse repo or securities financing. It is assumed that they will be rolled over rather than being paid back at maturity. Also, deposits held at other financial institutions for operational motives custody and so on have a zero inflow in the calculation of net inflows.

> Derivatives cash inflows: the sum of all net cash inflows should receive a 100% inflow factor. The amounts of derivatives cash inflows and outflows should be calculated in accordance with the methodology described in paragraph 116.
>
> (BCBS, 2013, p. 158)

In the calculation of net outflows, interbank loans are penalized as well as contingent credit lines, while derivatives are not so penalized as only net exposures are considered, although during a crisis counterparties may not be reliable. The entries that are more penalized are interbank loans and other credit commitments to special purpose vehicles. On the other hand, repos between financial institutions are not penalized in so far as they are properly collateralized; unsecured funding instead has a high outflow ratio.

The reasoning underlying these prescriptions is not very clear as, on one hand, residential mortgages and other securitized products are included among the list of highly liquid assets if they are provided with adequate rating while, on the other hand, the credits or debts between the banks that originate the loans and the special purposes entities or trusts that intervene in the process of securitization are punished by imposing a very high outflow ratio in the denominator of the ratio. So it could be argued that the new regulation aims at encouraging banks to keep the residential mortgage-backed securities (RMBS) on their balance sheet, although this is not the general orientation of the whole Basel III package. Moreover, the regulation again trusts external rating agencies that should, with their rating, determine whether a mortgage-based security is liquid just as it was before the crisis of 2007.

The liquidity ratio does not penalize derivatives at all, thus implying that they must be considered always highly liquid. Although derivatives are not part of the high liquid assets and are therefore not included in the numerator, their outflow on the denominator is 100 per cent on a net basis, which is as usual very small. BCBS (2013) states that banks should calculate by using existing valuation methodologies the cash inflows and outflows expected. Then it adds that these inflows and outflows must be calculated on a net basis, when a valid master netting agreement is available. In this prescription there are many problems. For some derivatives, existing methodologies to calculate inflows and outflows are very weak – for example, for derivatives that are not traded on any market. Further, they are quite complex. It must be added that the acknowledgement of master netting agreements means that the net outflow on the denominator of the ratio will be very small. Finally, the regulation does not require consideration in the denominator outflows deriving from 'increased collateral needs due to market value movements or falls in value of collateral posted'. So this increased outflow deriving from the necessity of maintaining unchanged the value of the collateral will not contribute to the total outflow in the denominator. In BCBS (2013, p. 119), the last question is clarified. If the posted collateral is cash or a security with zero risk weight in Basel, then there is no need to increase the outflow and the denominator arises; if instead the collateral posted is a security with higher than zero risk weight, then '20% of the value of all such posted collateral, net of collateral received on a counterparty basis (provided that the collateral received is not subject to restrictions on reuse or rehypothecation)' will be added to the required HQLA. This means that if government bonds are not considered to be carrying an all-zero risk weight in Basel III, then not only will they be less useful as liquid assets for the numerator of the ratio, but they will contribute to an increase in the amount required of them if they are used as collateral for securities financing transactions. Once again, 20 per cent is just a number taken from nowhere; that 20 per cent is calculated on a net basis and the same collateral can be used to secure many transactions. Further, to make things more complicated, another requirement is added as to market valuation changes on derivatives or other transactions. It is required that another addition is made to the outflow on the denominator to take into account valuation changes of derivatives and other transactions that may cause an increase in posted collateral:

> Any outflow generated by increased needs related to market valuation changes should be included in the LCR calculated by identifying the largest absolute net 30-day collateral flow realised during the preceding 24 months. The absolute net collateral flow is based on both realised outflows and inflows.

Here the regulator requires that the banks add some outflow that may arise from the change in the value of the derivatives that may require an increase in collateral. The outflow due to market valuation changes should be considered by calculating the largest absolute collateral flow realized in 30 days over the last two years. This will require a small addition to the required liquidity.

Once again, the ergodic principle prevails that the future will be like the past. So the variation in derivatives valuation occurred in the last 24 months is considered a safe indicator for liquidity requirements. If the past two years are tranquil times, in which no serious crisis nor problems in the money market have occurred, the maximum net outflow will be very tiny; this, however, does not predict anything on future net outflows.

The implicit assumption is that derivatives are liquid by definition. The same netting out does not apply for other contractual relations. For example, a depositor who is also a borrower of a bank cannot net out its obligations automatically. If the bank has a deposit at another bank and also is indebted to the same bank because the latter has bought a bond issued by the former, the second bank cannot consider only the net value of the two transactions. The deposit will weigh with a high discount in the outflow in the denominator, while the bond purchased will not be considered highly liquid.

Conclusions about the theoretical underpinnings of the ratio

The main consequence of the introduction of the ratio is that banks that have more loans than securities are penalized because by definition loans are not liquid, so they are induced to securitize them in order to get liquid assets. Of course, in order to be considered liquid an adequate rating must be obtained, but it is still possible to pool together different types of loans and mix them in a way that warrants a high rating by relying on statistics on past default rates by borrowers. None of these techniques has been forbidden after the crisis, so it can be easily reused after the memory of past disasters vanishes.

Moreover, the reliance on repo markets as sources of liquidity in the ratio encourages further the use of secured funding based on collateral which, according to Minsky, was very likely to result in lower liquidity when the value of collateral falls and margin calls will compel financial institutions to sell assets (Minsky, 1982, 1987, 2008; Tropeano, 2010). Minsky (2008) writes:

> A need by holders of securities who are committed to protect the market value of their assets (such as mutual or money market funds, or trustees for

pension funds) may mean that a rise in interest rates will lead to a need by holders to make position by selling position, which can lead to a drastic fall in the price of the securities.

(Minsky, 2008, p. 3)

The treatment of liquidity in the new regulation is consistent with the main feature of the risk-weighted capital requirements in the EU version: the stress on proportionality between capital charge and measured risk. So here again the lack of liquidity beyond its systemic risk characteristics is treated as a new risk that can be measured exactly for each single financial institution. So no systemic risk, by which it is meant that the risk of the financial system as a whole might be higher than the sum of the exposures of single institutions, is taken into consideration. This is evident in the European Banking Authority (EBA) considerations on the new regulatory tool, as the EBA calls it explicitly liquidity risk, and states that it has played a big role in the financial crisis (EBA, 2013, p. 71). EBA (2013, p. 72) states that if all risks were properly priced, public funds would not be needed for bail-out transactions. So, regulation of liquidity risk is highly necessary. According to the EBA (2013), the new liquidity requirements would favour stable, traditional banking rather than non-traditional banking activities. Smaller banks would be less affected than investment banks, with universal banks falling in between.

In order to respect the proportionality mandate for this additional liquidity risk, the regulation, as has been clear in reporting the articles, has specified exactly the liquidity risk that each single asset in the portfolio of a bank poses, and then has compared this liquidity risk with the potential estimated outflows in the 30 days' chosen period. So the liquidity risk depends on the type of assets; it is higher for some assets, while it is lower for others and also depends on the outflows structure of the portfolio of the bank. Liquidity risk is lower if the rating attached to an asset is higher. This concerns the numerator of the ratio. This is the main method to assess liquidity risk in the legislation. The denominator calculates in detail the runoff rates for any security. The runoff rates are arbitrary and reflect normal conditions that were ruling in the past. For example, deposits that normally have low runoff rates may experience high runoff rates if a new law on the resolution of banks that penalizes depositors in the resolution procedure is approved.

On the other hand, complex structures of interconnectedness through derivatives and secured financing are not considered as impairing liquidity. This view is reflected in the weights of liquidity assigned in the numerator and in the runoff rates for assets in the denominator. In the regulation, it is explicitly stated that the LCR is designed to reduce *unsecured* interbank interconnectedness as this will reduce the 'too-interconnected-to-fail' problem in the European banking sector and interbank contagion. So the problem with interconnectedness is limited to the unsecured segment, while the secured one does not create any problem.

While this may be true for the single institution, it does not hold true for the whole financial system. This is another example of how the regulation on liquidity does not tackle systemic risk and does not consider uncertainty in a non-ergodic world. The logic underlying those measures is that the risk of liquidity can be faced by imposing on each bank or financial institution an adequate cost. So the fact that no liquidity can exist for all banks, as Keynes already wrote in *The General Theory of Employment, Interest and Money*, is ignored. Behind these measures lies the idea that every bank must be liquid in order for the whole financial system to be liquid, which is just an illusion. The liquidity of the whole system is not the sum of the liquidity of each unit.

EBA's studies on the application of the BCBS designed liquidity coverage ratio to the EU banking system

EBA studies (EBA, 2013, 2014) on the possibility of implementing the LCR in the European Union found that the banks would have had no difficulty in meeting the ratio as they were holding plenty of sovereign bonds and reserves at the central bank. EBA (2013, 2014) assesses which assets should be considered highly liquid in the European Union in order to fulfil the criteria proposed by the Basel Committee (BCBS, 2013).

The principal criterion for liquidity is sale or repo-ability. Then the EBA looks at the evolution of markets in the European Union and discovers that mortgages in the European Union have performed well in the past, so they can be included among the HQLA. Moreover, even repo markets have been very active after an initial stop in 2007, regaining the same volume of the period before the crisis, so they can be relied upon to ensure liquidity through the possibility of pledging the assets in a repo transaction to obtain money. Then it goes further to suggest that even rehypothecated assets may be included under certain conditions among the HQLA assets. The main message is that since mortgage securities markets and repo markets have performed well in the EU both before and after the crisis, we can believe that they will do so in the future too. That the extraordinary intervention by the European Central Bank may have contributed to this good performance emerges here and there, but is not considered particularly relevant.

The past is considered a reliable guide for the future as always in all finance studies based on the belief in an ergodic world (see Davidson, 2009) and the role of monetary policy in codetermining results in conjunction with regulation is neglected. Two main points of Keynes and Minsky's theories are ignored.

In EBA (2013), it was stated that changes in a few components were responsible for banks adapting on a voluntary basis to the LCR regulation. On the nominator, these were increasing the shares of drawable central bank reserves and sovereign bonds (zero risk-weight and non-zero risk-weight domestic) and covered bonds over the period Q2 2011 to Q4 2012. On the denominator, decreasing shares of short-term, non-operational deposits by non-financials, undrawn liquidity lines and short-term fixed term deposits of retail and SME customers, short-term stable deposits from retail and SME customers, contributed to improving LCRs over the same period. Changes in loans did not contribute instead (EBA, 2013, pp. 90–1).

What is missed in this assertion is that in many South European countries, financing to microenterprises and small firms is extended by allowing overdrafts on deposits and granting flexible liquidity lines. These arrangements have been changed, contributing thus to the credit crunch for micro and small enterprises. This way of adapting to the ratio could have caused a reduction in their financing during a crisis even if loans were not cut.

It is worth noting that the LCR voluntary exercise as well as its final implementation regards all banks without size exemptions, so smaller banks lending to small firms may have chosen this way of complying. On the contrary, in the US it applies only to internationally active depository institutions (with US$250 billion in consolidated assets or more, or total on balance sheet foreign exposure of at least US$10 billion) and depository institutions holding companies, as well as their depository institution subsidiaries exceeding US$10 billion in total consolidated assets.

In the second report by the EBA (2014), the way of adapting to the ratio has already changed with respect to the first report (2013):

> Since December 2011, the main strategies used by banks to improve their LCR are: Swapping non-HQLA with HQLA by increasing central bank deposits (especially for non compliant banks); buying covered bonds and, to a lesser extent, Level 1 securities; *Reducing the exposures to retail and SME counterparties*, but this impact might have been mitigated by (1) an economic climate with contracted demand and (2) a competitive environment where banks that are LCR compliant have seized the opportunity to gain market shares, and (3) could have been distorted by external economic factors such as the timing of the financial crisis and the introduction of the LCR negotiation. Swapping unsecured debt and interbank funding with retail deposits (especially for banks that became compliant).
>
> (EBA, 2014, p. 66 [emphasis added])

Thus, in the second report, EBA (2014) acknowledges that compliance with the LCR may have led to a credit crunch towards the small and medium enterprises and to a cut in retail exposures.

EBA (2014) adds that it is evident that the most common strategy used by banks to meet the ratio was that of selling non-liquid assets and increasing their deposits at the central bank: 'Sell/cut non eligible assets to place the proceeds at the central bank and/or purchase eligible assets.' Another less used technique was to swap unsecured debt and interbank funding with retail deposits.

Since the main non-liquid assets for commercial banks are loans, cutting loans and increasing liquidity held at the central bank would be adequate. On the liabilities side, it would be convenient instead to cut interbank borrowing and other exposures to financial institutions and increase retail deposits. This has actually happened as loans have been cut in many European countries, particularly those of the southern periphery, while deposits collected have increased.

A bank that collects deposits and holds government bonds as assets would very easily fulfil the liquidity coverage ratio, but it would not be a bank according to Minsky's definition because it would not accept anything – it would not be a merchant of debt (see Minsky, 2008).

In the design of LCR by EU authorities, a function of banking can be preserved – namely, that of financing real-estate as RMBS are included among the HQLAs. Given that in many countries before the crisis there has been a bubble in the price of real-estate, this appears a dubious choice.

The main result of the crisis in switching from unsecured to secured financing is thus approved and blessed by the regulation. In article 31 (BCBS, 2013), it is stated that assets received in securities financing transactions can be used as liquid assets to fulfil the ratio:

> Assets received in reverse repo and securities financing transactions that are held at the bank, have not been re-hypothecated, and are legally and contractually available for the bank's use can be considered as part of the stock of HQLA. In addition, assets which qualify for the stock of HQLA that have been pre-positioned or deposited with, or pledged to, the central bank or a public sector entity (PSE) but have not been used to generate liquidity may be included in the stock.

(BCBS, 2013, p. 31)

So while unsecured lending and credit commitments and guarantees between banks and non-bank financial institutions or other entities are discouraged as they weigh heavily both on the numerator and on the denominator of the ratio, lending through repo agreements is the cheapest way of lending within the financial system. This is because, according to the valuation of the BCBS and EBA, the repo market has proved to be resilient to the crisis and because only unsecured lending, according to the BCBS analysis, contributes to the too-interconnected-to-fail problem. The fact that without extraordinary interventions by the central bank, this market may not be liquid at all, and that changes in the value of collateral and margin calls may initiate a process of contagion across all units in the economy is not taken into consideration. Repo counterparts can withdraw very easily and the introduction of central counterparties concentrates the risk, requiring again the intervention of the central bank to ensure their liquidity and solvency.[2] For example, a bank that on the assets side has fewer loans and more securities, and on the liabilities side has deposits and repo and derivatives in any amount, will meet the regulation more easily than a bank with a higher share of loans on the assets side and other banks' bonds and equities on the liability side.

While direct lending between banks, and between banks and other financial institutions is discouraged, any lending that occurs through complex derivatives structures or through repo with rehypothecation is considered as liquidity enhancing. For example, if a bank swaps the total return of a government bond with the total return of a corporate bond or a bond issued by another bank with a low credit rating, it will be able to fulfil the ratio because on its balance sheet only government bonds are recorded. The inflow and outflow deriving from the swap should be considered in the denominator of the ratio. Their amount, however, would depend on the methodology used, which may be internal. The impact on the denominator would depend on the maturity of the swap, on its value during the 30-day period and on the net value of other derivatives with the same counterparty. The main message is that in case of necessity – which is not the case at the present moment as all banks are flooded with liquidity at the central bank – instead of having a high liquid asset, according to the definition given in the metric, the banks could have a combination of a derivative and highly liquid assets, whose effect on the balance sheet would be different from having just a highly liquid asset.

Moreover, as we read in BCBS, 2013, p. 119, no new liquidity requirements are required if the mark-to-market value of a derivative is secured with collateral that is considered safe, such as government bonds and other public entities bonds that are subject to zero-risk weight in the Basel agreement. This means that if an institution has government bonds with zero-risk weight and swaps their return with the return of risky assets such as corporate bonds, then the eventual variation on the mark-to-market value of the swap would not require further liquidity according to LCR rules if a government bond is used to secure the eventual loss to the counterparty. This government bond may not be the same held as liquidity coverage, however, because the latter must be unencumbered. Yet it would be possible to use a government bond that has already been used as collateral once in another transaction because of the permitted practice of rehypothecation. It would further be possible to borrow that government bond[3] for a period if regulation constraints were binding.

So the incentive to have one's cake and eat it is very high. If an institution has government bonds, it can fulfil the liquidity coverage ratio while at the same time entering into a risky transaction. It can fulfil the liquidity ratio while increasing the return on equity if the bets made through derivatives are successful. Given those rules on derivatives, any attempt by regulation to affect the quality of assets on banks' balance sheets is destined to be unsuccessful.

The net stable funding ratio

The rationale for the introduction of a net stable funding ratio is the experience made during the great financial crisis of the fragility of funding structures by banks and other financial institutions. Most of them had long-term assets financed by short-term liabilities that were frequently rolled over. During the crisis, those liabilities were no longer rolled over, causing problems with funding and inducing the banks to dump assets in a falling market. While the problem could be cast as a mismatching between assets and liabilities, the legislation goes beyond the simple requirement of a similar maturity of assets and liabilities.

It describes the problem as an externality that arises when banks choose an excessively fragile funding profile because they do not sufficiently internalize the costs; these costs would be paid by others. So policy intervention is needed because of the externality. The tool used acts both on the assets and liabilities sides and rather than being a maturity, mismatching metrics tends to reduce the risk of both funding instability and asset illiquidity in the balance sheets of financial entities. The reason is that both funding instability and asset illiquidity matter during a run on a financial entity. The run in turn is described as 'a coordination of creditors who rush to the exit in order to avoid being trapped in a bankruptcy or resolution'.

The success of the run depends on two factors: (1) the ease with which assets could be pledged or sold without impairing the bank's business model or going concern value; and (2) the total amount of funding that could potentially be withdrawn in a run. The objective of the externality limiting policy should be to ensure that each bank has stable funding sufficient to finance the assets that cannot be sold or used in a repo transaction without causing solvency problems. Thus, in order to calculate the ratio a review of all assets, liabilities and off-balance sheet commitments is needed in the horizon of a year. This review must measure the stability of liabilities and equity (available stable funding at the numerator of the ratio), how likely they are to be withdrawn or whether they can be withdrawn because of business commitments or lack of sale or repo markets. It must measure too the need to stable fund assets (required stable funding at the denominator of the ratio). These two metrics, one for liabilities the other for assets, should be compared to determine the mismatch.

The reason for using two metrics to calculate the ratio is that it can be applied to any business model. Then, as in the case of calculating the capital requirements, weights are required in order to value each of the components in the numerator and denominator. The measure for both metrics is behavioural, not just maturity based. For example, sight deposits are very short term as they can be withdrawn at any time, yet they are liabilities accepted as available stable funding with a very high weight of 90 per cent; long-term governments bonds, the long maturity notwithstanding, are assets that do not require a high percentage of stable funding. They require only 5 per cent stable funding if they are issued by European countries, depending on the rating.

An element of systemic instability is added to the ratio by considering that the illiquidity of assets and the instability of liabilities are interlinked. Therefore, the weights should take into account the resilience of the financial system as a whole. An example of why systemic risk does matter is rehypothecation. Chains of rehypothecation in which collateral is transferred between financial intermediaries to secure short-term funding may lead to fire sales. Thus, 'setting higher weights for these transactions when they are recorded as assets, compared to when they are recorded as liabilities', is a device studied to take into account such risk. This is the only measure introduced in the NSFR ratio regulation to tackle systemic risk.

It is ironic to think that this tiny difference would save the financial system from the interconnectedness problem, but the financial institutions' associations strongly oppose it because it disrupts their careful constructed netting sets. If the weight on the asset is higher than that on the liabilities, the two values cannot be netted out. If netting contributes to interconnectedness, it should not be allowed in the first instance, while if it is not so, the 20 per cent add-on rule is not justified. As far as the 20 per cent add-on is concerned, it is foreseeable that the Basel Committee and the European Commission will adhere to the industry protest and thus will stop fighting systemic risk.

These considerations guide the method for setting ASF (numerator) and RSF (denominator) factors. Requiring that a bank's total ASF is sufficient in relation to its total RSF is equivalent to imposing the condition that the ASF/RSF ratio be no less than 100 per cent.

With regard to assets, the sum of all stable funding requirements is calculated by summing up the various quantities of assets weighted by some parameters. Required stable funding for loans to non financials varies according to the riskiness of the loans. The bracket is between 65 and 80 per cent.

Derivatives require 100 per cent stable funding, but only on a net basis. If liabilities are higher than assets, no stable funding is required. The detailed prescription is as follows:

> For the treatment of derivatives in the NSFR, 100% of stable funding is required for the net derivative assets position (as a result of deducting derivative liabilities – net of all variation margins posted – from derivative assets – net of cash variation margin received). If derivative liabilities exceed derivative assets, the difference will be considered 0% stable funding. As an add-on, 20% of the total derivative liabilities would be required as stable funding to limit its offsetting power and its stable funding consideration, thus ensuring a minimum RSF.
>
> (EBA, 2015, p. 39)

So once again, while netting is not contemplated for other assets categories, such as loans and securities, this occurs for derivatives only.

The treatment of derivatives and repo in the NSFR and the discussion with industry representatives

In order to mitigate this drastic difference in treatment, the law foresees an exception in so far as it requires a 20 per cent add-on as '20 per cent of liabilities would be required as stable funding'. The reason for this exception to the netting rule is explained in the European Commission document launching a consultation on the proposal for NFSR:

> Finally, gross derivatives liabilities are subject to a 20% RSF factor (§43(d) of the BCBS NSFR standard). As explained in the EBA NSFR report (p.166), this RSF aims at capturing 'to some extent, future funding risks arising from negative mark-to-market movements that ultimately result in net requirements

to post collateral. [.] This add-on allows covering this potential unfavourable evolution over one year (be they due to losses on derivative contracts or increases in the proportion of derivative liabilities where the bank is asked to post margins)'. The RSF therefore seeks to capture an additional funding risk related to the potential increase of the derivatives liabilities over a year, implying that more margins would have to be posted (for uncollateralised derivatives this funding risk is potentially more material but more hypothetical since it is conditional in the event that the counterparty requires the institution to post margin within a year) and that other derivative cash-flows have to be paid to the counterparty. The RSF then requires that 20% of the current gross derivatives liabilities be stably-funded on a one-year horizon.

(EC, undated, p. 3)

Another point on which the discussion with the industry representatives has been intense is the prohibition of subtracting margins posted from the replacement cost value of derivatives in order to lower the required stable funding of assets unless they are in cash.

In calculating NSFR derivative assets, collateral received in connection with derivative contracts may not offset the positive replacement cost amount, regardless of whether or not netting is permitted under the bank's operative accounting or risk-based framework, unless it is received in the form of cash variation margin and meets the conditions as specified in paragraph 25 of the *Basel III leverage ratio framework and disclosure requirements*.[16] Any remaining balance sheet liability associated with (a) variation margin received that does not meet the criteria above or (b) initial margin received may not offset derivative assets and should be assigned a 0% ASF factor.

(BCBS, 2014 (35), p. 8 (emphasis in original))

A footnote specifies that the NSFR derivative assets are equal to derivative assets minus the cash collateral received as variation margin on derivative assets (BCBS, 2014, p. 8, footnote 16).

Various associations' (International Swaps and Derivatives Association (ISDA), Association for Financial Markets in Europe (AFME) and Institute for International Finance (IIF)) representatives of interests in the financial industry oppose this article, arguing that it will increase costs and that those increased costs will in the end penalize end users. In response to the question about which activities will be particularly hit by the new measure, the ISDA, AFME and IIF point decisively at derivatives and ask for major changes:

We respectfully request that the calibration of the combined derivatives funding required, as envisaged within the BCBS standard, be reconsidered.

In particular, the recognition of variation margin received by banks, which has been aligned to the Leverage Ratio, is inappropriate in a long term funding standard. The restriction on the netting of high quality securities variation margin, and the application of the leverage ratio netting rules for cash variation margin, could severely impact the availability of derivatives for end-users. Furthermore, the application of the 20% add-on, in its current form, compounds this issue.

(AFME, ISDA, IIF, 2016)

The legislation rests on a contradiction. On one hand, it fully acknowledges the risk-mitigating character of derivatives; it accepts the way that collateral is treated among private financial institutions and assigns bankruptcy remote status to repos and derivatives; on the the other hand, though, it tries to avoid bank runs starting from collateral or repo counterparties by imposing a stable funding ratio that is based on the same logic of the previous measures.

The timing is important, too. The proposed LCR and NSFR have not yet been implemented after eight years on from the financial crisis, while capital regulation changes are already in place. As discussed in Chapter 2, the introduction of a capital regulation based on risk-weighted assets has penalized mainly the residual banking system, which has been focused on lending as its main business, while the measures that should have restrained the trading and wealth management activity have been postponed. The repo market, which shrank in the US after the crisis, in Europe has recovered the same volumes of contracts that were registered before the 2007 crisis (see ICMA 2017). Now, after eight years from the crisis, some norms that may hit the financial industry, though to a small extent, are going to be introduced, but it is likely that the vibrant protests of the associations will be heard and the legislation modified.

The International Capital Market Association complained as follows:

Given the role of repo and collateral markets at the heart of the financial system, this would have negative implications for the smooth functioning of broader financial markets – which would, in turn, lead to increased costs and risk for market participants, including those corporates and governments borrowing to finance their economic needs. At the same time there would also be a detrimental impact on the effectiveness of many of the measures put in place to improve the stability of the financial system, dependent as they are on high quality collateral.

(ICMA-ERCC, 2016, p. 2)

The same association in 2017 gratefully acknowledges that some requests to water down the content of the previous quoted article of BCBS, 2014 have been received by the European Commission, such as the inclusion in HQLA Level 1 of the variation margin received to be taken out of the NSF required derivatives assets, but further pushes for new changes. The rationale is given in the following statement:

> The ICMA ERCC also observes that collateral now plays a key role in financial markets, in no small part as a result of official policy interventions designed to mitigate the risks of financial market activities. For these measures to work as intended, it is essential that there is sufficient collateral fluidity – such that the right amount, of the right type, of collateral can be available whenever and wherever needed. This needs a good infrastructure for the movement of collateral, but also a robust repo market, since the repo market provides the principal mechanism for the transfer of collateral.
>
> (ICMA-ISDA, 2017, p. 2)

The ICMA then proposes to exempt all the short-term repo assets up to six months from the required stable funding. Since the majority of repo are very short term, this would mean exempting almost all of them from required stable funding. Of course, if this request were received, it would increase the availability of short-term financing as those who have repo claims are, in fact, the lenders. Repo claims are already favoured with respect to loans, as they do not carry capital charges. The pleading is justified as follows:

> The ICMA ERCC's own considered view is that the best way to adapt the NSFR would be to re-calibrate it such that short-term – in this context, say those of up to six months – secured financing transactions, such as repo, are exempt. Short-term cash and collateral liquidity management activity is governed by the liquidity coverage ratio (LCR) requirements which have been imposed, already leading banks to far more carefully and actively manage their liquidity needs out to at least 90 days and affording supervisors with a high degree of visibility in relation to these activities. *Such an exemption would avoid that the NSFR imputes an element of long-term funding costs into the financing of short-term assets.* The ICMA ERCC also sees that a broadly equivalent set of considerations lead logically to the conclusion that all short-term money market activities should be exempt from NSFR's imposition of an element of long-term funding costs. Money market activities will not be able to bear such costs and absent targeted relief central banks will be left having to intermediate liquidity.
>
> (ICMA, 2016 (emphasis added))

The specific argument on the inclusion of an element of long-term funding in the financing of short-term assets is not consistent, as the rules are not intended to avoid mismatching. For example, short-term deposits are considered as available stable funding for long-term assets, which should lead to a mismatching if the maturity of assets is compared to the maturity of liabilities. In the same way, also short-term assets may require long-term funding if they are deemed sufficiently illiquid. In the latter case, again a mismatching in the opposite direction would occur, but the aim of the ratio is not to avoid that mismatching. Instead, the ICMA is right to observe that once it has acknowledged the repo market and the presence of high-quality collateral as a benchmark for liquidity[4] (recall that the valuation of collateral is still a task assigned to private rating agencies), it does not make sense to try to slow its growth or make more expensive the use of collateral in financial transactions.

The ICMA (2017) opposes totally the 20 per cent add-on that paradoxically was the only measure introduced in order to take account of systemic risk and announces that a new metric which is being studied by its experts will be proposed to replace it. They write that the 20 per cent add-on would result in an estimated funding requirement of €340 billion for the financial industry. They do not think that the option of using SA-CRR will result in a lower number and are preparing a new proposal for a metric to be used to replace both the 20 per cent add-on and the SA-CCR. On the other hand, AFME and ISDA (AFME-ISDA, 2017) are happy with the EC's proposal for the recognition of all cash variation margins received, as well as with the proposed recognition of Level 1 HQLA as the received variation margin. Further, they suggest that the rehypothecable initial margin should be recognized as stable funding for assets.

In a proposal presented in November 2016 by the European Commission containing various changes to previously issued regulation, as well as new regulation on some fields (i.e. total loss-absorbing capacity, minimum required eligible liabilities, leverage ratio), the discussed 20 per cent add-on that should have taken into account systemic risk has been lowered to 10 per cent (see BBVA, 2016). The main reason why the European Commission with its new proposals has decided to surrender to many of the requests by the representatives of the industry is that of preserving the successful functioning of the government bonds market as most of the repo contracts have government bonds as collateral.

Behind those worries about the working of the government bonds market and their liquidity is the rejection of the role of the central bank in stabilizing government bonds prices. As Gabor (2016) has shown clearly, the growth of repo markets is linked to the introduction of autonomous central banks. Although the ECB has actually stabilized government bond prices after 2011 and is now engaged in quantitative easing operations, this is considered an exceptional intervention and the autonomy of the central bank in normal times has to be preserved. The normal way of working before the introduction of autonomous central banks and repo markets was for the banks to lend and borrow from each other while relying on central bank facilities – which were more expensive than interbank borrowing – in stress conditions. The European Central Bank does not wish to revert to that type of intervention.

The BCBS proposal introduced in the EU legislation instead insists on giving legitimacy and importance to secured lending and collateral use, and acknowledges the repo market as a provider of liquidity. The 20 per cent add-on, as well as the limitation in the recognition of collateral for the determination of the values of derivatives to be stable funded, were in contradiction with these basic principles, which is why they will very likely disappear. However, if they disappear it is implicitly argued that no systemic risk needs to be faced and it is possible to go on as though it were not there. Why, then, should these new metrics be introduced? Why are risk-weighted capital requirements not sufficient?

What type of banking does the NSFR favour?

At this point a question arises. What type of banking does the NSFR encourage or favour? As the latter is no simple mismatching rule, answering the question requires an analysis of stylized balance sheets patterns. The claim (see EBA, 2015) is that the ratio should favour traditional lending activity as the required stable funding for loans is 65–85 per cent, while the available stable funding for deposits is higher at 90–95 per cent, thus creating a positive available funding in this activity (see Marco, 2016). In what follows, other potential balance sheets compositions are examined to answer his question.

The classical and most common pattern of balance sheet is one in which deposits are entered on the liabilities side and on the assets side high-quality assets such as government bonds are rated AAA. The bank with such a balance sheet would easily fulfil the 100 per cent ratio between available stable funding and required stable funding. This would be called a narrow bank (discussed in Chapter 1). This bank would be very safe, but it would not fulfil the main task in Schumpeter's and Minsky's view of creating credit and liquidity (see Kregel, 2012; Minsky, 2008). Instead, a bank that creates credit would have bigger problems in fulfilling the ratio as loans are surely risky, although their credit rating may vary. As any regulatory measure depends on credit rating, the bank would not be asked to make any assessment of the applicants for the loans' future prospective yields, but would offer loans to companies that have a good rating. The latter in turn may not need credit at all as they already have plenty of finance. Thus, a safe and stable-funded bank may also be useless.

Despite the industry's complaints, it appears that the net funding need is higher, according to the weights assigned to required stable funding in the proposed document by the Commission, for a bank that has deposits as liabilities and loans as assets, rather than for a bank that has deposits as liabilities and derivatives, and highly rated securities and repo as assets. The RSF weight of loans is between 65 and 80 per cent, while the RSF weight of repo assets is just 10–15 per cent, depending on the quality of the collateral; the RSF for derivatives is 100 per cent on a net measure if there is neither an offsetting item on the liabilities side, nor collateral. Thus, the biggest RSF comes from loans even if they are backed by deposits on the liabilities side.

If, on the liabilities side, there is a mix of deposits and not highly rated government bonds, the ratio of 100 per cent may be difficult to reach. A portfolio of repo assets and matched book derivatives with some deposits and highly rated bonds on the other side would ensure complying more easily with the ratio. In the European Union, most southern European countries' banks have the majority of their assets made up of loans, while the liabilities are a mix of deposits and domestic government bonds (which are not highly rated). So, if the long-term and full-allotment refinancing by the central bank as well as its quantitative easing programme end, those banks will have more difficulties in complying with the ratio.

The tendency is the same for all metrics linked to Basel III – capital with respect to exposure at default (leverage ratio), risk-weighted capital requirements, liquidity coverage ratio and stable funding ratio. Loans are penalized simply because in all these metrics they cannot be offset by any other asset on the other side to lower the exposure and because they are subject to risk assessment according to criteria fixed by external private agencies. Repo assets and mortgages under certain conditions may be included in the high-liquid ratio numerator; the required stable for funding for repo and derivatives as the metric is calculated on net values and is lower than that for loans. If loans are collateralized, the value of collateral cannot be subtracted to calculate the net stable funding ratio. At the time of writing, repo liabilities do not enjoy good treatment as available stable funding, as their weight is zero.

Conclusions

The liquidity coverage ratio and the net stable funding ratio were introduced after the great financial crisis with the aim of avoiding liquidity crises and a run on banks. The liquidity crises and run on banks in turn were associated with a systemic risk that goes beyond the sum of individual risks. Yet those measures are based on the same mechanism on which risk-weighted capital requirements were built – that of pricing the risk deriving from different sources in the right way and thus penalizing those who take excessive risk. The principle that capital charges must be proportionate to risk is maintained, even when designing weights for high-quality liquid assets, runoff rates, weights for available stable funding and for required stable funding. Those weights are often arbitrary, based either on valuation by external rating agencies or the preferences of the European Commission, the European Central Bank and the European Banking Authority on which assets should either be promoted or discouraged.

Derivatives and secured financing emerge as the top assets in this hierarchy because they weigh little both in the liquidity coverage ratio and in the net stable funding ratio. Loans instead are at the bottom in the hierarchy because they are among the less liquid assets and because they are assigned a high required stable funding.

The regulation, on one hand, acknowledges the repo market as a provider of liquidity and tries to preserve its integrity and efficient functioning by lowering the costs that are charged for accessing it, totally ignoring the contagion mechanism that may arise in repo markets based on secured financing through margin calls and the sale of assets. On the other hand, the regulation tries to mitigate the systemic risk attached to it by including special clauses – for example, the 20 per cent add-on – that should limit the level of netting allowed for derivatives and securities lending (which comprises repo). At the time of writing, the contradiction seems to be resolved by explicitly giving up the aim of reducing systemic risk.

In conclusion, these new additional regulations, starting from the experience of recent crises, continue to ignore the existence of systemic risk in a non-ergodic world, and add new risks to the list of those already known and cured with risk-weighted capital requirements. Those new risks have to be faced by constraining leverage and funding maturity. The ratios that are used to measure them, however, are full of weights that are not justified by any theory and that cannot be defended on any ground.

Notes

1   The proposal of reforming the regulatory status of exposures to sovereigns has been warmly supported by German economists belonging to the German Council of Economic Experts (Andritsky *et al.*, 2016). They link the opportunity of reforming this risk exposure to the implementation of the new resolution regime for banks. Banks that are no more burdened with a high share of domestic governments bonds would have a bigger total loss absorbing capacity and would thus become more bail-in-able. The issue has been raised in relation to the last stage of the banking union, the common deposit insurance fund. Before entering into a common deposit insurance, the Germans want to be sure that the southern countries' banks, which are burdened with domestic government debts, are not going to fail, so they have first to require them to be free of that debt. Further discussion on the issue of sovereign risk and capital requirements can be found in ESRB (2015), European Commission (2015), Visco (2016), Lanotte *et al.* (2016).
2   A discussion whether central counterparties increase or decrease risk is taking place among economists (Duffie and Zhu, 2011; Duffie, 2014; Wendt, 2015). For the financial solidity of existing central counterparties both in the US and the EU, see Armakolaa and Laurent (2015).
3   The securities lending market at the world level has been growing in the last few years, as the data collected by the International Securities Lending Association show (ISLA, 2016).
4   This has happened in the definition of the assets that are considered highly liquid for complying with the Liquidity Coverage Ratio.

References

AFME–ISDA (2017) CRD 5: The net stable funding ratio. Available at: www.afme.eu/globalassets/downloads/briefing-notes/afme-prd-bn-nsfr-note-final-march-2017.pdf (accessed 31 March 2017).

AFME, ISDA, IIF (2016) Joint Associations – EC DG FISMA Consultation Paper: On further considerations for the implementation of the NSFR in Europe.

Andritzky, J., Gadatsch, N., Körner, T., Schäfer, A. and Schnabel, I. (2016) A proposal for ending the privileges for sovereign exposures in banking regulation, VOXEU. Available at: http://voxeu.org/article/ending-privileges-sovereign-exposures-banking-regulation (accessed 2 April 2017).

Armakolaa, A. and Laurent, J.P. (2015) CCP resilience and clearing membership. Available at: www.ceps.eu/system/files/CCP%20resolution%20SSRN-id2625579.pdf (accessed February 2017).

Basel Committee on Banking Supervision (BCBS) (2013) Basel III: The liquidity coverage ratio and liquidity risk monitoring tools. Available at: www.bis.org (accessed October 2016).

Basel Committee on Banking Supervision (2014) Basel III: The net stable funding ratio. Available at: www.bis.org (accessed October 2016).

BBVA, Regulation Watch, 23 November 2016. Available at: www.bbvaresearch.com/wp-content/uploads/2016/11/New-package-of-banking-reforms2.pdf (accessed 2 April 2017).

Davidson, P. (2009) Can future systemic financial risks be quantified? Ergodic vs nonergodic stochastic processes, *Brazilian Journal of Political Economy*, 29(4): 324–40.

Dirks, M., de Vries, C. and van der Lecq, F. (2014) Macroprudential policy: The neglected sectors, in D. Schoenmaker (ed.) *Macro-prudentialism*. London: CEPR Press, pp. 73–85. Available at: http://voxeu.org/sites/default/files/file/macroprudentialism_VoxEU_0.pdf

Duffie, D. (2014) Resolution of failing central counterparties. Working Paper No. 3256. Graduate School of Business, Stanford University, Stanford, CA.

Duffie, D. and H. Zhu (2011). Does a central clearing counterparty reduce counterparty risk? *Review of Asset Pricing Studies*, 1: 74–95.

EBA (2013) Report on impact assessment for liquidity measures under Article 509(1) of the CRR.

EBA (2014) Second report on impact assessment for liquidity measures under Article 509(1) of the CRR.

EBA (2015) EBA report on net stable funding requirements under Article 510 of the CRR. Available at: www.eba.europa.eu/documents/10180/983359/EBA-Op-2015-22+NSFR+Report.pdf (accessed 31 March 2017).

ESRB (2015) ESRB report on the regulatory treatment of sovereign exposures, European Systemic Risk Board, Frankfurt am Main.

European Commission (EC) (undated) DG-FISMA consultation paper on further considerations for the implementation of the NSFR in the EU.

European Commission (2015) Further risk reduction in the banking union, Five Presidents' Report Series, Issue 03/2015, European Political Strategy Centre, Brussels.

Gabor, D. (2016) The (impossible) repo trinity: The political economy of repo markets, *Review of International Political Economy*. DOI: http://dx.doi.org/10.1080/09692290.2016.1207699

ICMA European Repo and Collateral Council (2016) Impacts of the net stable funding ratio on repo and collateral markets. Available at: www.icmagroup.org/assets/documents/Regulatory/Repo/ERCC-NSFR-230316.pdf (accessed 31 March 2017).

ICMA (2017) European repo market survey, No. 32.

International Securities Lending Association (ISLA) (2016) ISLA Securities lending market report, September. Available at: www.isla.co.uk/wp-content/uploads/2016/10/ISLA-SL-REPORT-9-16-final.pdf (accessed 2 April 2017).

Kregel, J. (2012) Using Minsky to simplify financial regulation. Levy Economics Institute of Bard College, New York.

Lanotte, M., Manzelli, G., Rinaldi, A.M., Taboga, M. and Tommasino, P. (2016) Easier said than done? Reforming the prudential treatment of banks' sovereign exposures, *Banca d'Italia, Questioni di Economia e Finanza* (Occasional Papers), 326.

Marco, I.I. (2016) The net stable funding ratio: Theoretical background and analysis of the Spanish banking sector Banco de España 65 Revista de Estabilidad Financierea, No. 31, pp. 65–96. Available at: www.bde.es/f/webbde/GAP/Secciones/Publicaciones/Informes BoletinesRevistas/RevistaEstabilidadFinanciera/16/ (accessed February 2016).

Minsky, H.P. (1982) Central banking and money market changes, in H. Minsky, *Can it Happen Again?* New York: M.E. Sharpe, pp. 162–78.

Minsky, H.P. (1987) Securitization. Hyman P. Minsky Archive, Paper 15. Available at: http://digitalcommons.bard.edu/hm_archive/15 (accessed March 2017).

Minsky, H.P ([1986] 2008) *Stabilizing an Unstable Economy.* New York: McGraw Hill.

Toporowski, J. (1999) *The End of Finance*. London and New York: Routledge.

Tropeano, D. (2010) The current financial crisis, monetary policy, and Minsky's Structural Instability Hypothesis, *International Journal of Political Economy*, 39(2): 41–57.

Visco, I. (2016) Banks' sovereign exposures and the feedback loop between banks and their sovereigns. Available at: www.bancaditalia.it/pubblicazioni/interventi-governatore/integov2016/Visco_Euro50_Bank_Sovereign_Exposure_02052016.pdf (accessed 2 April 2016).

Wendt, F. (2015) Central counterparties: Addressing their too important to fail nature. IMF Working Paper No. 21.

Woods, J.E. (2017) On the political economy of UK pension scheme regulation, *Cambridge Journal of Economics*, 41(1): 147–80. Available at: https://doi.org/10.1093/cje/bev048

5 The new resolution regime for banks and the euro

Introduction

We have seen that starting from the new Basel III capitalization rules and going on the proposed and not yet implemented rules on leverage ratio, liquidity coverage ratio and net stable funding ratio, to lend has become, rather than the main task of banks, an activity that requires more regulatory costs as it is not easy to optimize risk to cut those costs. The same does not apply to securities and derivatives as their risk can be mitigated through the use of other derivatives and collateral in order to save regulatory capital and to calculate exposure at default in the leverage ratio. As to the liquidity coverage ratio, it was obvious that loans could not be liquid and are not useful to satisfy the ratio. In the application of net stable funding ratio, we have seen that loans require higher stable funding than other assets such as reverse repos and mortgage-backed securities.

The problem with loans is that it is not allowed to net them against anything else on the other side of the balance sheet in order to show a lower exposure to risk. The only option to save regulatory capital is to securitize them. This is also encouraged by the inclusion in the definition of high liquid assets of securitized loans that satisfy the safe securitization criteria. In turn, those safe securitization criteria do not foresee any significant change with respect to the pre-financial crisis habits. The tranching of loans and their pooling are allowed. The external rating agencies are still allowed to rate them by using statistical measures of risk.[1] The use of derivatives in order to cover risk such as interest rate risk and foreign exchange risk is mandatory (BCBS and IOSCO, 2015: 8–9; footnote 15:10).

Most studies claim that the securitization in Europe performed much better than in the US before the great financial crisis, although they do not explain why. One of the reasons is that the securitizations in Europe were made according to more prudent standards and did not involve a great use of derivatives as risk mitigation tools. This avoided the spreading of price falls during the crisis from one security to many others that had the initial loan as underlying. The new safe securitizations instead have imported all the technology (rating, tranching, risk mitigation to rise rating) that has contributed to their failure in the US. They require a long chain of derivatives to be attached to the securitized assets, so safe securitizations may not perform better than unsafe ones.

The vanishing of the distinction between money, claim and security

While loans may carry higher regulatory costs than securitized mortgages, the same is true of the other side of banks' balance sheets. Due to the joint effects of commercial law carve-out and new regulation changes, deposits risk becoming less safe for investors and less convenient for banks than other liabilities such as repos.

There is an ongoing debate whether repo liabilities should be considered as money or shadow money (Ricks, 2016; Gabor and Vestergaard, 2016a). In order to answer the question, an economic or legal definition of money must be provided. Surely repos, like other short-term liabilities, cannot be used as a final means of payment, so they are not money in that meaning. According to Ricks (2016), they have other features of moneyness because they can be converted into money easily preserving their nominal value. Gabor and Vestergaard (2016a) instead argue that repo liabilities are essentially shadow money. From the legal point of view, repos enjoy particular privileges that may help maintain their perception of quasi-money. This is related to their being bankruptcy-remote as they enjoy safe harbour status. Their quasi-money perception is constructed through a series of legal constructs that innovate the same legal definition of money.

As Paech (2015, p. 15) writes:

> The risk mitigation techniques of master agreements (as protected by the safe harbour rules) are used to abolish established legal boundaries. ... This high degree of flexibility is nothing less than revolutionary, overthrowing traditional legal restrictions on the use of assets with a view to obtaining cash and creating liquidity more generally. This is the result of the combined use of the techniques available under safe harbour rules, notably enforceable termination and netting of contracts, enforceable collateral and limitation of insolvency avoidance. The EU Financial Collateral Directive contains a paradigmatic blueprint for this phenomenon.[59]

He stresses that the difference between owning a security and having a right on it disappears:

> First, the differences between full title and security interests disappear because the safe harbours sanction the use of title transfer collateral, netting and 'margining'.[60] Under such arrangements, while the collateral provider (the borrower) is protected as efficiently as it would be under a traditional security interest such as a pledge or mortgage, the collateral taker (the lender) enjoys far greater freedom to use the collateral assets than it would under a traditional security interest, in that it becomes the legal and beneficial owner of the asset and can therefore dispose of it, without being obliged to return that specific asset as long as the asset returned is of the same kind.
> (pp. 15–16)

In this new world, there is no difference between owning an asset or just disposing of it as collateral received. The consequence is that no difference exists between claims, money and security (Paech, 2015, p. 16). I think the author intends that no difference exists between payment in cash, through a claim (a promise to pay) in the future and a security. The collateral provider may give another security in replacement of that pledged or just cash for securities collateral or securities collateral for cash. The specificity of collateral becomes as irrelevant as is the distinction between money, claim and security.

From the legal point of view, then, repo liabilities may be considered as money, though from the economic point of view, they are not if money is defined as the final means of payment for the purchase of goods or settlement for securities. This change in rules is not neutral. It is motivated by the increased profits that this management of collateral yields. As Paech (2015) observes, the vanishing of the distinction between money, claim and security makes it possible to assign to these positions a monetary value which is the current market value. Thanks to the existence of safe harbour rules, a derivatives and repo portfolio can look like a balance of assets and liabilities, each booked at current market value that can be summed up to show a net exposure. This leads to big savings in regulatory costs as the 'exposure at default', which is the denominator in both the risk-weighted capital requirements and the leverage ratio rule, becomes a smaller number. This explains why any attempt to apply the same standard – for example, when calculating the net stable funding ratio – to loans on one side and derivatives and repos on the other side results in favouring the latter with respect to the former. It is not permitted to subtract the deposits from the loans to get a net exposure.

To summarize the discussion on the moneyness of repo liabilities, and more generally of liabilities issued by non-bank financial institutions (Poszar, 2014), it is true that they are not a final means of settlement (Michell, 2017), or, put in a simpler way, people can't buy an underground ticket by using them. Similarly, non-bank financial institutions can't create credit out of nothing.

That said, the rules that stay behind the master netting agreements contracts create reciprocal obligations that do not need the settlement by cash or need it only for a tiny portion of the notional amounts written in the contracts. Most papers on the moneyness question (Michell, 2017; Gabor and Vestergaard, 2016b) use diagrams that represent balance sheets of financial institutions and look at how repo agreements change them. The hotly debated issue is whether non-bank financial institutions or even banks can expand credit by using repos. The examples represented in the diagrams deal with single bilateral transactions. Yet the contracts that link these financial institutions to each other collect many transactions between the same counterparties into one single contract, thus reducing the use of cash or deposit money as a means of settlement. Cash settlement would be needed only if this sand castle of netting rules had fallen apart. This is what all the organizations involved try to avoid by protecting their contracts.

Beyond that, the repurchase agreement presents many advantages for the buyer (lender). He lends without having to record a loan in its balance sheet with all the regulatory charges linked to it (capital, leverage ratio (LR), liquidity coverage ratio (LCR) and net stable funding ratio (NSFR)). He earns a profit from that lending. He receives also a security as collateral of the loan that becomes its ownership and of which he can dispose (selling, rehypothecating). He may need the security specifically for purposes such as netting some other security or introducing it in a hedging set or shorting another security. This may in turn yield saving in regulatory costs and reduce potential losses in speculation. The security, however, is not on his balance sheet but still in the balance sheet of the seller (buyer) because the cash paid for the collateral is added as an asset to the seller's balance sheet (balanced on the liability side by the repayment due to the buyer at maturity). The latter's balance sheet will expand, signalling that he has increased his leverage by borrowing. The asset on the seller's balance sheet is cash or a regular bank deposit, while the obligation to repay it is the same as a loan to be repaid, although it is not recorded as a loan but as 'collateralized borrowing liability' (ICMA, undated).[2]

So the buyer (lender) can lend without having recorded a loan. He may need the security specifically for purposes such as netting some other security or introducing it in a hedging set or shorting another security. Another advantage is that when the security is no longer needed, he can resell it, making a profit, or provide another security or a cash compensation. So the buyer needs the security not for its resale value, but just as the means of carrying out regulatory arbitrage, speculation or simply complying with new rules. The demand is increased by the introduction of the new regulation on counterparty credit risk on high liquid assets and so on. He could have bought the security on the market, but by combining its purchase with a loan to the seller, he makes a profit that would not have been there by simply buying it. Yet, if the aim of the whole process is to game regulation and to reduce the risk of speculation, why should such a contorted construction be protected? A repurchase agreement could exist and has always existed without the legal ownership of the collateral by the buyer (lender).

Repo markets and leverage

As Paech (2015) writes, the use of repos increases profits as it permits increasing leverage. Collateralized lending and repo based on safe harbour rules and master netting agreements recognized in the regulation increase the profit possibilities to those investors who want to bet on the value of assets by borrowing short term. In that respect, since their claims are senior with respect to those of long-term investors like bond holders and depositors, they are favoured with respect to these other categories of investors who stand to lose in case of bankruptcy, and the more so after the introduction of so-called bail-in procedures for the resolution of banks.

The necessity of complying with margin calls on collateral may cause big fluctuations in the price of assets and fire sales. Of course, these fluctuations may be mitigated by prompt interventions by the central banks to protect the value of those assets, but that intervention would be simply a subsidy to leveraged investors aiming at speculative profits. In this way, the equivalence between cash and repo liabilities vanishes, as both are stable in terms of nominal value, but this stability is maintained through a public subsidy. The same holds even if repo transactions are cleared by a central counterparty. In the EU, the few central counterparties that exist are banks and thus are entitled to central bank liquidity provision, thus depending on some outside source of stability.

So in the new world of banking in which everything must be secured with a good collateral, a collateral that has a good rating and whose oscillations in value are protected by margin calls, then the very mechanism to ensure that the creditor in repos is not damaged, causing a fall in the value of the collateral. Rating agencies' downgrades lead to fluctuations that lead to a change in haircuts that in turn lead to the sale of assets. If the parties to a repo contract have already reached their maximum leverage, the sale in assets causes a great reduction in their positions (Sissoko, 2014). This in turn may cause further downgrades and start the whole process again through a feedback effect.

As Sissoko (2016) points out, the repo markets are what makes it possible for one side of the market to hold a safe cash-like asset without relying on the banking system. The other part, however, provides the insurance on the safety of the asset through agreeing to post variation margins.

The whole structure is fragile because everything is marked to the market while traditional loans are not; they may sit for a while on the banks' balance sheets without causing changes in the value of deposits. In traditional banking, bank owners bear the credit risk of bank loans, and the banking system bears liquidity risk by making it possible for temporary declines in asset values to lie hidden on the balance sheets of banks. The banks in turn are the beneficiaries of central bank support until the under-valuations disappear. The banking system, in her opinion, would prevent liquidity strains from being transmitted directly to the real economy.

In our economy, repos are replacing deposits as investment for big cash pools, while traditional deposits persist only in some countries for retail consumers. Sissoko (2016) argues that the repo lenders are always safe, while the repo borrowers bear the risk of big losses. In the context of modern financial markets, the repo borrowers are often institutional long-term investors such as pension funds and insurance companies, while repo lenders are cash pools whose investors seek a replacement for deposits. Repo lenders in a bilateral repo contract have the right to rehypothecate the collateral received and thus may gain from increased leverage. The amount of allowed rehypothecation varies according to the jurisdictions. In the UK, there is no limit to the number of rehypothecations, while in the US it is not so. It is the same as if a bank that lends through a mortgage could then sell the house before a breach of the contract occurs or use it as collateral for its own borrowing.

Sissoko (2016) argues that the insurance by repo borrowers to repo lenders may lead to big oscillations in the price of long pool shares or in their mark-to-market values. In the case of exchange-traded funds (ETFs), for example, this may lead to heavy redemptions, which in turn lead to a liquidation of the assets to which ETFs refer as underlying and therefore to a further decline in their prices. Sissoko observes that even if a long pool investor knows that market prices are falling due to a liquidity event and will over time rise again, it will be rational for the investor to be among the first to exit. The insurance of repo borrowers may cause at the macroeconomic level dangerous consequences. This is another instance in which Minsky's belief that the investor who cares about his own gain will indeed disrupt the whole economy rather than increase welfare for all.

Further, while the characterization of repo borrowers and lenders applies well to the US financial market or to the dollar-denominated repo assets, the situation is slightly different in Europe as most repo borrowers and repo lenders are themselves banking institutions. In Europe, most repos are bilateral repo contracts, so the lenders are free to rehypothecate the collateral received from the borrowers, thus increasing their leverage. The borrowers that are doomed in case of a fall in the value of the collateral and have immediately to post margins are themselves banks that, if their dimension is such to pose a systemic risk, need to be saved by the state. In turn, their share prices would reflect the losses suffered in their repo borrowings.

Repos, securities lending and derivatives in the Banking Recovery and Resolution Directive

According to the new EU legislation on the resolution of banks that tries to avoid the involvement of state finances through the so-called bail-in, the losers would be the shareholders, holders of subordinated and even senior debt, as well as some of the depositors. In this case, given that the bankruptcy-remote status of repos and derivatives must be respected, the repo lenders' claims would be ensured by the sacrifice of all other groups of claimants.

It has been claimed (Paech, 2015) that this special status of repo claimants will change with the introduction of the new resolution regime in the European Union. The novelty introduced so far is that the early termination rights are suspended for two days after the beginning of the resolution and afterwards they are resumed only for those repos that remain on the balance sheet of the old (bad) bank, while those that are transferred to the new supposedly healthy bank are not restored unless the new bank proves to be less healthy than it should be:[3] 'Even where master agreements provide for termination and close-out upon reorganisation or restructuring,[114] resolution regimes eschew the route of privileged treatment through a safe harbour-like mechanism (Paech, 2015, p. 28). The same idea is more strongly stated in the following sentence: 'Resolution regimes are more clear-cut in this regard than insolvency laws. There are no exceptions from the administrative stay comparable to safe harbour rules in insolvency law' (Paech, 2015, p. 28–9).

To sum up, the claim is that the privileged status of securities enjoying safe harbour status in bankruptcy law are negated by the new laws introducing resolution regimes, so the repo creditors would no longer be privileged against other types of creditors. This view neglects the fact that according to EU Directive (2014), repos with a maturity of less than one week are excluded from the bail-in. Repos in the new resolution regime still deserve a privileged treatment as they are exempted from being either written down or converted into equity.

Paech (2015) considers that safe harbour rules may no longer be needed in the new resolution regime. Zhou *et al.* (2012) are even more explicit on the topic:

> More importantly, *by eliminating insolvency risks*, the pressure on distressed financial institutions to post more collateral against their repo contracts could be significantly reduced, thereby minimizing liquidity risks and preventing runs on repos or other contracts. Equally important is that bail-in would reduce the need for assisted mergers and therefore, provide an alternative to even larger SIFIs.
>
> (p. 9, emphasis added)

We have already discussed the asymmetry between borrowers and lenders that shifts on the side of borrowers the burden of making repo liabilities maintain a fixed monetary value through margin calls. In the quotation above, it is assumed that this problem can be overcome just by eliminating insolvency risks through bail-ins.

Article 71(5) states that upon the end of the termination stay, the contracts transferred to the new institution can be terminated only if the condition for bankruptcy or resolution of the new institution are met. Instead, if the contracts are left in the old institution, they may be terminated. It is supposed that the new institution will be healthy, so no need to terminate the contracts arises, according to Paech (2015).

So the dividing line is between the contracts that will be transferred to the new institution and those that remain in the old one. The important point is which investors claims will be still valid or will be instead cancelled in order to guarantee the health of the new institution. In the BRRD (2014), article 44(2), it is written that the resolution authorities shall not exercise the write down or conversion powers to some liabilities and among them are listed:

> Resolution authorities shall not exercise the write down or conversion powers in relation to the following liabilities whether they are governed by the law of a Member State or of a third country:
>
> (a) liabilities to institutions, excluding entities that are part of the same group, with an original maturity of less than seven days;
>
> covered deposits;
>
> (b) secured liabilities including covered bonds and liabilities in the form of financial instruments used for hedging purposes which form an integral part of the cover pool and which according to national law are secured in a way similar to covered bonds;
>
> (c) any liability that arises by virtue of the holding by the institution or entity referred to in point (b), (c) or (d) of Article 1(1) of this Directive of

client assets or client money including client assets or client money held on behalf of UCITS as defined in Article 1(2) of Directive 2009/65/EC or of AIFs as defined in point (a) of Article 4(1) of Directive 2011/61/EU of the European Parliament and of the Council (1), provided that such a client is protected under the applicable insolvency law;

(d) any liability that arises by virtue of a fiduciary relationship between the institution or entity referred to in point (b), (c) or (d) of Article 1(1) (as fiduciary) and another person (as beneficiary) provided that such a beneficiary is protected under the applicable insolvency or civil law;

(e) liabilities with a remaining maturity of less than seven days, owed to systems or operators of systems designated according to Directive 98/26/EC or their participants and arising from the participation in such a system;

(Regulation no. 2014/59 EU, Article 44(2))

There is a long list of securities that are excluded from the conversion and thus are not subject to the bail-in. Most of them are related to hedging and netting processes. It is an explicit goal of the regulation, not to split netting and hedging sets as they are shaped by the existing rules:

In order to preserve legitimate capital market arrangements in the event of a transfer of some, but not all, of the assets, rights and liabilities of a failing institution, it is appropriate to include safeguards to prevent the splitting of linked liabilities, rights and contracts, as appropriate. Such a restriction on selected practices in relation to linked contracts should extend to contracts with the same counterparty covered by security arrangements, title transfer financial collateral arrangements, set-off arrangements, close out netting agreements, and structured finance arrangements. Where the safeguard applies, resolution authorities should be bound to transfer all linked contracts within a protected arrangement, or leave them all with the residual failing institution. Those safeguards should ensure that the regulatory capital treatment of exposures covered by a netting agreement for the purposes of Directive 2013/36/EU is not affected.

(Regulation no. 2014/59/EU, Recital (95))

If this non-splitting principle prevails, then the derivatives securities lending and repo contracts will be either transferred to the new institution, thus being saved or in theory they could also be written down but on a net basis (Ashurst, 2016).[4] If instead they are left in the old bank, the usual safe harbour rules will be reactivated after the two days' stay, so they can be terminated.

The whole structure of contracts designed by private institutions such as the ISDA, ICMA and others will be maintained untouched, even during the resolution processes. Other contracts like deposits and bonds may be broken – i.e. converted into equity of the new institutions or cancelled outright.

In practice, securities lending and repos with a short maturity that are the majority of repo contracts are excluded from the bail-in. Other long-term repos and derivatives may be subject to it, but only on a net basis, as all the linked contracts must not be split up. This contrasts with the treatment of other investors and even of depositors.

This treatment supports the perception that repo liabilities are, if not cash, something very similar to it (Ricks, 2016; Gabor and Vestergaard, 2016a). This is confirmed by their treatment and by the intervention of central counterparties in their clearing. Central counterparties are becoming the next too-big-to-fail institutions. Their eventual losses will require another bail-in with the same rules. So the legislation protects this tool more than deposits that are the legal means of payment for the economy.

From this viewpoint, the difference between insured and uninsured deposits is not relevant because both are legal means of payment and used to discharge debts and pay taxes. If someone writes a cheque on their account in a bank, the people that accept it do not make enquiries about whether the deposit on which the cheque is written is uninsured or insured. In addition, repo liabilities are privileged with respect to deposits independently of their size. While deposits are written down to the extent that their size is bigger than the insured deposit threshold, repo liabilities cannot be written down whatever their size is. So depositors' insurance is limited in size, while the implicit insurance of repo liabilities is not. This will induce both banks and depositors to prefer repos liabilities/assets to traditional deposits. And, since repo liabilities are also used widely by non-bank financial institutions as a replacement for bank deposits, their status as quasi-money will be reinforced by this preferential treatment. The counterparties of repo assets, which are other financial institutions – either banks or non-banks – have a preferential treatment with respect to retail investors and firms.

This disrupts the trust relationship, which is at the basis of banking. Then, in order for the competition between banks and non-bank financial institutions that are free to create quasi-money to be based on a level playing-field, the state should ensure directly all deposits, irrespective of their size (Minsky, 2008; Ricks, 2016). In turn, the possibility of being written down or converted into equity should concern repos and other short-term lending instruments, too.

In European countries all this contributes to disadvantage traditional banks that lend to the non-financial sector with respect to investment banks or big universal banks. It is as though the repo liabilities would enjoy an insurance without limits, while deposits are insured only up to a certain threshold. This happens even if they are not recognized as legal means of payments and cannot be used either to discharge debts or to pay taxes.

Possible disruptions to the payments system during bank resolution procedures

Writing down deposits of any size constitutes a blow to the orderly working of the payments system, as previous cases of application of this tool before the introduction of the BRRD have shown. The intensity of the disruption will depend on the structure of the banking system. The more that firms finance themselves from banks and have deposits at them to keep cash reserves used to pay subcontractors and workers, the more the system will be hit.

Particularly dramatic is the case in which firms entertain multiple relations with banks, being indebted to more than one bank, usually for small amounts. This happens in Italy, for example, where there are no long-term relationships between banks and firms in the tradition of the German Hausbank, but instead every firm borrows from several banks at the same time and each bank lends only a small amount following a sort of insurance strategy. In that case, writing down the deposit of firms means that they are not able to continue business and to repay loans due to other banks that have not failed. So, through the resolution mechanism, the crisis of one bank may spread to others with a domino effect. This is what happened in Cyprus, where this type of resolution was first experimented before being established as a common rule for Eurozone countries. At the time of writing, notwithstanding the exit from the ESM programme and the macroeconomic recovery due to tourism, the rate of non-performing loans in Cypriot banks is around 45 per cent. This is a clear legacy of the bail-in process. The damage was very large because the Cypriot banking system, although oversized with respect to the country's gross domestic product, was a traditional banking system in which most of the assets were loans and most of the liabilities were deposits.

The same threshold for insured deposits is questionable in Europe as the bank resolution legislative framework for the whole Eurozone is not yet accompanied by a common backstop mechanism whose scheme has been postponed, as many contrasting views exist on the way it should work. In this situation, even the safety of deposits under the insurance umbrella is doubtful. As Kregel (2013, p. 5) writes, referring to Minsky's own opinion:

> But, as Minsky observed, the ability of the scheme to meet its commitments implicitly requires the central bank to validate the insured deposits of any failed bank. It is a contingent liability represented in the United States by the existence of a line of credit with the US Treasury should the fund fall short of needs. The central bank must then provide the reserves necessary to meet the needs of the scheme, which is a contingent liability of the central bank.

In the EU, the European Central Bank is not committed to provide lines of credit to deposit insurance schemes in the various countries.

In Regulation (EU) No. 806/2014, the common resolution fund should start with each country building its own resolution fund to which the banks have to pay the insurance fee. After this first stage, in which no resources are mutualized, a part of the funding of the single funds would be pooled, but the details on how and when this would happen were linked to an intergovernmental agreement that had to be signed.[5] Initially, the contributions should be raised at the national level and later on they should be pooled at Union level after an intergovernmental agreement on their transfer and mutualization had been signed. In 2015, the Commission made a new proposal for a European Deposit Insurance Scheme. This scheme should proceed in three successive steps: a reinsurance stage, a co-insurance stage and a European system of deposit guarantees. The last step should be completed in 2024. However, this new tool, the European deposit insurance scheme, does not require any intergovernmental agreement, because banks contribute directly to the European Deposit Insurance Fund (EU Regulation No. 806/2014). There is no transfer of funds already collected at national level to the European level.[6] In this last proposal, a pure private insurance mechanism would be at work through a reinsurance scheme, just as it happens for private insurance companies. Regulation No. 806/2014 has been amended (European Commission, 2015) to incorporate this deposit scheme and the new regulation was enforced on 30 June 2017.

However, the reinsurance can hardly work without a fiscal backstop. Gros (2015) acknowledges that the resources of any normal deposit insurance will be insufficient in a systemic crisis. He imagines that the European Stability mechanism could act as a fiscal backstop (p. 4). Nieto (2016, p. 146) also discusses the lack of a fiscal backstop for both the Single Resolution Fund and the European Deposit Insurance Scheme.

In the case of the European Union, in which no government has the power to issue money, even a fiscal backstop would not be sufficient as the governments of the countries hit by a banking crisis would not succeed in raising money from the markets. So again, the only resource left is the central bank. However, the European Central Bank is not involved in any way in these proposals. None of these proposals, however, includes the commitment by the central bank to a credit line to the fund and this is their major drawback (Kregel, 2013).

In the current situation, the central bank is not committed to provide credit lines to insurance schemes for deposit, yet it is committed to provide liquidity lines to central counterparties dealing with the clearing of repos, securities lending and derivatives.[7] LC Clearnet, which is one of the major central counterparty entity for this type of business, is a licensed bank in France and surely is entitled to receive central bank liquidity assistance (Gabor and Vestergaard, 2016a). This is badly needed as the current risk management of clearing houses is not very reliable. Their own stress tests show that they would not have sufficient liquidity in a crisis scenario (see BIS-IOSCO, 2016). To the template question, what was their likely move in case all the previous liquidity provisions would be insufficient, the answer is always to get central bank funding. So it seems that the central bank backstop becomes more a hidden subsidy to the activity rather than a simple emergency liquidity provision. Although there is currently a discussion on living wills for central counterparties and clearing houses, they have not yet been introduced into the legislation.

From all this, it seems that the public interest is more concerned with the protection of repo derivatives and securities lending contracts among financial institutions than the protection of the system of payments in the real economy that works mainly through the legal means of payments such as deposits. This means further that the application of such rules will protect the counterparties to repos and secured lending that are overwhelmingly financial institutions and may destroy the productive structure of the economy.

Within the Eurozone countries to which the directive applies, the banking system which has the more traditional business model will be hit the most, while banks that have a business model more oriented on securities and derivatives will be hit less. If the former are also repo borrowers and the latter are repo creditors, the advantage will also assume a geographical and political feature. Moreover, the repo lending and borrowing model places a great importance on the safety of collateral, so the price of the collateral that is accepted more easily or with a lower haircut by repo lenders increases, while that of collateral considered riskier decreases. In the context of the Eurozone countries where the most used collateral are government bonds of member countries, but there is no real risk-free asset as no country retains its own money, it becomes a race to get the government bonds of the country that is considered safer, so the countries with lower deficits and debts will enjoy a higher price of their bonds and a lower return. The spread in the yield between stronger and weaker countries' government bonds could increase, not only because government bonds of weaker countries are considered less safe, but simply because the demand for the safest asset has increased with respect to the available supply. In the Eurozone, no state is sovereign, so the competition between different countries' government bonds becomes a competition among private assets in which rating agencies will have the major influence. So the repo borrowers that have their own country's debt as assets will be able to borrow at a lower price with respect to those that have a higher valued government bond at their disposal. This will increase the difficulties for weaker countries' financing and decrease the costs of stronger countries' financing.

Margin calls in turn will cause frequent oscillations in the prices of government bonds if the banks that are called to provide more margins are liquidity constrained and thus are compelled to sell those same bonds in order to get cash to comply with the call. What Sissoko (2016) correctly identifies as fluctuations in the value of mutual funds and other long cash pool investors in the Eurozone context become fluctuations in the prices of government bonds of weaker countries and in the share prices of their banks. This pattern has emerged during the financial crisis of 2011 in Europe, but has been stopped by the European Central Bank emergency liquidity provisions, particularly the long-term refinancing operations that have, in fact, replaced the interbank market and the reciprocal secured lending. Obviously, when these extraordinary measures, now continued by the quantitative easing, will cease, then the same pattern will re-emerge.

The failure to regulate the repo market in the EU

As Gabor and Vestergaard (2016b) point out, there has been a failure to regulate the repo market in the EU after the great financial crisis. Attempts at regulation have been made and are testified by several reports published by the Financial Stability Board and the European Commission. Those reports clearly showed how the repo market increases leverage of financial institutions and is a primary factor behind systemic risk. The rehypothecation chains which are unwound during a crisis period cause a spread of losses in the financial system. In the EU, the problem was compounded by the circumstance that after the crisis the volume of repos had not meaningfully declined as it had in the US.

The proposals presented by the FSB and the EC were aimed at increasing haircuts on repos by imposing a minimum floor on their level. At the same time, there was a discussion whether to introduce a financial transaction tax in the EU. It was calculated by a Goldman Sachs report that the major contribution to this tax revenue would come from the repo market, which in the EU was much bigger than that for securitized assets. The organization that defended the repo against both the mandatory floor haircut and the transaction tax, the European Repo Council, issued various reports and answered to the consultations launched by the European Commission, claiming that these measures would have a great impact on the liquidity of the government bond markets in Europe, so they would have increased the governments' financing costs. In 2014, with the arrival of Jonathan Hill at the European Commission, the Capital Markets Union programme was launched with the aim of unifying the capital markets in the European Union.

The International Capital Markets Association and the European Repo Council jumped on to it. They claimed that in order to foster the integration of capital markets in Europe, it was essential to provide for the free movement of any capital and particularly of collateral. They coined the expression 'free flow of collateral' and argued that any restriction to the repo market (minimum haircut, financial transactions tax) would hinder the free flow of collateral that was a prerequisite for the liquidity of capital markets (Gabor and Vestergaard, 2016b).

An interesting observation by the European Repo Council (ERC, 2014) was that indeed no tax should be levied on repos because repo liabilities are indeed the new cash, in which credits and debts among financial institutions are cleared. So repos being money, they should be protected in order to hinder a fall in the volume of financial transactions. This overlaps with our previous discussion on how the safe harbour status and the seniority with respect to uninsured deposits in banks' resolution procedures actually makes repos a close substitute for money. In fact, in banks' resolution procedures, repos are on the same foot as insured deposits.

Another point made by the European Repo Council was that repos were put at the centre stage and thus were blessed by many just introduced regulatory measures like the liquidity coverage ratio and the net stable funding ratio. We add that even the leverage ratio in the way it calculates the denominator of the ratio exposure at default recognizes all the hedging constructions and collateral structures built in both the balance sheet and off-balance sheets of financial institutions. In the definition of liquid assets, the existence of a liquid repo market was considered as the main characteristic of liquidity. So the European Repo Council is right in arguing that if the whole regulatory apparatus is built upon rules that increase interconnectedness and systemic risk, then it is not consistent first to foster its expansion as a positive thing and then to try to reduce its size. We have stressed that the equivalence between money, claim and security warranted by the Financial Collateral Directive paved the way to this treatment of repos as though they were money. Further, in the European Union, there is no common rule to limit rehypothecation, while in the US a Security and Exchange Commission (SEC) rule limits the rehypothecation by brokers of their customers' collateral to 140 per cent.

Another reason why the prospected regulation of repo markets was no longer pursued resides in the attitude of the ECB on the question (Gabor and Vestergaard, 2016b). The ECB was aware that reducing the size of the repo market would require a return of unsecured lending between banks and that there was no sign that banks were ready to go back to the pre-crisis pattern of reciprocal lending. The freezing of the interbank market and the downsizing of the repo market would have required again the direct intervention by the ECB in financing banks through new extraordinary liquidity injections that risked becoming ordinary routine. In order to avoid that outcome, the ECB, according to Gabor and Vestergaard (2016b), opposed the minimum haircut and the transaction tax.

Thus, the final picture that emerges from the puzzle is that in the European Union and in the Eurozone in particular the traditional hierarchy of monies has changed, putting at the top of the pyramid repo as the most important type of money that serves to maintain high the leverage and the profits of financial institutions by ensuring that repo lenders are whole on their money, even if this causes heavy fluctuations in government bonds prices, which are the most common collateral used in Europe. Deposits both insured and uninsured come after that because their invariant monetary value is not ensured in the case of a banking resolution. Their value would then depend on the emergency funds that the state may get from the European Stability Mechanism and from the intervention of the ECB to support the prices of government bonds. So, rather than being an asset whose nominal value does not change in contrast to other types of assets, they have become an asset whose value depends on a series of contingent circumstances. Ironically, derivatives that are traditionally defined as contingent claims have been insured, while deposits that are described as bank liabilities with fixed monetary value have become contingent claims.

This story on the regulation of repos in the EU contrasts with the story that has been taking place in the US where the Federal Reserve operated to constrain the leverage that can be pursued by this tool and therefore the growth of this segment of the money market. In the US before the crisis, most repos were intermediated through a bank that actively contributed to the expansion of the market by providing intraday credit to repo dealers. The banks thus were actively involved in the efficient functioning of the market by taking credit risk. The Fed, through its reform of the triparty repo market, decreased the permitted share of risk that banks were taking, and probably for that reason the repo market volumes declined.

In the EU, most repo contracts are bilateral contracts between banks and so have remained after the crisis, too. Since banks are on both sides of the deal, it is actually a secured interbank market. The ECB has not tried to control its expansion, presumably because the disruption of the unsecured interbank market made it essential. The consequence has been that after a small decline in 2007–8, the market has thrived and enjoys the same level of transaction as before the great financial crisis. Since the counterparties are banks, they are entitled to the liquidity provision by the central bank, which provides a backstop to it. As Gabor and Vestergaard (2016b) show, any attempt to decrease leverage by imposing a minimum mandatory haircut or constrain rehypothecation has been given up. The ECB's only intervention in the repo market has been in redesigning the haircuts for Eurozone countries' government bonds in 2011 by differentiating their treatment as collateral for financing by the central bank. This move actually created a segmentation in the use of collateral in repo between core countries and peripheral countries' government bonds, thus reinforcing the ongoing tendency of the latter to fall in price. From this viewpoint, it was exactly the opposite of the Fed intervention to support the value of the less valued collateral in the market (Mehrling, 2010).

Consequences of the recent regulation changes on the nature of the common currency

In the particular circumstances of the Eurozone countries, in which no country is sovereign – that is, can create its own money – the world that regulatory changes jointly with supervisory common practices and mandatory resolution procedures shape is one in which private assets compete with each other as, for example, in the free banking period in the US. Then the notes issued by private banks were competing with each other based on the perceived solidity of their issuers. The system was not very stable, however, as frequent runs on banks were taking place. In stress periods, private clearing houses contributed to stop the panic and later, in 1913, a federal central bank was introduced.

In the new European legislative framework, deposits are no longer guaranteed as neither the state with its fiscal capacity nor the common central bank backs them. However, what is guaranteed is that the reciprocal claims among banks and other financial institutions based on collateralized lending will always be honoured. This might cause a fluctuation in the prices of the assets underlying the claims that secure them, the government bonds of the Eurozone countries. In this case, the European Central Bank could intervene using the newly introduced tool, Outright Monetary Transactions, and mitigate these fluctuations by buying the bonds whose market prices have been falling, but its intervention is linked to the obligation by the country whose bonds are bought to ask for emergency credit assistance from the European Stability Mechanism and to accept all the conditions attached to it. First, the central bank does not guarantee the normal working of the payments system, as resolution procedures may weaken it considerably, and second the integrity of the claims in the repo and securities lending markets is warranted, even if making whole the creditors in this market may cause big fluctuations in some of the underlying assets such as peripheral countries' government bonds. In turn, if this happens, the ECB may intervene to stabilize the latter's prices and so avoid the bankruptcy of banks that have government bonds issued by their own country as an important share of their portfolio. The collapse of the payments system that would follow is avoided, but only if the country concerned surrenders the power to tax and spend to external undemocratic agencies. The euro then would reveal itself as neither a purely private bank money nor a state money, but a contractual money (Strange, 1971; Ingham, 2004). The conditions of the contract are written down in the interplay of the various regulations, pacts and monetary policy tools.

As it is well known among lawyers (Gelpern and Gerding, 2016; Hockett and Omarova, 2016), but usually ignored by economists, safe assets, by which it is meant risk-free assets, do not exist in nature, but are constructed through institutions, and the law is one of those institutions. As Gelpern and Gerding (2016) argue, the state does provide the necessary infrastructure to make people behave as though some contracts were risk free. The law would thus construct and maintain safe asset fictions and would place them at the foundation of institutions and markets. The faith in the safety of some assets is built in those foundations and the decision to frame the safe asset construction in one way rather than another does depend on political choices, as it has distributive consequences.

Faith in the safety of bank deposits is being challenged in Europe as a consequence of the missing state dimension for law. Most decisions are taken at the level which is supranational and then introduced in national legislation. But the real meaning of deposit insurance is undermined by the lack of monetary backstop by the state. Moreover, in the hierarchy of assets to be considered safe, repo assets, securities lent and interbank secured assets as well as mortgage-backed securities of a certain rating are clearly put ahead of loans. This reverses a traditional hierarchy of safety that started with the introduction of deposit insurance and with the liquidity provision by the central banks to commercial banks to maintain the monetary values of deposits fixed. People are still behaving as though the previous conventions have held, but several episodes seem to point out that this persuasion will be challenged by the facts. This could be justified by the project of returning to a free banking environment, in which every depositor has to look carefully at the soundness of their bank, and through competition among banks only the best will survive. This is, however, very unlikely and difficult to put in practice in an environment in which financial statements are so complex that they are difficult to interpret, even for accountants and specialists. Moreover, the force of competition to select the best banks will not display itself in an environment full of too-big-to-fail groups that risk almost nothing from their bad behaviour. Shareholders may be punished, but given the governance structure, the dispersed property structure and the limited liability regime, managers will be able to leave without paying anything and retaining big emoluments.

In the European context, this project risks empowering the banks in the northern and central states focused on investment and trading with respect to the banks in peripheral states, focusing on traditional banking activities through various channels. As the stress tests and all the macroprudential actions will be based on the microprudential apparatus based on new designed capital requirements, leverage ratio, liquid coverage ratio and net stable funding ratio, they will be biased towards requiring more capital to the latter banks and less capital to the former by default. The next step will be to resolve the banks that do not comply with the new regulations and maybe the big banks of the core countries will buy those of the peripheral ones, thus becoming even bigger.

Meanwhile, the banks that will no longer be able to provide credit to their traditional customers like micro-firms and SMEs, and that will be abandoned by traditional depositors because of the unsafe status of deposits, will be replaced by other market entities like online deposit only banks or online lending only channels.[8] The centuries-long creation of a bank that both takes deposits and grants loans, and that warranties the safety of deposits with the contribution of the central bank and of the state could be destroyed.

Notes

1 For a detailed analysis of why the legislation retained the central role of credit rating agencies although they were severely disqualified by their performance during the great financial crisis, see Bavoso, 2016.
2 ICMA describes very well how the accounting goes for repo assets and liabilities in this answer to a frequently asked question: 37. Is repo used to remove assets from the balance sheet? This question has been prompted by incidents such as Lehman Brothers' 'Repo 105' or MF Global's use of 'repo-to-maturity'. In both cases, assets sold in repos were accounted for as disposals and removed (temporarily) from the balance sheets of the sellers. This disguised their true leverage. However, in both cases, use was made of provisions specific to US Generally Accepted Accounting Principles (GAAP). These have been closed.

 In Europe, such accounting options are not available and repo must be accounted for in the standard way. This follows the principle that balance sheets are intended to measure the value and risk of a company, not the legal form in which it has structured its transactions. In a repo, as the seller in a repo commits to repurchase the collateral at a fixed future repurchase price, he retains the risk and return on that collateral. Accordingly, the collateral remains on the balance sheet of the seller, even though he has sold legal title to the collateral to the buyer. The logic of this accounting treatment is confirmed by the consequence that, because the cash paid for the collateral is added as an asset to the seller's balance sheet (balanced on the liability side by the repayment due to the buyer at maturity), this will expand, thereby signalling that that seller has increased his leverage by borrowing. In order to make it clear to the reader of a balance sheet which assets have been sold in repos, the International Financial Reporting Standards (IFRS) require that securities out on repo are reclassified from 'investments' to 'collateral' and are balanced by a 'collateralized borrowing' liability.
3 The text of the law is as follows:

 5. Where a resolution authority exercises the power specified in paragraph 1 or 2 of this Article to suspend termination rights, and where no notice has been given pursuant to paragraph 4 of this Article, those rights may be exercised on the expiry of the period of suspension, subject to Article 68, as follows:
  (a) if the rights and liabilities covered by the contract have been transferred to another entity, a counterparty may exercise termination rights in accordance with the

terms of that contract only on the occurrence of any continuing or subsequent enforcement event by the recipient entity;

authority has not applied the bail-in tool in accordance with Article 43(2)(a)to that contract, a counterparty may exercise termination rights in accordance with the terms of that contract on the expiry of a suspension under paragraph 1.

(BRRD, Article 71(5))

4   At the end of a long legal discussion, Ashurst (2016) concludes:

Moreover, it may be that resolution authorities seek to absorb losses to the extent necessary for resolution by writing down or converting the institution's unsecured debt and/or capital instruments and not to use the bail-in tool in respect of derivative contracts, in order to avoid complex valuations and the accompanying risk of litigation or breach of the no-creditor-worse-off principle. Indeed, the Bank of England has been candid in saying that this would be its preference in a resolution scenario.

5   In the Regulation (EU) No 806/2014 it is written:

A single resolution fund ('Fund') is an essential element without which the SRM could not work properly. If the funding of resolution were to remain national in the longer term, the link between sovereigns and the banking sector would not be fully broken, and investors would continue to establish borrowing conditions according to the place of establishment of the banks rather than to their creditworthiness. The Fund should help to ensure a uniform administrative practice in the financing of resolution and to avoid the creation of obstacles for the exercise of fundamental freedoms or the distortion of competition in the internal market due to divergent national practices. The Fund should be financed by bank contributions raised at national level and should be pooled at Union level in accordance with an intergovernmental agreement on the transfer and progressive mutualisation of those contributions (the 'Agreement'), thus increasing financial stability and limiting the link between the perceived fiscal position of individual Member States and the funding costs of banks and undertakings operating in those Member States. To further break that link, decisions taken within the SRM should not impinge on the fiscal responsibilities of the Member States. In that regard, only extraordinary public financial support should be considered to be an impingement on the budgetary sovereignty and fiscal responsibilities of the Member States. In particular, decisions that require the use of the Fund or of a deposit guarantee scheme should not be considered to impinge on the budgetary sovereignty or fiscal responsibilities of the Member States.

(Recital, 19)

6   The transfer was foreseen in Regulation (EU) No 806/2014:

This Regulation, together with Directive 2014/59/EU, establishes the modalities for the use of the Fund and the general criteria to determine the fixing and calculation of ex-ante and ex-post contributions. Participating Member States remain competent to levy the contributions from the entities located in their respective territories in accordance with Directive 2014/59/EU and with this Regulation. By means of the Agreement, the participating Member States will assume the obligation to transfer to the Fund the contributions that they raise at national level in accordance with Directive 2014/59/EU and this Regulation. During a transitional period, the contributions will be allocated to different compartments corresponding to each participating Member State (national compartments). Those compartments will be subject to a progressive merger so that they will cease to exist at the end of the transitional period. The Agreement will lay down the conditions upon which the parties thereto agree to transfer the contributions that they raise at national level to the Fund and to progressively merge the compartments. The entry into force of the Agreement will be necessary for the contributions raised by the parties to be transferred to the national compartments of the Fund. This Regulation lays down the powers of the Board for using and managing the Fund. The Agreement will determine how the Board is able to dispose of the national compartments that are progressively merged.

(Recital, 20)

7 Mancini *et al.* (2015) explain how all the major electronic platforms that deal with repo in Europe are backed by the support of the central bank and this feature contributes to the resilience of the repo market even during stress periods (p. 27).
8 That the peer-to-peer lending platform or the other private initiatives to collect deposits will survive without a public backstop and that they will morph into real credit creation rather than pure intermediation are the open questions nowadays (Kregel, 2016). More likely they will give rise to another credit bubble before being subject to some formal public backstop (Hockett and Omarova, 2016, pp. 53–4).

References

Ashurst (2016) BRRD valuations and bail-in – how are derivatives treated? Securities and derivatives group update, 25 May 2016. Available at: www.ashurst.com/en/news-and-insights/legal-updates/brrd-valuations-and-bail-in-how-are-derivatives-treated/ (accessed February 2016).

Basel Committee on Banking Supervision (BCBS) and Board of the International Organization of Securities Commissions (IOSCO) (2015) Criteria for identifying simple, transparent and comparable securitisations? Available at: www.bis.org (accessed November 2016).

Bavoso, V. (2016) Simple transparent and standardized securitization business as usual? Brussels Foundation for European Progressive Studies.

BIS-IOSCO, Committee on Payments and Market Infrastructures, Board of the International Organization of Securities Commissions, 2016. Consultative report: Resilience and recovery of central counterparties (CCPs): Further guidance on the PFMI, August 2016. This publication is available on the BIS website (www.bis.org) and the IOSCO website (www.iosco.org). Bank for International Settlements and International Organization of Securities Commissions, 2016.

ERC (2014) Collateral is the new cash: Systemic risks of regulating repo. European Repo Council International Capital Markets Association (ICMA).

EU Directive 2014/59/EU, Directive 2014/59/EU of the European Parliament and of the Council of 15 May 2014, establishing a framework for the recovery and resolution of credit institutions and investment firms, published in *Official Journal of the European Union*, 12 June 2014.

EU Regulation No. 806/2014 of the European Parliament and of the Council of 15 July 2014, establishing uniform rules and a uniform procedure for the resolution of credit institutions and certain investment firms in the framework of a Single Resolution Mechanism and a Single Resolution Fund and amending Regulation (EU) No. 1093/2. Available at: http://eur-lex.europa.eu/legal-content/EN/TXT/PDF/?uri=CELEX:32014R0806&from=EN (accessed 10 March 2017).

European Commission (2014) European Deposit Insurance Scheme (EDIS) – Frequently asked question, No. 21. Available at: http://europa.eu/rapid/press-release_MEMO-15-6153_en.htm (accessed 30 March 2017).

European Commission (2015) Proposal for a Regulation of the European Parliament and of the Council amending Regulation (EU) No. 806/2014 in order to establish a European

Deposit Insurance Scheme, Strasbourg, 24 November 2015, COM(2015), 586, final 2015/0270 (COD). Available at: http://eur-lex.europa.eu/legal-content/EN/TXT/PDF/?uri=CELEX:52015PC0586&from=EN (accessed 11 March 2017).

Gabor, D. and Vestergaard, J. (2016a) Towards a theory of shadow money, INET Working Paper.

Gabor, D. and Vestergaard, J. (2016b) Capital Markets Union and the free flow of collateral, Foundation for European Progressive Economic Studies, Brussels.

Gelpern, A. and Gerding, E. (2016) Inside safe assets. Working paper published in *Yale Journal on Regulation.*

Gros, D. (2015) Completing the banking union: Deposit insurance, CEPS Policy Brief no. 335, December. Available at: www.ceps.eu/system/files/PB335%20DG%20 Completing%20BU_0.pdf (accessed 10 March 2017).

Hockett, R.C. and Omarova, S.T. (2016) The finance franchise (8 August). *Cornell Law Review*, Vol. 102 (2017); Cornell Legal Studies Research Paper No. 16–29. Available at: https://ssrn.com/abstract=2820176 or http://dx.doi.org/10.2139/ssrn.2820176

Ingham, G.K. (2004) *The Nature of Money*, Cambridge: Polity.

International Capital Markets Association (ICMA) Frequently asked question, No. 37. Available at: www.icmagroup.org/Regulatory-Policy-and-Market-Practice/repo-and-collateral-markets/frequently-asked-questions-on-repo/37-is-repo-used-to-remove-assets-from-the-balance sheet (accessed November 2016).

Kregel, J. (2013) Lessons from the Cypriot deposit haircut for EU deposit insurance schemes. Levy Economics Institute of Bard College, New York, Policy Note 2013/4.

Kregel, J. (2016) Public financial institutions after the financial crisis: A new deal in the making? Prepared for the MINDS – BNDES – Conference on The Present and Future of Development Financial Institutions. Available at www.minds.org.br/media/papers/kregel-minds-bndes-financial-i53d557d967047.pdfhttp://www.minds.org.br/media/papers/kregel-minds-bndes-financial-i53d557d967047.pdf (accessed 28 February 2017).

Mancini, L., Ranaldo, A. and Wrampelmeyer, J. (2015) The euro interbank repo market (30 July). Swiss Finance Institute Research Paper No. 13–71; University of St Gallen, School of Finance Research Paper No. 2013/16. Available at: https://ssrn.com/abstract=2331355 or http://dx.doi.org/10.2139/ssrn.2331355

Mehrling, P. (2010) *The New Lombard Street. How the Fed became the dealer of last resort*. Princeton: Princeton University Press.

Michell, J. (2017) Do shadow banks create money? Financialisation and the monetary circuit, *Metroeconomica*, 68(2): 354–77.

Minsky, H.P. ([1986] 2008) *Stabilizing an Unstable Economy*. New York: McGraw-Hill.

Nieto, M.J. (2016) Bank resolution and mutualization in the euro area, *European Economy*, 2: 431–54.

Paech, P. (2015) The value of insolvency safe harbours, LSE Law, Society and Economy Working Papers 9/2015, published in *Oxford Journal of Legal Studies*, 2016, 36(4): 855–84. Available at: https://doi.org/10.1093/ojls/gqv041

Pozsar, Z. (2014) Shadow banking: The money view. Working Paper 14-04, Office of Financial Research.

Ricks, M. (2016) *The Money Problem Rethinking Financial Regulation*. Chicago: University of Chicago Press.

Sissoko, C. (2014) Shadow banking: Why modern money markets are less stable than 19th c. money markets but shouldn't be stabilized by a "dealer of last resort". Legal Studies Research Papers Series No. 14–21.

Sissoko, C. (2016) The economic consequences of "market-based" lending. Available at: http://ssrn.com/abstract=2766693 (accessed November 2016).

Strange, S. (1971) The politics of international currencies, *World Politics*, 23(2): 215–31.

Zhou, J., Rutledge, V., Bossu, W., Dobler, M., Jassaud, N. and Moore, M. (2012) From bail-out to bail-in: Mandatory debt restructuring of systemic financial institutions, International Monetary Fund Discussion Note.

Part II

Financial regulation and the European crisis

Some case studies

6 Financial fragility in the European crisis

Three episodes

Introduction

Fragility, according to Minsky (1982), cannot be measured through simple metrics. It has a peculiar systemic dimension. It relates to interconnectedness and layering in the financial system and depends on history and institutions. I am starting from this viewpoint to analyse the fragility that built up in the European financial system after the big financial crisis of 2007. I am arguing that fragility in the aftermath of that crisis has taken a different shape with respect to the previous period ranging from the early 2000s to 2007. Behind this transformation is the feedback between the financial system and changes in rules and institutions. In the post-crisis period there were several changes in regulation to overcome the legacy of the 2007 crisis and in institutions to face the new challenges of the European 'crisis'. Minsky stressed that a major force behind the evolution of the financial system is financial innovation. In a competitive system, bankers and non-bankers will strive to reap profits by inventing new products and new strategies (see Ferri and Minsky, 1991).

I am sharing with Nesvetailova (2014) the idea that the financial system is a complex ecology where individual microeconomic decisions and actions interact. The result of the interaction is often different from the targets of the parts. Further, bricolage is a feature of financial innovation in so far as actors do not behave as having a thought structure behind them, but rather tend to exploit profit opportunities that emerge under particular and often unforeseen circumstances (see Engelen *et al.*, 2010).

The plan of the work is the following. As derivatives are the main channel of product innovation in finance, a collection of data on the issue of old and new derivatives products has been assembled in the first section. In particular, it is highlighted how the London financial centre has gained in influence. In the remaining sections, three episodes of financial fragility will be examined. The first episode deals with the turmoil in the prices of government bonds and the birth of a new market for Western European credit default swaps for the same bonds. The second deals with the second bail-out of the bank Dexia that contains some paradigmatic elements of the behaviour of big core countries' banks in 2010–11. In Dexia's case, it is shown that the bail-out and the liquidity problems were not due, as argued by existing research, simply to a carry trade gone awry, but rather to an unsuccessful hedging strategy involving interest rate swaps. The third focuses on an episode of extraordinary regulatory policy implemented by a new institution, the European Banking Authority, in November 2011 that acted as a transmission chain of the crisis from core to peripheral countries' banks.

Financial innovation in Europe after 2007: new and old derivatives

The notional amounts of derivatives, after having registered a slight fall after the 2007 financial crisis, are now rising again worldwide. Data from the Bank for International Settlements (2013) latest survey show that the total notional amount should be around $700 trillion. The relative weights of particular derivatives over the total as well as their geographical distribution have changed. As this chapter is related to the issue of financial fragility in Europe, I will examine data that refer to various dimensions, such as the currency denomination of derivatives, the development of particular instruments having as underlying securities issued by European entities, the actual balance sheet holdings of derivatives by European banks, the location of the issuing financial institutions and the nationality of the counterparts. No such measure in itself is exhaustive, but it is necessary to have a framework to start a discussion of how derivatives may contribute to fragility in the current environment. The most common derivatives issued, CDS (credit default swaps) and IRS (interest rate swaps), show contrasting trends in the years after the crisis. CDS as a notional amount fell after 2007, but then recovered during the global financial crisis, particularly the CDS indexes, while IRS show a rising trend and high year-on-year positive rates of change.

The market for CDS having as reference entities European entities existed before the financial crisis and was very active in the years before it. It is difficult, however, to have data for this period because the market was over the counter and it is difficult to have data on the European dimension of the phenomenon. In the years before the crisis, European banks were participating in the shadow banking network in the US (see Poszar *et al.*, 2010). Since 2004, CDS indexes having as reference entities a basket of European entities have been created. In 2007, two separate series of indexes were unified and Markit, a London-based company, became their owner and manager. New indexes were created and for the first time an index was launched referencing developed Western European governments debt, called *ITRAXX Sovereign Western Europe*. The global index CDS experienced a boom in the period between 2003 and 2007 when the global crisis erupted. Originally, in 2004, the success of these indexes was linked to their use in the global securitization chain. Proprietary trading desks of banks and hedge funds, according to Cousseran and Rahmouni (2005), took advantage of the liquidity and the flexibility of standard CDS index tranches to take long or short positions according to their views on levels of default correlation in the underlying portfolios (correlation trading). There were many advantages of the trading of CDS index tranches for the CDO market: improved transparency, liquidity and risk management, increase in market liquidity, narrowing of bid/ask spread, improvement in the management of market participants' risk (see Cousseran and Rahmouni, 2005). The market enjoyed increasing trading volumes in the years preceding the big financial turmoil of 2007. Unfortunately, data are available only for the indexes issued by Markit from 2008 onwards. Before 2008, there are data on the world's total notional amounts of CDS, but it is not possible to infer the share of those amounts in which the reference entities are European. From the narrative of the crisis that has prevailed, it seems that European banks' branches, subsidiaries and special investment vehicles were massively participating in the securitization of US-originated mortgage loans. Securitized assets have always been smaller in Europe with respect to the US, both before and after the financial crisis of 2007. In fact, most CDOs and CLOs issued in Europe are synthetic. Synthetic securitizations do not require that loans are removed from banks' balance sheets. After a drop following the crisis in 2007–8, the issue of CDS has recovered, but showing lower notional amounts. This recovery may be motivated by banks seeking regulatory capital relief against corporate loans in their portfolio. The most common way of doing it was to use balance sheet CLOs (collateralized loans obligations) that would shift the risk outside the bank and thus allow it to save capital by lowering the share of risk-weighted assets over total assets. The key drivers of Balance Sheet CLOs were the management of regulatory capital and funding (see Green Street Capital Research, 2010). In particular, as Pollack (2012) stresses, between 2011 and 2012 there has been an increase in the CDS indexes referencing European corporate debt that were tranched. Tranching allowed protection to be bought for a particular section of the index with a determined degree of risk. In this case, the same use of the indexes was made as before the financial crisis. Pollack (2012) adds that those deals were mainly made by big banks to earn fees from issuing structured products, while second- and third-tier banks would use these products for regulatory relief. The rise in the exposure to the tranched index between the end of 2011 and the start of 2012 is peculiar to Europe as the corresponding Markit index for US corporates has registered only a negligible rate of growth (see Pollack, 2012). A new product that was launched by Markit after the big financial crisis was a CDS index referencing Western European sovereign debts. The index was called *ITRAXX Sovereign Western Europe*. The notional amounts of CDS issued under this name are shown in Figure 6.1.

As shown in Figure 6.1, notional amounts were in the order of €200–300 billion. They were much lower than those of other CDS indexes like the ITRAXX Europe referencing debt issued by European private entities that enjoyed notional volumes in the order of various trillion euros. This, notwithstanding the *ITRAXX Sovereign Western Europe*, was very important during the period of higher financial distress because it registered the cost of insuring against sovereign defaults. The premia paid by the purchasers of insurance became a widespread measure of the risk involved in the holdings of the underlying government bonds. This happened even if the market was very thin and totally over-the-counter (OTC).

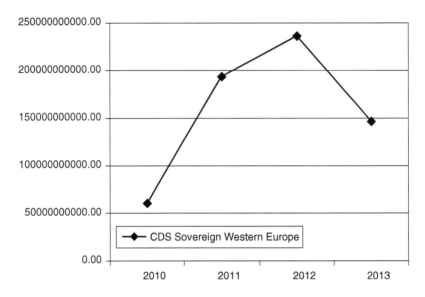

Figure 6.1 The index ITRAAX CDS Sovereign Western Europe in notional values of euros

Source: DTCC data repository.

The premia were fixed by the banks that acted as dealers for the owning company, Markit. The dealers were all big transnational investment banks. Daily quotes were available on the Markit website and were frequently reported in newspapers and magazines. In Markit's customer information leaflet, the process through which the quotes were made is described as 'very similar to the Libor's fixing'. This small market was, however, very important for the diffusion for the crisis in Europe. As we can see in Figure 6.1, the notional amount rose very strongly in 2010 and 2011. The fall from 2012 onwards is due to a policy change. In November 2011, a European Union regulation, Regulation (EU) No 236/2012 of the European Parliament, forbid the purchase of naked CDS, having as reference entities European Union governments; although the regulation was binding only from 1 November 2012, it immediately caused, according to ISDA (2014), a reduction in weekly notional volumes that continued after its implementation. In this way, the demand for CDS has been discouraged. Although this particular section of the indexes has suffered a contraction, the notional amount of CDS outstanding, both single name and indexes, is still high and a high share of it is related to Europe. According to BIS (2013), most CDS are issued in the London offices of financial institutions, while the counterparties to deals of the size of $13.011 billion (out of a total $24.349 billion of notional amounts) are located in Western European developed countries (BIS semi-annual survey, June 2013, Table 8, p. 26).[1] It has also declined the share of CDS that has been traded among reporting dealers of BIS, the major banks, while it has increased the share traded

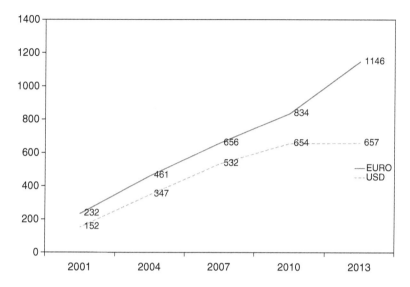

Figure 6.2 Global over-the-counter interest rate derivatives market turnover by currency. Net-net basis, daily averages in April, in billions of US dollars

Source: Bank for International Settlements (BIS).

between reporting dealers and other financial institutions, which are either non-banks or smaller banks.

While the resurgence of CDS after the big financial crisis has been relevant, in particular for the creation of new products that were used in the new European crisis such as the *ITRAXX Sovereign Western Europe* index, the most striking development in the derivatives world has been the enormous increase in the issue and daily trading volumes of interest rate derivatives. In Figure 6.2 we see the daily turnover of OTC derivatives interest rate swap respectively in dollars and euros.

We can observe that the turnover of IRS in euros has increased very rapidly in the period after the global financial crisis. In 2007, the value of the turnover was $656 billion, while in 2013 it reached $1,146 billion. It almost doubled in six years. Most of the rise happened in the period 2010–13 when the crisis in Europe became deeper. The turnover of IRS in dollars rose from 2007 to 2010 from $532 to $654 billion, while staying almost unchanged in the period between 2010 and 2013, increasing by just $3 billion. Since the data on turnover are published in dollars, the difference could eventually be due to a change in the exchange rate. The BIS in a footnote to the tables adds that the exchange rates used for the conversion are the average exchange rates of April. From the observation of the average monthly April exchange rates dollar/euro in the years of the triennial surveys, however, it is not possible to ascribe the change in turnover values to exchange rates changes only.

Figure 6.3 shows the data on interest rate derivatives notional values collected by the semi-annual surveys of the Bank for International Settlements. The notional values of interest rate derivatives in euros are steadily rising in the period

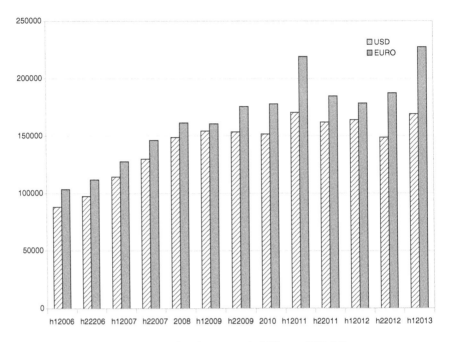

Figure 6.3 Interest rate swaps notional amounts, in billions of US dollars

Source: Bank for International Settlements (BIS).

being considered, reaching in June 2013 a value higher than $200,000 billion. The growth of the corresponding IRS in dollar is much slower.

The extraordinary growth of the European Union segment of the interest rate derivatives market is confirmed in the data on turnover by country. In Figure 6.4, we see that the UK has the highest turnover in the trading of interest rate derivatives in the world followed by the US. This reflects presumably the leading role of the London financial centre. As we see in Figure 6.3, even before the crisis in 2007 the turnover in London was much higher than in the US. After the crisis, however, the rate of growth in turnover of the two big financial centres diverged even more. While the US experienced a very slight fall in turnover in the last survey in 2013, with respect to the 2010s, the UK increased its share of global turnover to a very high amount. The highest increase happens in the time span 2007–10. While the other European Union countries contribute little to the statistics, an exception is France, which shows an increasing turnover throughout the period, reaching in 2013 almost $200 billion.

The rise in trading in the London financial centre may be linked to the rules on rehypothecation of collateral that are more favourable to financial institutions with respect to the US. Moreover, there are internal incentives within the financial institutions for the increase in trading volumes. Bowman *et al.* (2012) write that compensation ratios are important for the incomes of senior investment bankers in the City. Thus, higher pay comes from higher trading volumes.

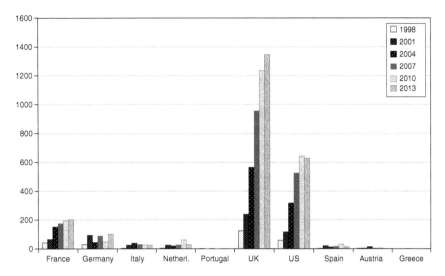

Figure 6.4 Over-the-counter interest rate derivatives market turnover (by country) 1998, 2001, 2004, 2007, 2010, 2013, in billions of euros

Source: Bank for International Settlements (BIS).

Although these elements may have mattered, the size of the increase calls for an explanation that includes the demand side. *All these interest rate derivatives would not have been created without a rising demand for them.* So the question to be answered is whether the evolution of the European financial system in the aftermath of the big financial crisis has generated this increased demand for interest rate derivatives. Among interest rate derivatives interest rate swaps have contributed massively to that increase. IRS may be used for a variety of reasons. The most obvious one is to protect the value of a portfolio of bonds. Sometimes, however, their use arises from the diffusion of other practices such as collateralization. The value of the collateral is marked to the market and its changes may cause margins calls. Thus, in the case of government bonds, IRS may be used to protect themselves from these calls. Another disguised form of the same practice is possible in repurchase agreements. The bond sold and then repurchased is a sort of a collateral for a loan and may involve also margins that change with the value of bonds. Therefore, again IRS are useful to face those margin calls. After the 2007 financial crisis, the market for unsecured loans in Europe among banks has almost disappeared and all loans tended to be secured through collateral. Repo agreements were of the order of €5–6 trillion on average in the years 2010–13 (see ICMA, 2014). Moreover, new financial products might have required entering into IRS contracts. A case in point are synthetic exchange-traded funds (ETFs). ETFs are exchange-traded funds and are considered by EU legislation as investment funds and thus subject to UCIT regulation. The difference from traditional investment funds is that they can be traded at any moment and do not charge a redemption fee or minimum tenure clauses. They were launched in the US as a tool to avoid high management fees and to provide flexibility to retail investors. In the US, the market is made mainly of retail investors and is successfully competing with the mutual funds industry. In Europe, instead the market is concentrated on financial institutions, which trade the ETFs among themselves. A share of 70 per cent of all trades happens over the counter. Another specificity of the European market is the preference for synthetic ETFs with respect to physical ones. For example, if an ETF is referenced to a bond, the seller may hold the bonds as physical assets or use instead the swap market. This type of ETF is easier to be arranged by big investment banks; for them, the process involves an internal transaction between two different departments of the same firm – the investment and the derivatives desks. As a business report explains:

> In these cases, there is no "separation of powers"—a single entity, usually a bank, designs the fund, selects the collateral, vouches for its quality and value, writes a swap contract to make up the difference and then makes payments to keep the swap current.
>
> (Kremer, 2014)

In that case, entering into an interest swaps is part of the process of origination of a synthetic ETF. If the supply of synthetic ETFs increases, so does the demand for IRS. Synthetic ETFs have been scrutinized by the Financial Stability Board for their potential destabilizing impact on the financial system (see FSB, 2011). The volume of ETFs outstanding at end 2013 was €303,061 million. The increase has been noteworthy since in 2005 the volume was only $70,000 million (see FSB, 2011, Graph 1, p. 2). Synthetic ETFs represented 17 per cent of North American ETFs as of June 2013, but 69 per cent of European ETFs.

The increase in derivatives seen in aggregate data is also visible in bank balance sheets data. The big banks of core countries like Germany, Great Britain and France have the major share of derivatives in their balance sheets, in the range 20–33 per cent, while peripheral countries' big banks have a lower share, in the range 6–10 per cent (see MBRS, 2012). The ratios of derivatives to capital are indeed very high. Capital, in fact, is very low for some core countries' banks. A fitting example is Deutsche Bank, which in 2012 had a total notional amount of derivatives of €55.605.039 million, of which €45.337.568 million were 'interest related' – i.e. they were interest rate derivatives. A big part of the interest rate derivatives, €41.264.732 million, were over the counter. The regulatory capital was 2 per cent of total assets (see Deutsche Bank, 2012). The value of 2 per cent, of course, is the ratio of capital to total assets, while the ratio considered in Basel III and in the European Union regulation is the ratio of capital to risk-weighted assets. European banks have ended up with enormous exposures in notional amounts and a tiny capital with respect to total assets.

Figure 6.5 shows ECB consolidated banking data on derivatives positions reported according to hedge accounting rules.

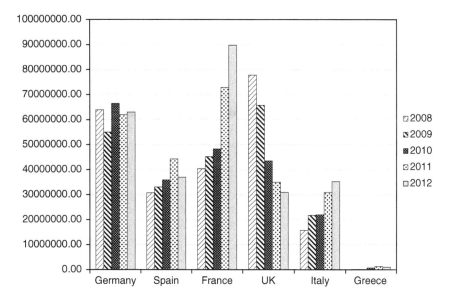

Figure 6.5 European banks' derivatives

Source: ECB consolidated banking data.

We see that for the UK derivatives holdings are declining; for France, Spain and Italy they are rising. The derivatives positions held by French banks are much higher than those of other countries. Moreover, they are also rising in the period 2008–12. On the contrary, the UK banks' derivatives positions are decreasing over the same period (see Figure 6.5). In the UK most derivatives were held in the balance sheets of non-bank financial institutions as the FSB writes:

> In the UK, a significant part of this growth is associated with an increase in derivative assets of NBFIs, which is matched by a commensurate increase in derivative liabilities, and is in line with trends in the gross market value of global OTC derivatives and London's large share of this market.
>
> (FSB, 2012)

From the consolidated data it seems that UK banks, which have suffered the most from the financial crisis, have lowered their derivatives position. This agrees with aggregate data showing the increase in the UK of the share of shadow banks' assets in the period 2007–2012 (see FSB, 2012). Instead, German banks have more or less maintained their positions throughout the period, while banks in France, Spain and Italy have increased their derivatives positions. The derivatives positions of French banks have more than doubled from 2007 to 2012, passing from €40 billion to €90 billion. The most pronounced increases have been registered in 2011 and 2012, the worst years of the European crisis (see Figure 6.5). Since the consolidated data collected by the ECB come from banks' financial statements compiled under the hedge accounting procedure, the relatively small numbers reflect the hedging process, although it is not known which are the hedged assets. According to Mügge and Stellinga (2011), hedge accounting involves designating a derivative, measured at fair value, as a hedging instrument and other items as the hedged instruments, measured at historical cost. Discretion by banks in choosing both the hedging and hedged assets is therefore allowed. What is certain is that hedge accounting[2] is useful in presenting an exposure to derivatives that is much lower than that which would result from notional amounts.

Summarizing, after the big world financial crisis, there has been a pronounced increase in the issue of interest rate swaps in euros linked to the expanding role of the London financial centre in this activity. This is seen in both the data on notional amounts outstanding and daily turnover volumes of IRS. The demand for interest rate derivatives has to be linked to the increase in secured lending among European financial institutions after the breakdown of the interbank market and to the practice of rehypothecation of collateral. A simpler use may have been that of protecting a bond portfolio, as we shall see on pp. 113–117 below, which discusses the problems of the bank Dexia.

Another important point is that, although the global amount of CDS issued at global level has strongly decreased with respect to the pre-crisis period, CDS having as counterparties entities in the European Union are in June 2013 more than half of the total CDS notional amount outstanding. Moreover, there has been strong interest among the investors to CDS indexes, and among them the series having as reference entities, Western European sovereign governments have played a role in the development and diffusion of the European crisis. Last but not least, there has been an expansion in the period 2007–12 of derivatives positions held by some European Union countries' banks. That expansion, according to ECB consolidated banking data, was very strong in 2011 and 2012 for French banks.

The evolution of markets changed the use of derivatives by European financial institutions. While in the pre-crisis era they were mainly involved in the securitization of US-originated mortgages and other debt, in the post-crisis environment they turned to the home market dealing in interest rate products that thrived because of the increase in the demand for secured lending and collateral due to the new regulations. Moreover, as we shall see, most core countries' European banks were developing a peculiar shadow banking activity that consists, according to Mehrling *et al.* (2013), of incurring short-term debt in order to buy longer maturity capital market assets. Interest rate derivatives were essential in order to protect the value of collateral and to protect also the value of the risky assets purchased. In the European environment after 2007, the risky capital markets assets were no longer mortgages or mortgage-backed securities, but the bonds issued by peripheral European countries' governments.

The CDS market and the fall in value of government bonds during the European financial crisis

We have seen that although CDS issue declined after the global financial crisis, a new market for Western sovereign European bonds CDS has developed. This market in quantitative terms measured as notional amounts outstanding is tiny. However, it has been very important for the transmission of the European financial crisis.

In this section we see how the market for CDS may affect the price of the underlying securities. This reasoning is applied to the case of the fall in price of peripheral countries' government bonds during the European crisis. While the use of CDS has been blamed for its potential of speculation and this fear has prompted the adoption of an European regulation that has stopped this market, it is argued that a higher premium on CDS may increase the uncertainty on the future course of the bonds and thus affect their spot price (see Figure 6.6). The increased demand for protection against default causes an increase in its price, the credit default premium. As this is seen as a sign of increased probability of default, the price of bonds falls and their yield rises. Uncertainty makes profitable speculative activities, too. This is exacerbated by the fact that all operators use models that define risk as depending upon volatility. If volatility rises, speculation

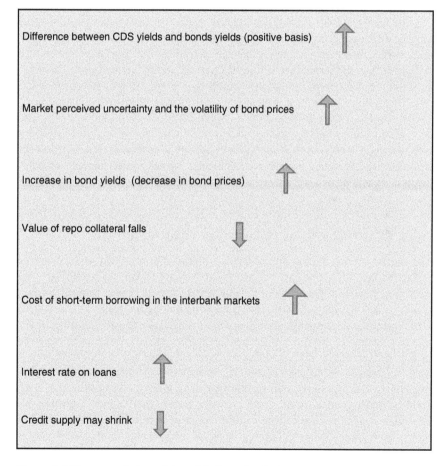

Figure 6.6 The transmission of the crisis from the CDS and bond markets to the credit market

is more profitable and the demand for protection rises too in a self-enforcing loop. In the market for sovereign bonds in the Eurozone such a feedback was based on the positive differential between CDS premium and bond yields spreads of the peripheral Eurozone countries' bonds. Many empirical studies have found that the CDS premium increases first and the bond yield follows (see, for example, Coudert and Gex, 2010; Arce *et al.*, 2012). Coudert and Gex (2010) argue that, undoubtedly, the CDS premium leads the bond yield in the case of southern European bonds markets, while the same does not hold for core European countries' low yield public bonds. Their interpretation of these findings is that the price discovery process in the market for southern European bonds happens in the CDS market, while in the core European countries it happens in the spot market. That CDS market leads the bonds market in a section of countries – the authors write – is puzzling because the latter is much less liquid than the former. They had found the opposite in the CDS spread with respect to the bond spread in the market for corporate bonds and had justified that result with the observation that the CDS market is more liquid than the bonds market.

If the feedback loop explanation matters, then it does not make sense to speak of price discovery process by the market for CDS. The CDS market is not discovering earlier than the spot market the right price based on fundamentals but it is making it. The spot market will follow. Once the high yield on bonds has worsened the macroeconomic situation in southern countries, then fundamentals will adapt themselves to the new, previously determined in derivatives market price. The process may take different routes. Surely, the increase in interest payments decreases domestic aggregate demand and gross national product, thus increasing the debt to GDP ratio. Moreover, since bonds are used in repo funding between banks, the fall in the value of repos will cause liquidity problems and probably credit contractions or higher interest rates for clients.[3]

Dexia's financial distress and its second bail-out in 2011

The second episode of fragility is Dexia's financial distress and its second bail-out in October 2011. The case is emblematic because Dexia had passed the stress tests run by the European Banking Authority in June 2011 and, according to the results, it had the highest capital to assets ratio among the banks in the sample. Dexia needed a second bail-out because it was unable to meet a margin call relative to a change in the value of derivatives in its portfolio. Changes in the value of derivatives, due to mark-to-market accounting, may act in the same way as interest changes in Minsky's original formulation of the financial fragility hypothesis. Dexia was rescued for the first time, in 2008, because of the losses suffered on the valuation of assets on its balance sheet. Dexia, like many big European banks, had participated in the boom of derivatives linked to the US mortgage market. Thus, it may be seen as emblematic of the evolution of European banks' fragility in the period between the great financial crisis and the so-called sovereign debt crisis. In the autumn of 2011, Dexia incurred losses on both its bonds portfolio and its interest swap position allegedly built to protect the same portfolio:[4]

> Dexia's derivative positions put even more pressure on short-term funding. Dexia was long fixed rate assets and hedged its positions using interest rate swaps. Between June and September 2011, Dexia had to post EUR 15 billion cash collateral due the fall in interest rates.
>
> (Acharya and Steffen, 2012, p. 17)

Acharya and Steffen (2012) explain that Dexia was long on peripheral European states bonds and it financed this position through short-term money market financing. Therefore, it was compelled to refinance frequently at the conditions prevailing on the market. Probably, Dexia, like many of its peers, used the bonds in its portfolio as collateral in repo financing. Clearly, when the value of collateral falls, the margins have to be increased. In 2011, peripheral states' government bonds depreciated in value due to the uncertain management of the Greek crisis. The losses that Dexia suffered were due to the sudden withdrawal of market funding and the higher margins on repos triggered by the fall in the mark-to-market value of the bonds. Acharya and Steffen (2012) found that all major European banks that had participated in the EBA stress test carried out in July 2011 invested in peripheral countries' government bonds pursuing gains from a carry trade strategy. They bought long-term bonds and financed this position on the short-term money market. The core countries' banks bet that the divergence in the yield of government bonds would soon disappear but their bet was wrong – so wrote Acharya and Steffen (2012). But the same authors wrote (see quotation above), that the banks protected themselves from changes in the price of bonds through interest rate swaps. So if the banks believed in the convergence of rates, they would not need any protection. Even if the carry trade strategy failed, the losses should be covered by the hedge. The problem, instead, was that the hedge did not work. The swaps that should have offset the bonds' depreciation did not provide any relief. In the new environment created by the explosion of the debt crisis, hedging strategies on sovereign bonds based on IRS linked to Euribor were bound to fail. In fact, before the crisis, the debts of all Eurozone countries' governments were considered equally risky because they were denominated in the same currency. The ECB, too, did not require different haircuts on European countries' government bonds used as collateral in refinancing operations until April 2010. Under this assumption, it was obvious that they should protect themselves from variations in the value of bonds by using IRS indexed to a single interest, the Euribor.

Actually, when the perceived risk of European governments' risks diverged, with peripheral countries being considered riskier and core countries less risky, hedging through a single interest rate could not offer protection from variations in bonds prices for all bonds independently of their nationality. For example, if the Italian bonds' price falls and their yield rises, the spot position of the investor in bonds will register a loss. In order to be hedged, then, the investor should gain on the derivative position, the IRS. In fact, if the trader is the fixed rate payer and the reference interest rate, the Euribor, rises, then its derivative position improves. However, since the Euribor is an interest rate that registers the variations in the cost of interbank credit among a certain number of European banks, it may not necessarily rise if Italian government bonds decline in value.[5] It may even fall, the turmoil in the market for government bonds notwithstanding. In the latter case, the investor would lose on both its spot position and its derivative position. More generally, since the ECB never acted as market maker for the European sovereign debts market, the yield of government bonds was not necessarily equal or near to the policy rate (see Terzi, 2014, p. 16). According to this reconstruction, there was no 'carry trade gone awry' (see Acharya and Steffen, 2012) but rather a hedging strategy that was bound to fail.

Dexia could have accessed the central bank liquidity facility but it should have pledged collateral that it did not have. Even the European Commission noted this point according to what reported in Acharya and Steffen (2012):

> The European Commission explicitly addressed its concerns with respect to the large amount of sovereign debt in Dexia's portfolio and the use of interest rate derivatives which 'probably requires significant collateral for Dexia, which may reduce its eligible collateral base for financing from the central banks or in the interbank repo market' (EC, 2010).
>
> (Acharya and Steffen, 2012, p. 8)

Another problem arising from the new legislation is that, due to the various repos, CVA (credit valuation adjustment) hedging and other similar transactions, unencumbered assets become very scarce on the banks' balance sheets (see Fender and Lewrick, 2013). It is worth recalling that the change in collateral policy by the ECB, started in April 2010, and continued with the decision from January 2011 to graduate haircuts on eligible collateral for refinancing operations in the BBB+ to BBB– range penalized the banks holding peripheral countries' bonds. The banks holding massive amounts of peripheral countries' bonds were, indeed, core countries' banks.

Acharya and Steffen (2012) argued that the case of Dexia is not an isolated phenomenon. Many European banks, particularly those in the core European states, they wrote, would have used the same carry trade in peripheral countries' government bonds to boost profits and similarly incurred in losses on their derivatives positions and in the necessity to restore impaired capital.[6] In particular, they found that larger banks (i.e. banks with more international focus, more wholesale funding and that are more systemically important) had larger sovereign exposures to Italy. They conclude that large banks, banks with more short-term debt as well as undercapitalized banks, were more likely to engage in carry trades, particularly among core countries' banks. Thus, core countries' European banks, just after having registered heavy losses linked to the US crisis, started immediately to engage in the same activities of borrowing short term on the wholesale markets to finance the acquisition of long-term, high-yield peripheral countries' government bonds.

Regulatory policy and the transmission of the crisis from core to peripheral countries' banks

We have seen in the previous sections how, through the increased use of derivatives, the practices of secured lending and collateralization, the shift to mark-to-market accounting, layering and interconnectedness have increased among European banks. This in turn raises fragility. What has been missing in the previous discussion, however, is the geographical dimension of that fragility. Both core and peripheral countries' banks have become more fragile; the interplay of their fragilities, due to the integration in European financial markets, has mattered for the diffusion of the financial crisis. In fact, the only aim of European Union legislative activity in the field of finance prior to the crisis has been that of favouring the integration among European banking and financial markets. This aim has been pursued through legislation that has made easier cross-border activities of domestic banks (see Posner and Veron, 2010). The process of European integration focused on the target of a single market for goods and services, including financial services. This process, however, happened in the framework of a world liberalization of markets. So the process of expansion of European banks has not been limited to the European Union countries. Most banks in Europe have merged with UK and US financial institutions. Core big countries like Germany and France have played the major role but some big banks from Spain and Italy have participated in this expansion, too. In every country, however, the target of a unified market has been seen as requiring an increase in the size of banks, which has been favoured through a process of mergers of smaller banks in order to achieve a size that would have allowed them to play a role in the new international and European free market. In fact, if we look at the data (see Borgioli *et al.*, 2013) we see that in most countries the majority of banks are big banks, in both the centre and the periphery. In France, Spain and Italy, more than 80 per cent of all banks are big. In Germany, there is a much wider presence of small and medium-sized banks. In Portugal, Greece and in the new accession countries most banks are small. Although banks in Europe have become similar because of size and common regulation, and the adoption almost everywhere of the universal banking model, differences still persist in their business models. Core countries' big banks have a lower ratio of deposits to total assets and depend more on wholesale money markets for financing (see Orsi and Solari, 2010). If we look at revenues, we see differences, too. Core countries' big banks depend more on trading and commission fee income and much less on interest margin (see Orsi and Solari, 2010). Big banks in the periphery rely instead more on interest income and have a higher share of deposits over total assets. Core big banks have a higher proportion of derivatives over the total of assets with respect to southern European banks (see pp. 109–11 above).

In the aftermath of the global financial crisis, core countries' banks, hit by loan loss provisions and impairment of assets linked to the US mortgage securitization process, started new profitable trades in peripheral countries' bonds. They entered into swaps contract to hedge their long positions in peripheral countries' government bonds. The increase in CDS spread and bond yields of peripheral countries caused problems to core countries' banks that heavily speculated on those bonds by borrowing short term in the wholesale money market. The liquidity problems were heavy and the protection through IRS did not work because the Euribor did not rise in the second half of 2011, so holders of peripheral countries' bonds were losing on both positions – the bonds and the IRS. Those same banks had successfully passed the stress tests organized by the European Banking Authority in July 2011, so their problems were considered as a proof that the stress test results were very unreliable. The link between big systemic banks (from core countries) and the policy recommendation is highlighted by Tröger (2012) who argues that, beyond supervision regimes, what matters to prevent big banks' financial distress are coordinated micro-prudential regulatory measures such as the one taken by European politicians and the EBA in December 2011:

> On October 26, 2011 European politics reacted to the dwindling confidence in the European banking system with far reaching coordinated measures. *Inter alia* a recommendation by the European Banking Authority (EBA) 46 sought to tighten relevant micro-prudential regulation to reestablish confidence in SIFIs' resilience.
>
> (Tröger, 2012, pp. 14–15)

The EBA recommended that the banks should have by June 2012 a Tier 1 common capital ratio of 9 per cent, which means Tier 1 capital as ratio to risk-weighted assets. The European Council of December 2011 approved that decision. Although it was just a recommendation, it was implemented.[7] The reason may be the reputational damage associated to non-compliance. In fact, according to Parliament and Council Regulation 1093/2010 (EU) of 24 November 2010, establishing a European Supervisory Authority (European Banking Authority), a formal recommendation addressed to member states' banking supervisors is not legally binding but subject to a comply-or-explain mechanism. This means that the national authority has to declare its non-compliance within two months after the issuance of the recommendation and communicate its reasons to the EBA, which has to make public this communication (see Tröger, 2012).

The recommendation also changed the way in which sovereign bonds' risks and hence capital should be calculated. The bonds included in the available-for-sale assets would be charged with capital after removing the previously valid prudential filters and those in the hold-to-maturity portfolio should be valued as of 30 September 2011. The removal of prudential filters meant that unrealized gains and losses in those assets would affect regulatory capital, while the valuation of the hold to maturity portfolio as of September 2011 values would further require capital to offset their fall in value. The removal of filters, although being a part of the Basel III proposal, has not been implemented in Europe so far – instead, the US has implemented it – and the option of opting out is still available to national supervisors (see Becker, 2013), so the 2011 recommendation antici-pated a rule that will never be implemented.

In Figure 6.7 we can see a map of the interactions that occurred among differ-ent sections of the European banking system through policy and their macroeco-nomic repercussions.

As Figure 6.7 shows, the recapitalization measures caused a credit crunch in European periphery banks that cut loans. Those banks had higher capital needs because of the higher ratio of risk-weighted assets, mostly loans, to total assets. As of June 2013, the ratio of risk-weighted assets to total assets was 45,4 for Italy, 46,9 for Spain, while it was much lower for Germany 20,4 and France 26,3 (see MBRS, 2013).

They were also hit by the falling values of their own governments bonds. Since their main assets are loans, they did cut loans particularly to small and medium enterprises independently of their merit of credit. At the same time, the

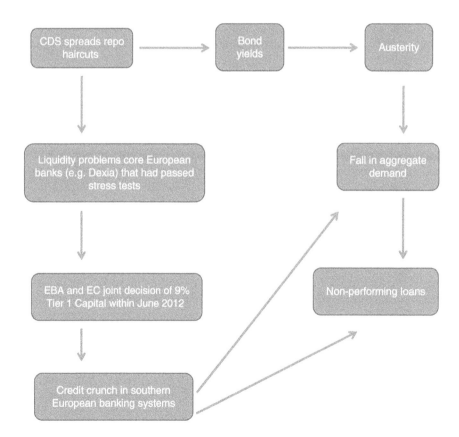

Figure 6.7 The European crisis

end of 2011, the increase in spread between European government bonds yields led either through moral suasion or direct impositions to change governments by replacing them with politicians willing to reduce public deficits and implement a whole range of austerity measures. The result was a fall in aggregate demand and an increase in non-performing loans. This in turn induced banks to further contract credit because of the increased lending risk. Demand for loans, in turn, declined in 2012 and 2013 because many enterprises either had defaulted or were closed. Therefore, the lower demand accommodated the initial supply contraction.[8]

Conclusions

This chapter has examined three episodes of financial fragility in the context of the European crisis. They have been chosen to highlight the various patterns of interaction among financial and policy actors that have occurred across time and space.

One pivotal episode of the financial crisis is the increase in the yield differential between core and peripheral countries' government bonds. In that case, the launch of a small but highly influential market for CDS indexes in sovereign bonds may have affected their spot price through the uncertainty channel. In turn, this would have caused an increase of the cost of financing for peripheral countries' banks that were more focused on credit than their core countries' peers.

The second episode showed how a transnational bank, Dexia, following a profit strategy that was pursued by many core countries' big banks at the same moment, suffered losses in both the valuation of peripheral countries' bonds and its interest rate swaps portfolio, which called for a rescue by various states. The reason why its hedging strategy failed was the particular institutional design of the European common currency and the role of its central bank. Another feature of this episode is the change in strategy of European banks that switched from being active players in the US shadow banking system to engage in a shadow-like strategy of borrowing short term to purchase longer maturity risky assets in the capital markets. These risky assets were no longer mortgage-backed securities but peripheral European countries' bonds.

In the end, a geographical dimension was added to the analysis. A centre-periphery feedback loop emerged as a plausible explanation for the last phase of the crisis. The connecting link, in this case, has been the sudden decision by the European Council and the EBA to force an immediate recapitalization on the Eurozone banks. The European banking authority was itself a new institution created after the 2007 crisis with no clear regulatory authority. The aim was to increase the resilience of big banks after the bail-out of Dexia and the widespread fear that many banks could follow suit. The extraordinary recapitalization hit two parts of the European Union – core and periphery – in a different way because of the composition of their banks' balance sheets. Core countries' banks with a higher share of securities and derivatives over total assets had to contribute only marginally, as this resulted in a lower share of risk-weighted assets over total assets. Banks in the periphery having more loans in their balance sheets were penalized instead. The interplay of different fragilities among centre and periphery banks has thus deepened the recession.

Notes

1 Unfortunately, the BIS has introduced in its survey questions on the geographical position of counterparties only in the last report issued in 2013, so it is not possible to make a comparison with the past.
2 Hedge accounting is a method of accounting where entries for the ownership of a security and the opposing hedge are treated as one. Hedge accounting attempts to reduce the volatility created by the repeated adjustment of a financial instrument's value, known as marking to market. This reduced volatility is done by combining the instrument and the hedge as one entry, which offsets the opposing movements.
3 Allen and Moessner write:

> For example, on 9 November 2011, presumably in response to market volatility in the wake of the European Council statement of 26 October, LCH Clearnet SA increased collateral margins on unsettled trades, including repos, in Italian government securities by between 3 and 5.5 percentage points. The increase caused a sharp fall in Italian government securities prices – an example of positive feedback created by the use of algorithms designed to manage risk.
>
> (Allen and Moessner, 2012, p. 16)

4 A fixed interest swap in its simplest form may be used to protect the value of a bond portfolio. In that case, the investor that is long on the bonds is supposed to buy an interest rate swap and to pay a fixed rate while the counterparty to the deal, the seller of the swap, will commit itself to paying a floating rate. The floating rate is linked to a benchmark interest rate, which for the European interest rate swaps with long maturity is normally the Euribor rate, a rate charged on interbank unsecured loans among 44 European banks. The value of the swap for the buyer is positively related to the interest rate while the opposite holds for the seller. From what is known for Dexia, its losses were due to both a fall in the value of European governments bonds and a fall in the value of the swap; the former was due to the increasing perceived risk of default of the issuing states and the latter was due to the fall in the Euribor interest rate. A lower interest rate may have unforeseen effects in a financial structure, in which derivatives constitute a large part of the financial institutions' portfolios. A lower interest rate may cause liquidity problems.
5 The Euribor at all maturities was rising for the first half of 2011 after the rise in the refinancing rate by the ECB decided by Trichet. In the second half of the year, the Euribor and also the refinancing rate fell. The fall was, however, much more pronounced for the short maturities (one week to one month), while it was negligible for the long maturities (12 months).
6 Dexia could be considered a shadow bank (see Mehrling *et al.*, 2013). The reason is that it used short-term money market funding to finance the acquisition of assets in the capital market – namely, long maturity public bonds, profiting from the difference between the cost of repo (haircut) and the yield on bonds.
7 See EBA (2011). The EBA was established to define common standards but had no legislative mandate to impose regulatory measures. Therefore, it issued just a recommendation called 'Recommendation of 8 December 2011 on the creation and supervisory over-sight of temporary capital buffers to restore market confidence'. This is an example of informal regulation in the European Union.
8 For an analysis of the determinants of the contraction in loan supply in Italy, see Del Giovane *et al.* (2013). The study uses the answers to the ECB Bank Lending Survey to

determine whether the contraction in loans has been due to demand or supply factors. The findings are that both have happened, although with a different timing. The supply factors were more relevant in particular episodes of strong financial stress like the second half of 2011, while the demand side mattered more in the second half of 2012. These findings fit well in the narrative of the crisis exposed in this section.

References

Acharya, V.V. and Steffen, S. (2012) The greatest carry trade ever? Understanding Eurozone banks risks. Available at: http://financeseminars.darden.virginia.edu/Lists/ Calendar/Attachments/153/Acharya%20paper%20for%202013%20-%20Carry%20 Trade.pdf

Allen, W.A. and Moessner, R. (2012) The liquidity consequences of the euro area sovereign debt crisis, BIS Working Papers No. 390.

Arce, Ó., Mayordomo, S. and Peña, J. I. (2012) Credit-risk valuation in the sovereign CDS and bonds markets: Evidence from the Euro Area Crisis, No. 22/12, Faculty Working Papers, School of Economics and Business Administration, University of Navarra. Available at: http://EconPapers.repec.org/RePEc:una:unccee:wp2212 (accessed February 2013).

Bank for International Settlements (BIS) (2013) Derivative survey, June.

Becker, L. (2013) Filter furore: EU countries set to shield banks from bond volatility, *Risk*, 4 November.

Borgioli, S., Gouveia, A.C. and Labanca, C. (2013) Financial stability analysis insights gained from consolidated banking data for the EU, European Central Bank Occasional Paper Series No. 140, January.

Bowman, A., Ertürk, I., Froud, J., Johal, S., Moran, M., Law, J., Leaver, A. and Williams, K. (2012) Scapegoats aren't enough: A Leveson for the banks? CRESC Policy Briefing.

Coudert, V. and Gex, M. (2010) Credit default swaps and bond markets: Which leads the other?, Banque de France, *Financial Stability Review*, 14: 161–7.

Cousseran, O. and Rahmouni, I. (2005) The CDO market functioning and implications in terms of financial stability, Banque de France, *Financial Stability Review*, 6: 43–62, June.

Del Giovane, P., Nobili, A. and Signoretti, F. (2013) Supply tightening or lack in demand? Is the sovereign debt crisis different from Lehman? Available at: www.bancaditalia.it/ studiricerche/convegni/atti/sovereign_debt/delgiovane.pdf

Deutsche Bank (2012) Annual Report. Available at: https://annualreport.deu tsche-bank.com/2012/ar/servicepages/downloads.html (accessed February 2014).

Engelen, E., Ertürk, I., Froud, J., Leaver, A. and Williams, K. (2010) Reconceptualizing financial innovation: Frame, conjuncture and bricolage, *Economy and Society*, 39(1): 33–63.

European Banking Authority (EBA) (2011) Recommendation of 8 December 2011 on the creation and supervisory over-sight of temporary capital buffers to restore market confidence. Available at: www.eba.europa.eu/documents/10180/16460/EBA+BS+2011+173 +Recommendation+FINAL.pdf/b533b82c-2621-42ff-b90e-96c081e1b598 (accessed March 2014).

Fender, I. and Lewrick, U. (2013) Mind the gap? Sources and implications of supply–demand imbalances in collateral asset markets. *BIS Quarterly Review*, September, pp. 67–81.

Ferri, P. and Minsky, H. (1991) Market processes and thwarting systems. Jerome Levy Institute, Working Paper No. 64.

Financial Stability Board (FSB) (2011) Potential financial stability issues arising from recent trends in Exchange-Traded Funds (ETFs), April.

FSB (2012) Global shadow banking monitoring report.

Green Street Capital Research (2010) Balance sheet CLOs: Why the rally?

International Capital Market Association (ICMA) (2014) European repo market survey No. 26, conducted December 2013. Available at: www.icmagroup.org/Regulatory-Policy-and-Market-Practice/repo-and-collateral-markets/ercc-publications/repo-market-surveys/

ISDA (2014) Adverse liquidity effects of the EU uncovered sovereign CDS ban, ISDA research note, January.

Kremer, L. (2014) 4 signs of a potential ETF apocalypse now. Available at: www.cnbc.com/id/101378179

MBRS (2013) *Le maggiori banche europee nel 1 semestre*. Available at: www.mbres.it

Mediobanca Ricerche e Studi (MBRS) (2012) *Dati cumulativi delle principali banche internazionali e piani di stabilizzazione finanziaria*. Available at: www.mbres.it

Mehrling, P., Pozsar, Z., Sweeney, J. and Neilson, D.H. (2013) Bagehot was a shadow banker: Shadow banking, central banking, and the future of global finance (5 November). Available at: http://ssrn.com/abstract=2232016 (accessed September 2014).

Minsky, H. (1982) *Can it Happen Again?* Armonk, NY: M.E. Sharpe.

Mügge, D. and Stellinga, B. (2011) Fair value limited: Contingent preference formation in international accounting standard setting. Working Paper. Available at: www.griffith.edu.au/__data/assets/pdf_file/0005/407804/Mugge-Stellinga-Fair-Value-Limited-V2.pdf (accessed September 2014).

Nesvetailova, A. (2014) Innovations, fragility and complexity: Understanding the power of finance, *Government and Opposition*, 49: 542–68.

Orsi, L. and Solari, S (2010) Financialisation in southern European economies, ICaTSEM, Institutional Change and Trajectories of Socio-Economic Models. Working Paper No. 2.

Pollack, L. (2012) The remarkable resurgence in synthetic credit tranches, *Financial Times FT Alphaville*, 30 April.

Posner, E. and Veron, N. (2010) The EU and financial regulation: Power without purpose?, *Journal of European Public Policy*, 17(3): 400–15, April.

Poszar, Z., Adrian, T., Ashcraft, A. and Boesky, H. (2010) Shadow banking, Federal Reserve Bank of New York Staff Report No. 458.

Terzi, A. (2014) When good intentions pave the road to hell: Monetization fears and Europe's narrowing options, Levy Economics Institute of Bard College, Working Paper No. 810.

Tröger, T.H. (2012) Organizational choices of banks and the effective supervision of transnational financial institutions, Institute for Monetary and Financial Stability, Goethe University, Frankfurt am Main, Working Paper No. 54.

7 Deleveraging in European banking and financial stability, 2010–13

Introduction

This chapter illustrates a point already stressed in the first chapters of this book – namely, that deleveraging in itself may not always be associated with a decrease in financial fragility as it may happen through ways that increase interconnectedness and layering.

The deleveraging that happened in Europe after the great financial crisis is an example of that. At the beginning there was no deleveraging at all; thereafter, starting from 2011 the deleveraging took the shape of cutting loans and external exposures, and increasing derivatives. Finally, as the data from 2013 show, there was perhaps some deleveraging in derivatives, too. This type of deleveraging induced heavy losses to the main core countries' banks that, however, were relieved by the extraordinary intervention by the central bank through the long-term refinancing operation. That intervention cannot be considered a thwarting system apt to achieve some shared societal goals.

Deleveraging in European banks

In Chapter 1, Minsky's idea of the interplay between economic dynamics and the thwarting systems as a key to interpreting the movement in time of a capitalist economy has been explained. It has also been discussed why the thwarting mechanism that had worked in the postwar period until the 1980s no longer worked, according to Minsky's own reflections in the latter works of the 1990s and according to other scholars inspired by Minsky.

In particular, it has been clarified how destabilizing movements in the prices of financial assets may occur when money is endogenous and investment is no more the main force behind the business cycles. The tendency of banks to expand their size in a money manager phase of capitalism had worried Minsky in the 1990s and the historical evolution after his death confirmed his worries. Recent proposals inspired by Minsky have been made (see Chapter 2) to stop this tendency and to limit the leverage by banks and the multiplication of their assets. In Chapter 2, it was argued that limiting leverage alone would not be sufficient as a mechanism to constrain the outcomes of market processes to viable or acceptable ones. In the quotation by Ferri and Minsky (1991), a thwarting system must be apt, which has been interpreted as able to achieve some shared public goals. So, some thwarting systems, though useful in counteracting the wild oscillations in some prices, may not be useful to get the goals that the public or the authorities or the government consider necessary for the development of an economy. Therefore, not all thwarting systems are alike from the economic policy perspective. There must be a hierarchy in which they are inserted in order to decide which one to pursue according to the objectives.

The interplay among regulation, monetary policy and fiscal policy in the European Union after the great recession can be studied as an example of adopting the wrong thwarting systems if the goal to be pursued is full employment and avoiding a deflation in wages and general price levels. If aggregate data on banking are looked upon, it seems that the goal of constraining the growth of banks' assets has been reached and that leverage has consistently fallen for European countries' banks. The decline in leverage has been higher for European banks than for the banks of other advanced countries such as the US, Canada, Australia (Caruana, 2017, Graph 4, p. 6). According to the data presented there, the European big banks' leverage fell from a peak of around 50 in 2007 to a very modest 15 in 2015. The decline was of enormous size. The leverage by US major banks fell from around 20 per cent to around 7 per cent, so the peak leverage for European banks was much higher than that for US ones. The same trend is present in the metric 'consolidated assets over gross domestic product' that falls in the Eurozone from 120 per cent at the peak to 80 per cent in 2015, in the United Kingdom from 160 per cent to 90 per cent, in Switzerland from 460 per cent to 200 per cent (Caruana, 2017, p.7, Graph 5). It is worth stressing that Caruana does not consider cross-border claims according to national accounting statistics but looks at consolidated data that include all assets by banks, including those booked in their branches and subsidiaries abroad that would not be present in banks' assets, as reported in national accounting data. So deleveraging is bigger in size if calculated by looking at consolidated data. Caruana (2017) concludes that 'deleveraging is a prerequisite for restoring sustainable growth after a financial credit boom' (p. 8). The deleveraging happened by squeezing foreign assets, particularly southern countries' assets by northern countries' banks after the European debt crisis and by increasing capital.

So one should conclude that a thwarting mechanism worked to constrain the instability arising from banks' expansion either nurtured by spontaneous forces or by policy interventions. The interventions to restore the solvency of some banks by recapitalizing them and the change in regulation may have acted in the same favourable direction. So, in a way, the proposals of changes in financial regulation quoted above or the still circulating idea of splitting the big banks or reshaping them through ring-fencing would be largely redundant as the main goal – that of having smaller banks – would have already been reached. Some are even worried for the decline of European investment banks and their loss of competitiveness with respect to US banks (Goodhart and Schoenmaker, 2016). Perhaps, therefore, that cure had not only been valid for the disease, but as a collateral effect it would have killed the patient.

So, in order to assess whether a thwarting mechanism has been finally found and the role that financial regulation and monetary policy have played in it, we have to look more carefully at detailed flow data on the changes in the balance sheet assets and liabilities of European Union banks after the Great Recession and during Europe's own crisis. The data collected will be flow data and consolidated. It is important to use consolidated data as the ones reported in national accounting do not reflect the international character of banking business, and do not represent the reality of multinational firms, composed of many legal entities with different statuses distributed throughout the world.

As will be evident in the rest of the chapter, the way in which the deleveraging has taken place is important to judge whether the new combination of internal dynamics and thwarting systems will deliver a stable environment and will serve well the capital development to paraphrase Minsky. It will appear that the change in regulation both implemented and simply announced to take place in the future jointly with the evolution of markets during the European crisis brought to a deleveraging in which the assets serving the normal working of the economy were cut and those that are used to gain fee commission incomes or interest income not deriving from the interest margins were indeed increased. The potential oscillations on the price of financial assets stemming from the interplay of these microeconomic choices have been tamed by the central bank intervention that has been instrumental in the portfolio reshuffling of northern countries' banks dumping the southern countries' private and public assets by refinancing the southern countries' banks with long-term operations so that they could buy their own government bonds. The deglobalization and home bias reappearance within the European Union, and particularly the Eurozone, has not been an accident of history following a worldwide trend but rather a conscious choice of the European Central Bank and probably of the most powerful governments of the Eurozone.

In the next section we will use the same method by Caruana (2017) and trace the changes in banks' assets and liabilities looking at consolidated data in the worst period of the so-called European sovereign debt crisis, 2010–13. In the remaining parts of the chapter, we will look at the evolution of regulation in the same period, focusing on the discussion among the authorities and the industry through public consultations that shaped the final form it took. In the last section, we will show how the portfolio choices of banks that deleveraged in a way that increased layering interconnectedness and the danger of cumulative price movements in financial assets that could bring losses to many financial institutions were offset by the extraordinary long-term refinancing operations by the ECB. It will be clear that the ECB through thwarting the instability arising from private entities' decisions did not act to foster the capital development of the economy, so this thwarting mechanism cannot be considered adequate.

Changes in banks' assets and liabilities, 2010–13

Changes in total assets and liabilities for the years 2010–11 are positive. This means that the crisis notwithstanding banks' balance sheets become bigger.

The pattern of growth of both assets and liabilities is very different in 2010 with respect to 2011. In 2010, loans increased by almost €400 billion. Securities holdings increased, too, while external assets decreased. In 2011, total assets increased by almost €1 trillion, but the biggest part of that increase went to remaining assets. Loans almost stopped growing. Therefore, the only source of growth in assets were derivatives. On the liabilities side, in 2010 the major source of growth in liabilities were deposits followed by capital and reserves. In 2011, in a symmetric pattern with assets the major item that increased instead were remaining assets, which were for the greatest part derivatives.

The overall picture in the aggregated consolidated data is a retrenchment from overseas markets and an increase in the holdings of securities issued by both general governments and other euro area residents. So far, what the aggregated data show is that banks have withdrawn from external markets perceived as riskier after the great financial crisis and have increased the holdings of securities issued in the euro area mainly by governments. The changes in their balance sheet might indicate a more prudent behaviour with respect to the pre-crisis period in which most European banks, especially those from the core countries, were actively engaged in the US shadow banking system (Poszar *et al.*, 2010). However, at the same time, European banks were heavily engaged in derivatives dealings, as the data on remaining assets show (see Figure 7.1).

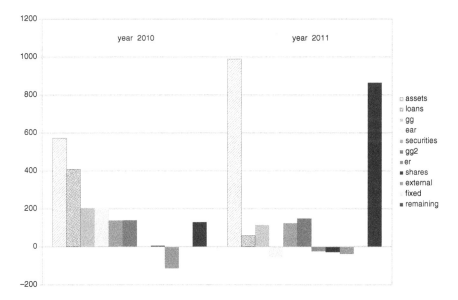

Figure 7.1 Changes in assets: European banks, 2010 and 2011. gg = general government, ear = euro area residents.

Source: ECB consolidated banking data, billion euro, flows.

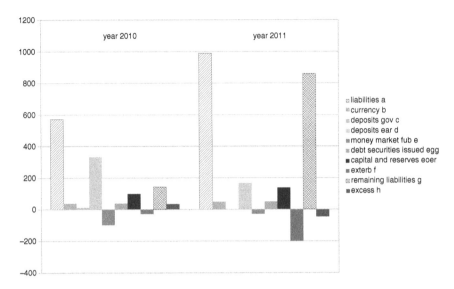

Figure 7.2 Changes in liabilities: European banks, 2010 and 2011.

Source: ECB consolidated banking data, billion euro, flows.

On the liabilities side, there was a decline in the increase of deposits and a decrease in external liabilities because of the retrenchment of European banking from foreign markets, while there was an increase in capital and reserves (see Figure 7.2). The decrease in external liabilities was again linked to the problems experienced by all financial institutions in the US money markets. The branches and subsidiaries of European banks were borrowing short term to buy all the products deriving from the securitization of loans in the US (MBS, ABS, CDO and CDS). In Europe, the traditional activity of banks, to lend and to accept deposits, had not been particularly shaken in the years before the great financial crisis.

Changes in banks' assets and liabilities, 2012–13

In 2012 and 2013, deleveraging – that is, a shrinking of banks' balance sheets – took place. In 2012, the growth of both assets and liabilities was very subdued, and banks' balance sheets almost stopped growing. In 2013, both the assets and liabilities of banks shrank, so a sort of deleveraging happened (see Figures 7.3 and 7.4). In 2012, loans growth was negative, while that of government bonds holdings was positive (see Figure 7.4, p. 129). In 2013, almost all items showed negative rates of growth. In particular, both loans and external assets fell. The fall in external assets might have been due to the selling of participations in institutions outside the EU. The selling of participations sometimes was due to the requirements entailed in bail-out interventions of distressed banks that took place

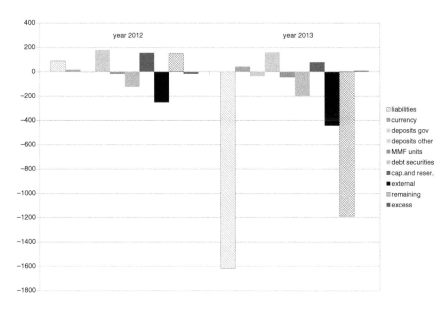

Figure 7.3 Changes in liabilities: European banks, 2012 and 2013.

Source: ECB consolidated banking data, billion euro, flows.

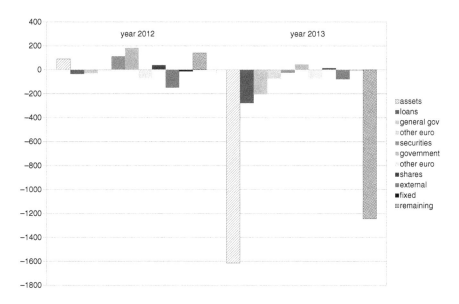

Figure 7.4 Changes in assets: European banks, 2012 and 2013.

Source: ECB consolidated banking data, billion euro, flows.

in the period 2008–10. In part, they were also linked to the necessity of deleveraging to face the new regulatory environment. The contractions in loans to other euro area residents were not large in those data, although disaggregated data show that there had been a severe credit contraction in peripheral countries.

In 2012, on the liabilities side, the deposits, capital and reserves have slightly increased. The same happened in 2013, but the most striking change in that year was the large fall in external and remaining assets. In 2013, the major change regarding liabilities (and assets as well) concerned 'remaining assets', which are reported derivatives held for trade and some margins for derivatives trading. This invoice shows a negative value of more than €1 trillion in 2013 (see Figure 7.3, p. 129).

In the ECB tables, a footnote informed that a change had happened in the reporting practice of one member state – Germany. A German law passed in 2010 that created a levy to deal with the banks' losses also required that they should report the gains and losses in the derivatives held for trade in the balance sheet.[1] The gains and losses from derivatives reported in German banks' balance sheets accounted for the main determinant of the changes in total banking assets for the whole euro area.[2]

In 2011 and 2013, the 'remaining' assets and liabilities balanced each other. This meant that the German banks acted as derivatives dealers; they had derivatives on both sides of their balance sheets (Mehrling *et al.*, 2013). The winners and losers in the game were those entities, banks, non-bank financial institutions, non-financial corporations and states that had derivatives either as assets or as liabilities. They might have been the protection demanders or suppliers.[3]

In 2013, the pattern of remaining assets is similar to that recorded in 2011 but with opposite signs. While in 2011 both remaining assets and liabilities balanced each other but had positive signs, in 2013 they balanced each other but displayed negative signs. This may have been due to the expiring of contracts previously registered either as assets because they represented a claim to others (they were actually a gain) or as liabilities – that is, a debt to others, due to the unfavourable change in prices. The change in signs in 2013 may have been due to the cancellation of old contracts because they had expired and to the fact that no new contracts were recorded. New contracts entered into, however, either had initial zero value (which is obvious for interest rate swaps) and so do not contribute to the aggregate, or their values were falling with respect to the previous years – 2010, 2011 and 2012.

Another possibility is that the derivatives that were previously registered as assets as they were increasing in value turned into liabilities because of the losses incurred and the same symmetrically happened for liabilities. The negative sign on both assets and liabilities derivatives may be also due to the compression of derivatives – that is, according to the definition given by the Bank for International Settlements (BIS): 'Compression is a process for tearing up trades that allows economically redundant derivative trades to be terminated early without changing each participant's net position' (see BIS, 2015, p.3, n.3). BIS (2015) adds that the compression and the increasing use of central counterparties are the main rationales for the reduction in notional volumes of derivatives registered in 2014 and 2015.

The increase in derivatives in the period 2010–12 seen in aggregate data is also visible in bank balance sheets data. The big banks of core countries like Germany, Great Britain and France have the major share of derivatives in their balance sheets, in the range 20–33 per cent, while peripheral countries' big banks have a lower share, in the range 6–10 per cent (MBRS, 2012, 2013). Further, European banks have ended up with enormous exposures in notional amounts and a tiny capital with respect to total assets (MBRS, 2012, 2013). This is confirmed by looking at the published balance sheet of the biggest German bank, Deutsche Bank. In 2012, Deutsche Bank had a total notional amount of derivatives of €55.605.039 million, of which €45.337.568 million were 'interest related' – i.e. they were interest rate derivatives. A large part of the interest rate derivatives – €41.264.732 million – were over-the-counter. The regulatory capital was 2 per cent of total assets (Deutsche Bank, 2012). The value 2 per cent, of course, is the ratio of capital to total assets, while the ratio considered in Basel III and in the European Union regulation is the ratio of capital to risk-weighted assets.

The same tendencies emerge in consolidated banking data on derivatives positions published by the ECB (see Figure 6.5). For the UK, derivatives holdings were declining; for France, Spain and Italy they were rising. The derivatives positions held by French banks were much higher than those of other countries. Moreover, they were also rising in the period 2008–12. It is interesting that banking systems belonging to countries that were not involved in the subprime loans creation in the US and its debacle, increased the derivatives in their balance sheets. Most of these derivatives were interest rate linked.

This change in portfolio strategy was reflected in the profitability of the banks. Profitability may be considered by looking at operating income and its sources. In 2012 and 2013, net interest income became the most relevant source of operating income for many countries' banking systems in both the core and the periphery. This income, however, did not come only from traditional lending activity, but it also came from financial assets designated at fair value through profit and loss, held for trading and derivatives (hedge accounting interest rate risk). In Belgium, Luxembourg, Germany, France and Italy, interest income contributed to operating income, in the range between 40 and 60 per cent. Interest income did not come only from loans and receivables, but also from financial assets and derivatives. The share of interest income from financial assets and derivatives was 50 per cent in Belgium and Luxembourg, 20 per cent in France and Italy, 30 per cent in Germany and 40 per cent in the Netherlands and Malta (ECB, 2013, Chart 32). The data on interest income and its sources changed little in 2013 (ECB, 2014, Chart 28). All data sources pointed in the same direction. Undoubtedly, the banking system in the aftermath of the US crisis and during the European one piled up more and more derivatives.

Changes in regulation in 2010–13

In this section we will look at the regulatory changes that may have favoured the switch from the involvement in the US derivatives market to the creation of

European home-made derivatives by European banks. Basel III was finalized in September 2010. The European Market Infrastructure Regulation (EMIR) draft and various amendments to the IAS (International Accounting Standard) 39 were published in 2010. Institutional actors could make expansion plans in derivatives, given that they were allowed as tools to mitigate risks and banks could make plans to optimize capital use through derivatives in the expectation of the new regulation too (see Härle *et al.*, 2010). IASB 39 (2010) updates efforts to accommodate the use of hedging through derivatives into accounting practice. So, while the banks in the period 2008–10 simply went on following the same strategy of the highest possible return on equity by enlarging their size, only changing the composition of their portfolios, in this new phase when many uncertainties on the new regulation were wiped out, they started organizing themselves for the future. Non-banks and markets took advantage of the opportunity to grow out of the new prospected regulations and changes in accounting rules. They just managed in the time between the publication of draft and proposals – namely, 2010 for Basel III, 2011 for Capital Requirements Regulation (CRR) (LCR, NSFR) and the European Market Infrastructure Regulation (EMIR). For all these measures, the implementation time was used by the industry's representatives to shape the regulations according to their needs. This is testified by the answers that they gave to the consultations launched by the European Securities and Markets Authority (ESMA) before defining the technical standards without which the regulations could not be put into force. So, even if the majority of this regulatory overhaul came into force only later (Capital Derivatives Directive IV), from 1 January 2014 and the mandatory clearing of derivatives in 2015, it is exactly in this period preceding the coming into force of the new legislation that the games are played. In the period between the publication of the drafts and coming into force of the new regulation, the industry successfully lobbied to get the new rules applied in a way that did not damage its interests, meaning that common practices in the big banks like CVA desks became embedded in the legislation. Further, the answer to the authorities implementing the technical standards was that the banks did not want to be constrained in their choice of mitigating instruments and had a pecking order in which CVA through collective management of collateral and derivatives was the preferred solution; hedging with derivatives was the second choice and the third and least preferred solution was initial and variation margins for uncleared derivatives.

From a Minskian viewpoint, the draft of EMIR published in 2010 should not be considered a thwarting strategy because it fostered a greater use of derivatives in the new environment. It was, rather, a deviation amplifying strategy as derivatives pricing amplifies the fluctuations in the prices of the underlying through various channels. This happens if the price of the derivatives affects the price of the underlying and vice versa with a feedback loop. This may happen if markets are not homogeneous (Mirowski, 2010) and arbitrage does not work. Furthermore, the increase in repo financing and the necessity of new collateral required also by the new regulation to avoid counterparty risk in transactions increased layering (Fender and Lewrick, 2012).

The use of derivatives for mitigating risks does not make sense if derivatives prices do not follow the price of the underlying, which in turn are supposed to be on average at their equilibrium prices according to rational expectations hypothesis. If the price of the securities underlying derivatives are not always at their presumed equilibrium level and if derivatives prices do not necessarily converge to them because arbitrage does not always work, then fluctuations in one set of prices may lead to higher volatility in the other set of prices with a feedback effect displaying itself. In this case, regulation policy, instead of acting as a thwarting factor, acts as a deviation amplifier system. This is what happened during the European crisis with both CDS premiums and peripheral countries' bonds yields rising and reinforcing each other. The thick web of interconnections created through leveraged funding backed by collaterals – namely, the same government bonds – was unwound by margin calls that could not be met in the second half of 2011.

The regulation transposed into law the recommendations by the Basel Committee on Banking Supervision on the revision of Basel II (see Masera, 2011). The aim of Basel III, the popular name for the new package, was to improve financial stability mainly by increasing capital that banks must keep available in case of financial stress or outright default. The increase in capital should be sufficient to cover eventual losses arising from various risks such as market and credit risks.

The theoretical apparatus is a recalculation of risks with weights that have been updated after the painful experience of the great financial crisis. During the last crisis, it became evident that financial institutions had underestimated counterparty credit risk associated to over-the-counter derivatives. Therefore, they suffered heavy losses that could bring them to default in the absence of public intervention. Starting from this observation, CRD IV foresaw a new charge called the Credit Valuation Adjustment (CVA) Risk Capital Charge. The charge was designed to cover losses that arose when the counterparty's financial position worsened. If this happened, the market value of the counterparty's derivatives obligation declines, even if no actual default occurred. The CVA capital charge would be greater for trades of long-dated derivatives. It would be related to net exposures, so one directional trade would be penalized more.

The size of the expected uncollateralized mark-to-market values would be the base to calculate the charge. If you had many over-the-counter interest rate swaps, or exchange-related swaps, or commodities swaps, all of which increased, it would be convenient to hedge through CDS. This meant, however, a demand for new CDS and an increase in the share of those assets in the portfolio. This increase could be masked in financial reporting by permitted 'hedge accounting'. Therefore, collateralization would help to save capital. Trading with lower rated counterparties would increase the capital charge instead. The capital charge would be reduced if the institution hedged its position through a CDS. Of course, trading with counterparties for which no liquid CDS market existed would be penalized. The CVA charge was very low for trades cleared through a central counterparty (CCP) because they were collateralized daily. At the same time, in the European market infrastructure regulation that was passed in 2012, it was foreseen that entities should hold an 'appropriate and proportionate amount of capital to manage the risk not covered by appropriate exchange of collateral'. The industry wanted neither to waste capital nor to be obliged to post initial margins and variation margins that are usually posted in cash, for collaterals in uncleared trades of derivatives (see BCBS-IOSCO, 2013). So, it referred to a practice that consisted in managing counterparty risks on a portfolio basis in which all the trades with the same counterparty would be collected to establish after the netting of reciprocal obligations what collateral would be posted and what residual risk should be hedged through other derivatives (this time not subject to CVA). In order to hedge the counterparty risk, the legislation allowed the use of both single name and index CDS.

In the text, it was not specified which type of margins should be used and the clarification of that point was left to subsequent work by the EBA on technical standards (see EBA *et al.,* 2012, 2014). The EBA launched a consultation, with a paper (EBA *et al.*, 2012) asking for feedback from the concerned industry. There was also some dispute regarding whether EMIR requirements for margining would overlap with CRD IV requirements for more capital. The industry through the International Swaps and Derivates Association (ISDA) made clear that it was fiercely opposing introducing mandatory initial margins for uncleared derivatives transactions and suggested that the financial institutions should be free of choosing among the many ways available to mitigate risk. They noticed that many banks had already CVA desks that were caring about credit valuation adjustment on a portfolio basis:

> In the period since the credit crisis firms have become much more sophisticated in managing counterparty credit risk. Credit Valuation Adjustment ('CVA') desks have been established to centrally manage and offset the credit risks arising from OTC derivatives and Secured Financing Transactions. Credit and market hedges are used to manage these risks, and have been very successful in offsetting the aggregate credit exposures in their books. In addition, valuation reserves are taken against illiquid positions. Also, firms have built integrated systems to manage counterparty risk and fund derivative positions. The forced segregation of IM threatens some of these models and should be a matter for agreement between the parties.
>
> (ISDA, 2012, Part B: The Background, n.p.)

Credit and market hedges means credit default and interest rates swaps. The most disliked measure was the initial margin on uncleared trades because this would have required cash and also the segregation of collateral that could have not been rehypothecated.

The practice of CVA desks was already present before the crisis but quite limited. After the crisis it became widespread at least for big institutions even before the new regulation was passed into law.

Calculating CVA risk is complex. Historically, institutions did not calculate CVA but it became more common in the early 2000s with some large institutions setting up dedicated CVA desks to hedge CVA risk often across the firm as a whole (but sometimes on a desk-by-desk basis). Following the financial crisis there has been a renewed focus on managing counterparty credit risk and managing CVA risk has become more common and more sophisticated.

(Allen and Overy, 2014, p. 6)

The whole design of this regulatory change would indeed increase layering and interconnectedness and, in fact, increase the notional outstanding of derivatives as well as the repo activity and securities lending more generally. This will contribute to fees and trading income of too-big-to-fail institutions while increasing the financial fragility in Minsky's definition (Minsky, 1982, 1992).

The initial margin will be mandatory from 2017, although the obligation will be phased in various years, each one corresponding to a certain level of derivatives notional volumes held in the balance sheets. The initial margin will be segregated and its calculation will depend on that of the future prospective value of the derivatives. So, the initial margin may simply be calculated as a percentage on the notional values which is provided by regulators. This percentage varies according to the type of derivative and to its maturity. More complicated instead is the use of internal models. They should use a 99 per cent one-tailed Historic Simulation Value-at-Risk (VaR), with at least a ten-day holding period. The historic period should be between three and five years. Some 25 per cent of the scenarios must represent a period of financial stress. The model must include scenarios of the most recent period. The periods of financial stress must be applied per asset class. Further, the model should be recalibrated every 12 months (Apers, 2016). IM models may account for diversification, hedging and risk offsets within well-defined asset classes such as currency/rates, equity, credit or commodities, but not across such asset classes and provided these instruments are covered by the same legally enforceable netting agreement (Citibank, 2014). So, again it will be possible to use derivatives to mitigate the risk of other derivatives in a sort of Russian doll structure. The initial margin should be applied only to new contracts.

Given that the initial margin was discussed but not decided, and it was implemented only much later for the new contracts, the adoption of this measure did not disturb the growth of derivatives dealing at that time. So both the rise of secured lending through repo as replacement for unsecured interbank lending and the widespread diffusion of CVA desks – spontaneously created before the crisis but being much boosted by the post-crisis environment and the new regulation drafts presented by international private organizations and then approved into law – required new derivatives having as underlying European securities. This in turn was a powerful incentive to securities firms and other financial services firms (as the index owners' firms) to provide new financial instruments that could be used to the above listed aims (see Chapter 6).

Long-term refinancing by the ECB as a thwarting mechanism in the European crisis?

As discussed in the first section, European banks have deleveraged with respect to their pre-crisis levels. The second section described the evolution of changes in banks' balance sheets. In the third section, the parallel change in regulation was reconstructed. This section will show how the extraordinary long-term refinancing by the ECB resolved the unhealthy situations in which banks of core countries had put themselves because of their choices after the US crisis erupted.

Core countries' banks had heavily invested in both public and private debt issued by peripheral countries' entities (Acharya and Steffen, 2012). During the crisis, when the trust in the solvency of peripheral countries entities vanished and in the expectation of regulation changes that would have required new protection (CVA) against risks arising from the counterparty, many of these banks exposed to peripheral countries' risk bought protection in the form of interest rate swaps and credit default swaps (see Chapter 6).

The situation could be described by using T-accounts representing the balance sheets of the various components of the financial system. The scheme used by Mehrling *et al.* (2013) to explain the operations of the shadow banking system (Poszar *et al.*, 2010) can be borrowed to show what happened within the European financial system in the years after the eruption of the US crisis up to 2014. Differently from Mehrling *et al.* (2013) in this case, the shadow bank's T-account is replaced by that of a chartered bank. In Europe, in fact, universal banks acted just as shadow banks in the definition that Mehrling *et al.* (2013) gave them: they funded themselves on the short-term money market to purchase longer maturity securities. The (shadow) bank[4] account has on the liabilities side short-term financing like repo agreements and on the assets side government bonds, corporate bonds and derivatives that should serve to offset various risks – mainly market and credit risks (see Table 7.1).

Between them and financial institutions with a higher risk profile are placed dealers that have on both the liabilities and the assets side derivatives, so they have a matched book (see Table 7.2).

Table 7.1 The (shadow) bank

(Shadow) bank assets	Liabilities
Peripheral countries' government bonds	Deposits
Peripheral countries' private debt	Repurchase agreements
IRS, CDS	

Table 7.2 The dealer bank

Dealer assets	Liabilities
Reverse repo	Repo
IRS	IRS
CDS	CDS

Table 7.3 The non-bank financial institution

Non-bank financial institutions' assets	Liabilities
High yield bonds	Repo
Other risky assets	IRS
	CDS

Other financial institutions exist and their balance sheet has derivatives on the liabilities side and risky assets on the assets side (see Table 7.3).

The latter sell protection to the (shadow) bank through the intermediation of dealers. In the institutional European environment the first two actors, the shadow bank and the dealer, were both chartered banks playing different roles while the sellers of protection may have been non-bank financial institutions. For example, in the European context, the shadow bank is Dexia and the dealer bank is Deutsche Bank. The heavy increase in derivatives dealing may have arisen out of this demand for hedging peripheral debt exposures because of the increased risk perception due to the unfolding of the European debt crisis.

Yet these hedging plans were unsuccessful due to unexpected circumstances. The rates on the interbank market did not rise in parallel with those on government bonds of peripheral countries. Interest rates swaps linked to the unique Euribor rate were not useful to hedge the interest rate risk on peripheral countries' government bonds. The crisis in the sovereign debt markets did not spill over to the interbank market.[5] Ironically, the lack of contagion worsened the financial situation of European (shadow) banks. This contrasted with what had happened in the US in 2007–8 and in Europe in 2008. The reason for this lack of contagion may be that the volumes in that market had heavily declined as most lenders and borrowers had moved to the secured market. In any case, whatever the cause, the consequence was that the interest rate swaps being linked to the Euribor did not compensate the losses on the holdings of government bonds. The protection bought was not sufficient to cover the losses. In some limited time periods, Euribor rates at certain maturities even declined making the (shadow) banks register losses on both the bonds and the swaps that were supposed to cover the losses arising from them. The (shadow) banks suffered big losses,[6] the dealers were in a balanced position and the sellers of protection were either untouched or even gaining on their swaps position. The banks hit by the losses obviously tried to sell their assets, contributing to the further fall in their prices and eventually receded from the swap contracts (which proved to be costly).

In this scenario, the extraordinary long-term refinancing operations by the ECB acted as a thwarting mechanism as it allowed to stop the fall in the prices of peripheral government bonds and at the same time favoured the transfer of the same government bonds from the core countries' banks to the peripheral ones. The latter used the funds borrowed from the ECB to purchase from the former the government bonds issued by their own governments.

Table 7.4 The peripheral country's bank

Assets	Liabilities
Loans	Deposits
Own government's issued bonds	Long-term refinancing from the ECB
	Loans from core countries' banks

The core countries' banks were thus able to shed their exposure to peripheral countries' debt, both private and public, while the peripheral countries' banks increased their exposure to their own sovereign debt. In the balance of the peripheral country's bank the exposure to core countries' banks was replaced by an exposure to the ECB through the long-term refinancing operation (LTRO) (see Table 7.4). This same process mirrors itself in the balance sheet of the core country's (shadow) bank as exposure to the peripheral countries' banks was cancelled or reduced, and the claims on the Eurosystem increased. This contributed also to the Target 2 accumulation of credits of the Bundesbank to the Eurosystem and corresponding increase in the negative position of peripheral countries' central banks towards the ECB.

Minenna (2016) convincingly argues by collecting data from banks' balance sheets, central bank refinancing demands and Target 2 balances, that the peripheral countries' banks used part of the long-term refinancing received by the ECB to return the funds they had previously borrowed to finance the trade imbalances of their countries with Germany.[7] He concludes that the ECB LTRO was used to transfer the credit risk of German banks to the Eurosystem. That risk was thus mutualized.

That the liquidity provision by the ECB through the long-term refinancing operations acted as a risk-shifting device is stressed by other scholars, too (see Cour-Thimann, 2013; Cecchetti *et al.*, 2012). Cour-Thimann (2013) writes that target balances positive and negative accumulations were possible only because of the intervention by the ECB through its long-term refinancing. Without that intervention creditors in surplus countries could not have recovered their claims on foreign debtors, while debtors in deficit countries would not have been able to service their external debts previously contracted (Cour-Thimann, 2013, p. 24). Core countries' residents would have not been able to withdraw their investments in peripheral countries. Cour-Thimann adds, however, that this risk sharing was taken into consideration when European states decided to share a single currency. Cecchetti *et al.* (2012) argue that Eurosystem credit has allowed the public refinancing of credit originally granted by German banks to peripheral countries. This may have happened also for credit granted by other countries' banks (Cecchetti *et al.*, 2012, p. 14).

At the time of writing, all banks in the EU, both in northern and core countries and in southern and peripheral ones, show poor profitability in comparison to their peers in the rest of the world, and their share prices are well below the book value of their capital. It appears that this is the result of bad deleveraging in which the shedding of assets has happened without a business strategy oriented neither to true investment banking – that is, the underwriting of shares and bonds issued by non-financial firms – nor to traditional lending with the monitoring of projects and screening of applicants. The only activity in which European banks have excelled is the issue of more and more securities linked to the trading of various risks – above all, interest risk and exchange rate risk (see BIS, 2013). To this activity is linked also the survival and thriving of repo markets.

Conclusions

The deleveraging that occurred in the European banking system after the great financial crisis did not reduce financial fragility. New regulatory rules intended to tame risks were used instead to increase interconnectedness and create potential losses for the banks, particularly those of the core countries. Those banks that had already been recapitalized with state funds discovered new ways of making profits that relied heavily on short-term financing through repo and derivatives hedges. In a stagnating macroeconomic situation, it was easy to try to profit from just fees and commissions deriving from the issue of securities not linked to the economic activity. Furthermore, most banks in core countries derived a great part of their operating income from interest income not linked to the lending activity but deriving from securities and derivatives, as is clear in consolidated banking data.

The European debt crisis revealed the weakness of such a strategy and exposed the core countries' banks to heavy losses. Those losses were reduced by the ECB intervening to provide the peripheral countries' banks the means to repay their debts to core countries' banks and to buy their domestic governments' bonds from the foreign core banks. The governments' debt and credit markets became domestic again with banks increasing their shares of domestic governments' debt over total assets.

The ECB LTRO could be seen as a thwarting policy, as it contributed to the fall in the spreads between the yields of core and peripheral countries' government bonds and could have constrained the outcomes of capitalist market processes. The outcomes that came out of the interaction between market processes and the ECB action, though, were not acceptable as they redistributed risk in a way that increased inequality rather than decreasing it. Therefore, the ECB jointly with the change in regulation did not fulfil the requirements for a thwarting system in the definition given by Ferri and Minsky (1991)[8] as it did not achieve any social goal like increasing employment or decreasing inequality. On the contrary, by mutualizing the risk of core countries' banks and transferring them to the whole system, it increased the burden of the weaker countries while relieving the losses of the strongest. This intervention was very different from a traditional lender of last resort policy. It was also different from the quantitative easing carried out by the Federal Reserve as it was a long-term refinancing that bound the financed entities to return the amounts borrowed at the loans' expiry date. Securities bought by the Federal Reserve instead were and are still sitting on its balance sheet as no unwinding has yet been foreseen.

Notes

1   The base for the levy (tax) was twofold: one base consisted of a balance sheet total, minus liable capital, minus liabilities to customers; the second consisted of the value of derivatives held off-balance sheet. The tax base of the levy will be balance sheet based. The method of reporting will be that prescribed by the German Commercial Code, so it is supposed that German General Accepted Accounting Principles (GAAP) will be used. Although fair value accounting is not used for most items, for financial instruments held for trading it should be applied (Freshfields *et al.*, 2010).

2   Financial derivative positions with gross positive market values are recorded in the remaining assets and positions with gross negative market values are recorded in the remaining liabilities. The market price of a derivatives contract values the claim of one party to the other. So, positive market values are claims of the monetary and financial institutions to some and negative ones are debts to others. As the market value may switch from positive to negative over the life of the contract, the same derivative instrument may pass from the remaining assets to remaining liabilities over the same time span (see ECB, 2012).

3   Dexia was a loser, for example, as it used derivatives to hedge (see Chapter 6).

4   Shadow banks/(shadow banks): when not in brackets, shadow banks are a financial institution that has no banking licence; when in brackets, (shadow banks) are regular banks that act as a shadow bank.

5   Recent statistical studies on measures of stress in financial markets have found that a metric of stress in sovereign debt markets in the Eurozone during the period 2010–13 is not correlated to the same metric for stress in other financial markets such as the money market. While before 2010 the two metrics were growing or falling in parallel to each other, since 2010 they have diverged markedly. In particular, in 2011 and 2012 the stress index for sovereign debt markets increased while the stress index for the other markets declined. No contagion would have occurred from the sovereign debt market to the other financial markets (see Garcia-de-Andoain and Kremer, 2016). The work by Garcia-de-Andoain and Kremer (2016) is based on a previous work on the construction of the metric by Holló *et al.* (2012).

6   In the years that followed the (shadow) banks succeeded in unwinding their risky positions in peripheral countries' debt and the demand for interest rates swap as well as their trading decreased in Europe (Ehlers and Eren 2017).

7   After the long-term refinancing finally expired and it was returned, the ECB launched the quantitative easing programme through which the national central banks purchased the government bonds of their own governments, thereby buying them from the banks and paying them. Some banks bought the assets in anticipation of their rise in price, thus pocketing a profit when selling them to the central bank. This is one of few sources of profit left since the interest margin is squeezed by the zero interest rate policy, and the gains from swaps concerns only a few large institutions while the majority of players are still losing.

8   See Chapter 1, pp. 4–7.

References

Acharya, V.V. and Steffen, S. (2012) The greatest carry trade ever? Understanding Eurozone banks' risks. Available at: http://financeseminars.darden.virginia.edu/Lists/Calendar/Attachments/153/Acharya%20paper%20for%202013%20-%20Carry%20Trade.pdf

Allen & Overy (2014) Capital Requirements Directive IV Framework Credit Valuation Adjustment (CVA) Client Briefing Paper 10, January. Available at: www.allenovery.

com/SiteCollectionDocuments/Capital%20Requirements%20Directive%20IV%20 Framework (accessed 1 March 2017).

Apers, B. (2016) Are you ready for uncleared derivatives margining? *Rocket*, Special Edition, April. Available at: www.clearstream.com/blob/80866/1207df083d1f45ce2662 9f44643e88ce/gsf-apers-1604-data.pdf (accessed February 2017).

Bank for International Settlements (BIS) (2013) Derivative survey, June.

BIS (2015) OTC derivatives statistics at end June. Available at: www.bis.org/publ/otc_ hy1511.pdf (accessed 20 June 2017).

Basel Committee on Banking Supervision (BCBS) and Board of the International Organizations of Securities Commissions (IOSCO) (2013) Margin requirements for non-centrally cleared derivatives: Second consultative document, February.

Caruana, J. (2017) Have we passed 'peak finance'? Lecture by Jaime Caruana, General Manager, Bank for International Settlements International Center for Monetary and Banking Studies Geneva, 28 February. Available at: www.bis.org (accessed March 2017).

Cecchetti, S., McCauley, R. and McGuire, P. (2012) Interpreting Target2 balances, BIS Working Paper No. 393.

Citibank (2014) The future: Margin requirements for uncleared derivatives. Available at: www.citi.com/securitiesandfundservices (accessed February 2016).

Cour-Thimann, P. (2013) Target balances and the crisis in the Euro area, *CESIFO Forum*, 14: 1–50, Special Issue.

Deutsche Bank (2012) Annual report. Available at: https://annualreport.deutsche-bank.com/ 2012/ar/servicepages/downloads.html (accessed February 2014).

EBA, ESMA, EIOPA (the ESAs) (2012) Joint Discussion Paper on draft regulatory technical standards on risk mitigation techniques for OTC derivatives not cleared by a CCP under the regulation on OTC derivatives, CCPs and Trade Repositories, No. 648/2012 14 (JC/DP/2012/1).

EBA, ESMA, EIOPA (the ESAs) (2014) Draft regulatory technical standards on risk-mitigation techniques for OTC derivative contracts not cleared by a CCP under Article 11(15) of Regulation.

European Central Bank (ECB) (2012) Manual on MFI balance sheets statistics. Available at: www.ecb.org (accessed January 2015).

ECB (2013) Banking structures report, October. Available at: www.ecb.org (accessed January 2015).

ECB (2014) Banking structures report, October. Available at: www.ecb.org (accessed January 2015).

Ehlers, T. and Eren, E. (2016) The changing shape of interest rate derivatives market, *BIS Quarterly Review*, December, pp. 53–65. Available at: www.bis.org (accessed February 2017).

Fender, I. and Lewrick, U. (2013) Mind the gap? Sources and implications of supply–demand imbalances in collateral asset markets. *BIS Quarterly Review*, September, pp. 67–81.

Ferri, P. and Minsky, H. (1991) Market processes and thwarting systems, Jerome Levy Institute, New York, Working Paper No. 64.

Financial Stability Board (FSB) (2012) Global shadow banking monitoring report.

Freshfields Bruckhaus Deringer (2010) Briefing: The German bank levy.

Garcia-de-Andoain, C. and Kremer, M. (2016), Beyond spreads: Measuring sovereign market stress in the euro area. Available at: https://ssrn.com/abstract=2805093

Goodhart, C. and Schoenmaker, D. (2016) The global investment banks are now all becoming American: Does that matter for Europeans? *Journal of Financial Regulation*, 2(2): 163–81. Available at: https://doi.org/10.1093/jfr/fjw012

Härle, P., Lüders, E., Pepanides, T., Pfetsch, S. and Poppensieker, T. (2010) Basel III and European Banking: Its impact, how banks might respond and the challenges of implementation, McKinsey Working Paper on Risk No. 26.

Holló, D., Kremer, M. and Lo Duca, M. (2012). CISS – a composite indicator of systemic stress in the financial system, ECB Working Paper No. 1426.

International Accounting Standards Board (IASB) (2010) International Accounting Standard, IAS 39, Financial instruments: Recognition and measurement.

International Swaps and Derivatives Association (ISDA) (2012) Industry response to the European Banking Authority, European securities markets' association and European Insurance and Occupational Pensions Authority, Joint Discussion Paper on risk mitigation techniques for trades not cleared by a central counterparty. Available at: www.esma.europa.eu/file/10446/download?token=3TpMeMlc (accessed 2 March 2017).

Masera, R. (2011) The Basel III Global Regulatory Framework: A critical review, *Rivista Trimestrale di Diritto dell'Economia*, 3: 199–256.

MBRS (Mediobanca Ricerche e Studi) (2012) Dati cumulativi delle principali banche internazionali e piani di stabilizzazione finanziaria. Available at: www.mbres.it

MBRS (2013) Le maggiori banche europee nel 1, semestre 2013. Available at: www.mbres.it

Mehrling, P., Pozsar, Z., Sweeney, J. and Neilsson, D.H. (2013) Bagehot was a shadow banker: Shadow banking, central banking, and the future of global finance. Available at: http://ssrn.com/abstract=2232016 (accessed September 2014).

Minenna, M. (2016) *The Incomplete Currency*, Chichester: John Wiley & Sons.

Minsky, H. (1982) *Can it Happen Again?* Armonk, NY: ME Sharpe.

Minsky, H.P. (1992) The financial instability hypothesis, Working Paper No. 74, The Jerome Levy Economics Institute of Bard College, New York. In P. Arestis and M. Sawyer (eds), *Handbook of Radical Political Economy*, Cheltenham: Edward Elgar, 1993.

Mirowski, P. (2010) Inherent vice: Minsky, Markomata, and the tendency of markets to undermine themselves, *Journal of Institutional Economics*, 6(4): 415–43.

Poszar, Z., Adrian, T., Ashcraft, A. and Boesky, H. (2010) *Shadow Banking*, Federal Reserve Bank of New York Staff Report, No. 458.

8 Italy's banking crisis

Introduction

Italy's banking crisis is different from all the other banking crises that have unfolded since the eruption of the great financial crisis in Europe. Many banks were recapitalized by their governments' interventions, which amounted to €1,400 billion without guarantees. Waivers from EU state aid rules were granted by default. The most severely hit were the United Kingdom and Germany.

The first crises were located in core countries and were caused by their big banks' entanglement with the US shadow banking system. They were managed by using extensive state aids with approvals conceded by the European Commission that derogated from the prohibition of state aid in the European Union. Successively came the crises of countries that were partially entangled with a US system, but were also experiencing the burst of the housing bubble at home, in countries such as Ireland and Spain. Ireland supported totally the failing banks and the state became the debtor in their place. The European Central Bank approved emergency liquidity assistance for the banks and prohibited any burden sharing in the losses with shareholders and bondholders with the rationale that the world financial markets would be shaken by such a move. In this case, however, no automatic recapitalization by the state was possible because of the incapacity by the states to get funding on the market at reasonable cost. So, the rescues were a mixture of emergency liquidity assistance by the national central banks to their own banks that did not have collateral to get funding from the European Central Bank and recapitalizations with funds provided by the newly created European Funds. Thus, the problems suffered by banks were dealt with without any restriction in the economic policy of big core countries, but with a heavy intervention of the European Commission, the ECB and big states in the management of peripheral countries' crises (see the letter by the BCE to Ireland threatening to withdraw emergency liquidity assistance (ELA) approval if certain conditions had not been met).

The Irish case is very interesting as it represents the start of the new role of the ECB as the enforcer of fiscal pacts rather than the lender of last resort. As Chopra (2015) and Whelan (2015) argue, the role played by the ECB in the Irish banking crisis stretches the limits of its mandate. The ECB would not allow the senior creditors of failed banks that had to be liquidated and would not continue their normal activity thereafter to be involved in burden sharing, and allowed Irish banks that did not have collateral to be financed directly by the ECB to rely on emergency liquidity assistance provided by the Central Bank of Ireland under the approval of the ECB. The conditions for getting this emergency liquidity assistance were linked to many economic policy indictments that were contained in a letter – at that time secret and now made public – that the ECB sent to the Irish government.[1]

Apart from that, the ECB took other measures that worsened the crisis in Ireland. Chopra (2015) recalls that in order to reduce its exposure to Ireland through ELA, the ECB pressed for a quick deleveraging of the Irish banking system that would have implied selling assets during a crisis at very low prices. Only after some time did the ECB agree to wait longer, but the continuous need for ELA approval every two weeks did not help in restructuring the Irish banking system.

An opposite decision was taken instead by the ECB in Cyprus. ELA was suspended until the parliament would not approve a plan that required burden sharing not only with bondholders but also with uninsured deposits. The reason may have been that depositors in Cyprus were nationals or Russian entities, while Western banks and other financial institutions were not involved. However, in both cases through the threat of the suspension of emergency liquidity assistance, the ECB succeeded in shaping the restructuring process on its own terms.

So, while banking crises in core countries of the Eurozone were handled only by increasing state expenditure to refinance the banks without introducing fiscal austerity, banking crises in peripheral countries had been managed as an occasion to impose fiscal austerity and reforms in other wide-ranging fields from labour law to other regulations. The tool used to impose such reforms was usually in the form of a letter by the ECB that played a specific political role beyond its mandate. The Cyprus case is simply a change in policy. While in Ireland ELA was granted on the guarantee that senior bondholders would not be involved in burden sharing, in Cyprus the involvement of depositors and other uninsured creditors was made a condition for liquidity assistance. Thus, the distress in the banking system was just an excuse to impose so-called reforms that aimed at debt stabilization and whose final result was the explosion of debts.

Italy's banking crisis is different from the previous episodes of banking crises in many respects. The first and most important one is that the origins of the crisis do not lie either in the country's bank involvement with the US shadow banking system or in a home-grown real-estate bubble. In Italy, banks were not involved at all with the international subprime mess and there was no excessive expansion of credit with respect to gross domestic product (GDP) before the crisis. The ratio of credit to GDP in the peak years reached 160 per cent, which is much lower than the ratios reached in other European Union countries. Italy's banking crisis is mainly the result of the macroeconomic policies followed after the banking crises in other countries had erupted and the consequent so-called sovereign debt crises. It is mainly due to the burden of non-performing loans granted to non-financial firms, so the fall in aggregated demand and profitability is in the background. Indeed, rather than being directly linked to the US crisis, it is rooted in the European defective answer to that crisis.

Another peculiarity is that the Italian banking crisis occurred after the approval of the Bank Recovery and Resolution Directive (BRRD) and thus in an environment in which the involvement of shareholders, bondholders and even depositors in the rescue of banks had become mandatory. Further, in Italy, many small savers invest in bank deposits or in bonds issued by the same banks.

The macroeconomics of the crisis

Behind Italy's banking crises lie many factors, both macroeconomic and microeconomic although the macro ones dominate. The fiscal retrenchment since 2007 made government expenditure in real terms fall, while new taxes were introduced, particularly hitting the real-estate sector and the wealth of middle-income families. Industrial production fell more than GDP. Many firms were closed or went bankrupt. Credit supply fell more than GDP, too, and it continues to fall even if the rate of growth of GDP has returned to low but positive values. The decline in GDP in the period 2009–7 was 7.6 per cent, while that of loans was higher at 10.8 per cent. The difference was larger for 2012–11: the decline of GDP was 2.5 per cent, while that of loans was 10.8 per cent (Rapacciuolo, 2013, p. 6).

Ferri and Rotondi (2016) find that the rate of defaulted loans is higher for non-core Eurozone countries with respect to core ones, and is inversely linked to the rate of growth of GDP over the period 2007–13 (Ferri and Rotondi, 2016, p. 20).

In a study from the Bank of Italy (Notarpietro and Rodano, 2016) an empirical simulation of what would have happened if the two crises had not happened is carried out. The results are that in the absence of the two recessions and of the economic policy decisions that were taken after them, non-financial corporations' bad debts at the end of 2015 would have reached €52 billion, instead of €143 billion. The ratio of bad debts to the total amount of loans to non-financial corporations would have reached 5 per pent, not higher than the pre-crisis value.

The bulk of non-performing loans increased from very low levels, both as absolute values and as the percentage of the total assets from 2011 onwards. The majority of non-performing loans by sector belongs to two main industries: manufacturing and real estate. Both sectors were heavily and negatively affected by the two crises (international and European), although the transmission channels were different. Manufacturing collapsed because of the fall in demand and production. Real estate was less influenced by events abroad and also at home because no real-estate bubble developed in Italy as, for example, in Spain, but it was negatively affected by the increase in taxes on real-estate property approved by the Monti government in 2011 that induced many middle-income families to sell their homes, which in turn caused a fall in prices.

In 2011, the spread crisis erupted and monetary policy for the most part of the year was restrictive with an increase of the interest rate repeated twice. Italy was invited by a letter from the ECB to conduct a restrictive fiscal policy:[2] a change in pension arrangements in order to increase the sustainability of public debt; a change in labour law to increase competitiveness; changes in the regulation of product markets; increasing deregulation; changes in real-estate taxes. All these prescriptions were executed with different timings by the governments of Monti, Letta and Renzi, causing a continuing depression and inducing a phenomenon already seen in the 1920s – debt deflation. With a negative rate of increase of nominal income and falling inflation (in 2016, the rate of increase of prices had become negative), the real value of debt increased (Tropeano and Vercelli, 2016). The curious thing is that Italy was induced to carry all these pernicious economic policies without having asked for financial support by either the European Financial Stability Fund or the European Stability Mechanism. The overwhelming argument for all these so-called reforms was that they would cause a fall in debt, an increase in competitiveness and would encourage regrowth. Just the opposite happened, as the ratio of debt to GDP was higher than ever, having reached the value of 133 per cent as a consequence of an increase in the nominal debt (due, among other factors, to the payments to the European newly established funds to save other countries, expenses due to losses on derivatives by the state, the increased expenses of unemployment benefits and various electoral gifts as tax credits offered to selective groups, especially entrepreneurs, by the Renzi government) and the decrease in the denominator GDP. A typical debt deflation process had been working, also causing the fall in the value of financial assets, among which are shares and also of real estate (Tropeano and Vercelli, 2016).

It is noteworthy that in Italy no excessive real-estate expansion of the type that occurred in Spain and Ireland had taken place, and most Italians had as a major component of their wealth real-estate property. Many middle-income families had two or three houses, which often were holiday homes. The extraordinary increase in taxes on property during the Monti government induced many people to try to sell their property, causing a fall in prices in a stagnating market and, of course, the impossibility of selling new apartments that were planned to be built and the bankruptcies of the building societies that were indebted with the banks. The fall in the value of guarantees increased the net value of non-performing loans in the balance sheet of banks[3] that therefore required more capital.

In such a context, the most reasonable thing would have been to change macroeconomic policy and reflate the country through public investment in the absence of private investment, but this was strictly prohibited by European fiscal arrangements that became more stringent exactly at the worst moment in 2012. The Treaty on Stability, Coordination and Governance of the Economic and Monetary Union (vulgarly known as 'fiscal compact') worsened the outlook for most countries. It was signed by all countries belonging to the European Union with the exception of Great Britain and the Czech Republic. Its requirements were very heavy, imposing a ratio of state budget balance to GDP of 0.5 per cent and the value of 60 per cent of debt to GDP to be achieved in ten years. It stated that the competitiveness of a country must be judged by the reduction of public and private wages and the sustainability of debt must be judged on the cuts made to health, pensions and public services. It required changes in labour contracting, with the demise of centralized labour contracts in which trade unions had contractual power, and the introduction of decentralized arrangements at the firm level between workers and employers. Furthermore, it required an amendment to the Constitution to establish a balanced budget. If a country did not comply with that rule, the European Commission could report it to the Council and to the European Court of Justice, which could impose a fine of up to 2 per cent of GDP.

The microeconomics of the crisis

An historical excursus on Italian banks

The microeconomic factors behind the crisis are related to the modalities in which the passage from a public separated banking system to a private universal one occurred. While Italian banks had never been particularly keen on credit analysis, their attitude to the matter was totally affected by the liberalization and the change from structural to prudential regulation, and by the run to form even bigger groups in order to exploit scale advantages and be able to compete internationally. Both factors cut the links between local industries and banks, and the Italian banks, now bigger and free of the strict rules that were valid under structural regulation, were able to do whatever the managers of the newly created limited liabilities companies decided to do, with little control either by shareholders or by supervisors whose strictness had declined in the new environment to fit in with the new corporate governance.

Italian bankers were accustomed to very strict legislation that specified, in a way that was reminiscent of socialist and planned economies, the conditions under which credits should be conceded. They had operated like this in the period from the 1930s until the early 1990s, in which the separation between commercial and universal banks and banks operating in firms' shares was predominant. At that time, commercial banks were taking current account deposits and giving only short-term credit to enterprises (with a maturity of up to one year). The short-term credits, however, were often rolled over, so sometimes the separation was fictitious. The Istituti di Credito Speciale had on the asset side long-term loans to enterprises as well as the latter's bonds and shares, while on the liabilities side they had savings accounts, their own issued bonds often with state guarantees and Treasury advances. Istituti di Credito Speciale were active, both at national and at regional level, and provided credit to large enterprises operating in particular sectors as well as to medium-sized enterprises in a way similar to development banks. Credit was also granted at preferential conditions for certain sectors and certain less-developed areas of the country like South Italy. Behind all these measures there was, however, no clear development policy, and the strict application of legal norms prevailed over planned economic intervention. The conditions under which credit was awarded were strictly prescribed by law, so the bankers did not develop any credit screening experience but rather decided as bureaucrats. Their attitude in the last phase of this period, the 1970s and 1980s, did not help as credit was given to enterprises suffering serious crises without worrying about their solvency. Stagflation and the oil shocks had hit enterprises heavily. Credit continued to be given according to the same bureaucratic rules, causing losses to the intermediaries. Those enterprises were described as having soft budgets (de Cecco and Ferri, 1996).

The system was dichotomous, consisting of a few big and many small commercial banks that gave only short-term credit and many specialized institutions that provided long-term financing to the industrial sector, and sometimes to agriculture and artisanship also by using state guarantees and abiding by strict rules. The system was stable as long as the macroeconomic conditions were good, but it lacked both the banking expertise and involvement in industrial groups of German-style mixed banking and the market regulation of Anglo-Saxon capitalism. It was based on a special intervention by the state through state-controlled but autonomous financial institutions (Barca, 1999).

The 1993 Banking Act and the return to universal banking

In the early 1990s, the system was totally demolished to create space for a modernized system that was meant to be able to adapt to the new world macro-economic conditions of liberalization and globalization, and to the European project of a common currency. The idea behind the overhaul was to finally achieve a liberal market economy that had never prospered in Italy, to establish market institutions such as the stock exchange and independent authorities according to the Anglo-Saxon example, and to make banking more market oriented by fostering new credit and risk-management practices.

In Italy, as elsewhere in Europe, financial liberalization was linked to the reception of European Union legislation, mainly directives that had to be introduced into national legislation with an element of discretion (Kattel *et al.*, 2016). European legislation aimed at unifying the level playing field among European financial institutions and introduced the operation of a unique banking charter. The main principle of the union was the free movements of goods, people and capital in the area, and the prohibition of state intervention in the economy, excluding particular exceptional circumstances. The European banking systems that were each in their own way shaped by the state presence had to move away from that model and take on new forms. Each country, however, transformed itself according to different modalities by following the same rules. Germany, for example, never abandoned the universal banking system, so did not need to return to it, but instead changed the business model of its largest universal banks by merging with Anglo-Saxon investment banks and learning their methods. Other countries, like France and Italy, turned to new forms of universal banking.

Ironically, Italian banks that were turning to a more market-oriented system in the new context did not need to develop screening and monitoring skills, but blindly adhered to the new rules for judging creditworthiness and evaluating risk that were readily provided by the new Basel Committee recommendations. Those recommendations were meant to be useful for big banks operating at the international level, but they were enacted in the European union for all banks irrespective of their size and diffusion in order not to distort competition (see Masera, 2013). So Italian banks passed from the detailed prescriptions of state-owned financial institutions to a generic quantitative assessment of risk according to the various versions of the Basel agreements. The ability to screen borrowers and monitor their activities was not required after the liberalization of the banks, just as it had not been needed before it.[4] Risk weights replaced administrative rules.

Notwithstanding their way of proceeding, this changed in many respects, as summarized by Piluso:

> Clearly, the return of universal banking has gradually produced three expected outcomes, typically related to credit de-specialization: (1) multi-loans have partially declined, opening the door to preferential banking relationships; (2) banks have acquired stakes in industrial medium–large firms as a result of strategic commitments or rescue operations as main inside investors; and (3) banks have tried to develop the exchange market in order to transfer risks, collecting resources via bonds or equity issuances for client firms, making profits from underwriting operations.
>
> (Piluso, 2010, p. 99)

Multi-loans had partially declined,[5] but no long-term bank–firm relationship based on shared investment plans was developed. Loans were used to finance mergers and acquisitions, and the purchase of the former public enterprises that were privatized. Those enterprises that were quoted on the stock exchange followed a shareholders' maximization strategy and retreated from the research and innovation that used to operate when they were public. Banks and large firms became entangled again through interlocking shareholdings, with the result that it was easier for big firms to get loans to finance any expansion project they wished to engage in.

Banks that had increased in size and changed their business models in order to be competitive in the international arena did not participate in the large speculations that were behind the subprime crisis in the US, and during the crisis they were confident that they did not need help due to their responsible behaviour. They used international short-term money markets to finance their assets beyond their deposit takings, as the ratio of loans to deposits was higher than one. So they continued to finance their big customers' projects during the years of the great financial crisis and before the so-called spread crisis erupted. Then the macroeconomic policy that was pursued amounted to both a fiscal and a monetary contraction and depressed aggregate demand. This had repercussions on the banks' balance sheets, but they continued to pretend, following the government's assertions, that recovery was around the corner.

After the separation had been removed, they did not try to do any credit analysis because they were adjusting to the new reality of the Basel agreement, in which what mattered was the rating assigned to the borrower, not the quality of the projects of the firm that had applied for loans. As most large firms had a higher rating than small and medium-sized ones, the credit supply was oriented towards this segment of enterprises and this preference has survived even during the two crises that unfolded one after the other and even during the credit crunch, when credit was reduced more often to small and medium-sized firms than to big ones. As long as the macroeconomic conditions were not too difficult, the amount of non-performing loans was reasonably low. The new banks were owned by the same few large groups that also owned the big firms after privatization. So, a structure of interlocking shareholdings prevailed and remained with some adjustments. In this context of intersections between political, economic and information-dominating groups, it was easy for big firms to get loans – even very large amounts – while the traditional links – for example, subcontracting and financing, between big and medium-sized and small firms within the industrial districts – weakened because of internationalization and globalization.

For this reason, the credit crunch that started in 2011 affected different groups of firms in different ways. The cut in credit was more severe for micro-firms and medium-sized companies, so that the most profitable and successful ones began to look for alternative forms of financing, such as minibonds or online financing platforms. These new financing channels were encouraged by the political and monetary authorities as they believed that Italian firms relied too much on bank credit as a source of financing. The contraction in credit to small enterprises resulted in many bankruptcies since the start of the crisis and contributed to an increase in unemployment as small firms are more labour intensive than big ones.

So the new rules that required tougher capital, and above all a new redefinition of capital, were implemented exactly when the Italian banking system was hit by the depression following the spread crisis. The Bank of Italy and the various governments simply ignored the scale of the problem, proudly asserting that the Italian banking system had survived the subprime crisis without any damage thanks to the good supervision that was in place in the country. They were also convinced that the problem of bad loans would disappear as soon as the economy recovered and started to grow again, which it was assumed would happen very soon. Yet, as growth never materialized, thanks to the continuing restrictive fiscal policy and bleak expectations on the future that they nurtured, bad loans accumulated into a vast amount. However, the government's narrative as well as that of the Bank of Italy did not change.

So, contrary to what had happened in the US or in other European countries, the Italian banks had to face an increase in the capital required by the new regulation at the same time as the non-performing loans were mounting. In between, any recapitalization on the market was perceived as a sign of weakness and caused a fall in share price that cast many doubts on the health of the banks. The tricks used by the banks to comply with the new regulation were to extend deadlines and pretend that they were being more prudent in the granting of new loans and economizing capital by all means. So, for example, extending deadlines to non-performing customers was a device to avoid the recognition of bad loans, and another device was cutting altogether the loans to certain segments of business that required more capital irrespective of their profitability.

So now Italian banks are competing with each other to give credit to firms that are best rated according to the Basel requirements; yet those firms often do not need any credit because they do not have investment plans for the future or have sufficient funds of their own.

Smaller firms continued to be rationed instead in their daily commercial operations, finding it difficult to obtain even basic self-liquidating loans like discounts on receivables and factoring.

While the major single determinant of the increase in non-performing loans was the macroeconomic condition of the double crisis in the period 2009–16, there is no doubt that the process of liberalization of finance and privatization of the big public enterprises created a change in the bank–enterprise relationship in Italy. The practice of granting multiple loans was not completely relinquished, and in the context of big firms and big banks, the increase in the maximum loan that could be obtained by one bank also caused an increase in the sum of the loans obtained from numerous banks. The model of multiple loans from many banks was the historical heritage of the 1930s and of the repeal of mixed banking according to the German model, as underlined by Brambilla and Piluso:

> The new Bank Act requested a sharp separation between commercial banking and investment banking. Besides, as universal banking was formally banned, it encouraged banks to modify their relations with industrial firms and clientele. Before the Bank Act of 1936 all major German-style mixed banks tended to have long-term relations, as insiders, with their industrial clientele. Afterwards, banks were pushed to abandon exclusivity with industrial firms and manufacturing firms were encouraged to multiply banking relations, even if that goal was pursued more through moral suasion rather than via formal banking regulation.
>
> As a result, in the late 1930s banking relations were only partly shaped by the new regulatory scheme. Indeed, the former mixed banks did not completely cease to operate as universal banks in their day-to-day relations with industrial firms. The main change was the end of exclusive relations between the major banks and the largest industrial groups. Thus, multiple loans (i.e., when a firm was able to obtain a plurality of loans from a number of banks) transformed the specific kind of relationship banking prevailing in Italy after the brand new Bank Act of 1936, even if this emerged in a more clear way only after the second world war, that is to say during the Golden Age.
>
> (Brambilla and Piluso, 2008, p. 6)

The relationship between the big banks and firms that had disappeared as a consequence of the change in regulation and of the moral suasion of the 1930s re-emerged after the introduction of the new Banking Act in 1993 (Legge Amato that replaced the 1936 Banking Act) and liberalization. Those links, however, were not based on long-term relations in the tradition of the German mixed bank based on an exclusive relationship and the financing and monitoring of investment projects, but rather on personal connections deriving from the presence in the boards of the new banking companies quoted in the stock exchange of representatives of the major non-financial firms in a structure of interlocking shareholdings. So, financial and real capitalism were closely intertwined after the privatization of both public enterprises and banks.

The banks that were privatized followed shareholders' value maximization strategies as well as the new privatized enterprises. The means by which this goal was pursued did not foster growth, however. The big firms privatized reduced research and development efforts that had been thriving under public ownership and focused on profit from lowering wages and deregulating labour. The new banks tried to increase profit by cross-selling financial products to the public and by increasing fees and commission income. The fragility of such a structure was painfully revealed by the crisis.

The return to universal banking: a Minskian reading

The distribution of non-performing loans according to their size and the consequent redistribution of loans according to the size of the banks that were the lenders reminds us of some warnings that Minsky gave on the eventual repeal of the Glass–Steagall Act in the United States. The majority of non-performing loans are larger than €1 million in size, which reveals that they were granted to big firms. Barbieri (2014) calculates that a small number of borrowers (precisely the 0.42 per cent), who had borrowed sums between €5 million and €25 million, accounts for more than 23 per cent of the total non-performing loans of the Italian banking system, which means that fewer than 5,000 borrowers are responsible for €40 billion non-performing loans, with the average size of each loan being roughly €8 million. He finds that in the period 2009–14 the biggest increase in non-performing loans – 422 per cent – occurred for the loans larger than €25 million, while the smallest increase – 57 per cent – was registered for smaller size loans – i.e. between €30,000 and €250,000. The increase may have been caused by an increase in the supply of big loans or an increase in the non-performing loans in that size class. The rate of increase of non-performing loans increased through all loan sizes, although the amounts supplied have been constantly falling. The increase in non-performing loans was caused by an increase in the ratio of non-performing loans, which increased more for the biggest loan size classes. A higher percentage of big loans are not returned than are loans of smaller size.

The distribution of non-performing loans among the various types of banks shows that the first five groups account for two-thirds of total non-performing loans, while the other groups – big and small banks – account for the remaining one-third.

The first five banking groups' share of loans was 51 per cent. Their total assets are 40 per cent of the sum of the assets for all banks. The 90 per cent of their loans are granted to medium-size large firms (see Demma, 2015, p. 12).

The predominance of big loans among the defaulted or non-performing ones is linked to the transformation of the Italian banking system from one in which commercial banks and investment banks were separated to form one in which structural separation was abolished. This is a reminder of the observations that Minsky made while commenting on the opportunity for the US to repeal the Glass–Steagall Act and return to a universal banking system. He was worried that such a move, by relaxing the prohibition on having branches outside a state, would increase the size of banks and create units that were too big to fail. In particular, he conjectured on the likely increase in the average size of loans that this move would cause, under the assumption that the common rule of thumb on great exposures, as a percentage of 10–15 per cent of bank capital, were maintained.

This conjecture applies very well to the case of Italy, *mutatis mutandis*. In Italy, unlike in the US, the increase in the concentration of banks was a goal intentionally pursued by the Bank of Italy in order to enable them to compete in the European and global markets. In the US, however, it was simply the consequence of the removal of limits to the territorial expansion of the banks. In Italy, the increase in the size of the banks, just as Minsky foresaw, went hand in hand with the increase in the size of loans. The Basel regulation paid little attention to large exposures, which were more a tool of the old structural regulation, although limits on large exposures are still maintained and are now being made more severe.[6] These limits, however, as Minsky correctly argued, were related to a bank's capital that usually increases with its size.

Minsky (1994) recalls that the prudent banker's rule of thumb was that no more than 10–15 per cent of equity could be allocated to any one loan. This 10–15 per cent of capital loan determines the natural loan size habitat of a banking group. An 8 per cent total capital rule would imply that a $100 million bank should have $8 million in capital. The maximum credit line of this institution would be between $800,000 and $1,200,000. In the US in 1994, any bank with a maximum loans size of $1million or less was a bank for smaller businesses. The higher the total assets size, the higher the maximum loan size. With the relaxation of the prohibition of country-wide branching, smaller banks would become state, regional or national banks. He comments:

> Every case of amalgamation will increase the capital and therefore the maximum line of credit that can be given to any one customer. A movement of banks to higher natural habitats will take place. The progress to a small number of banks, each of which is too big to fail, with maximum credit lines so large that the conditions of supply of credit to large borrowers will improve relative to the conditions of supply of credit to small borrowers seems to be a most likely outcome of what is taking place.
>
> (Minsky, 1994, p. 14)

In Italy, the movement to higher natural habitats seems to have taken place. Likewise, the conditions of the supply of credit to large borrowers improved relative to those to small borrowers. The latter happened during the two crises. In order to counteract these tendencies, Minsky suggested a series of rules that could protect small banks and small borrowers. Regulation should differentiate between large and small banks. He recommended the creation of community banks with special privileges. Needless to say, in Italy, just as in any country in the EU (with the exception of Germany), the opposite happened, as all the rules were applied to any bank regardless of its size.

In Italy, during the two crises, the first following the 2007 US and global crisis, and the second starting in 2011, the contraction of credit to small firms was sharper than that to big firms, and the credit conditions for the former also deteriorated.[7] This occurred even though the performance of big firms' loans was much worse than that of small firms'.

The type of universal banking that emerged from the 1990s revision of the 1936 Banking Act, with the new regulation focused on a strict proportionality between capital and risk, has contributed to that result.

The problem of bad loans in Italy and their management after the approval of the BRRD

As bad loans were piling up in banks' balance sheets, the contraction of new credit notwithstanding, the idea of instituting a bad bank in order to relieve banks of their burden had been circulated. However, the government had to make a deal with the European Commission in order to create a bad bank that would not violate the European Union norms on state aid. The deal was concluded in January 2016 and the Italian Ministry of Finance praised it as the solution to the Italian banking problem. The terms of the deal were very complex and inadequate for the institutional circumstances of Italian credit markets (Barucci and Milani, 2016; Boda, 2016). In particular, the deal required each bank that had non-performing loans to create a special purpose vehicle (SPV) that had to buy the loans from itself. The special purpose vehicle in turn had to finance those purchases with the sale of asset-backed securities (ABS) in the market. The ABS to be sold on the market to willing investors was divided into tranches – senior, mezzanine and junior – with increasing levels of risk and yield.

A servicer independent of the bank was assigned the task of recovering the credits and to deal with the collateral sale. The quality of each ABS emission was assessed by a rating agency acknowledged by the ECB. The state was allowed to guarantee only the best tranche of the ABS – the senior one – if that tranche had received a rating higher or equal to BBB by a rating agency. The state should be remunerated for the guarantee and the price of the guarantee should be market determined. In order to fulfil this latter requirement, the price of the guarantee was linked to the average CDS premium paid by Italian issuers of securities carrying the same rating as the ABS. The SPV should not buy the loans at a higher value than that recorded in the banks' balance sheets.

As Barucci and Milani (2016) and Boda (2016) stress, the major shortcoming of this project was the splitting up of the bad bank into many different entities, each for each bank, which brought scale diseconomies, while not allowing a centralized management of the non-performing loans with the aim of recovering as much as possible and/or support of the insolvent firms.

In Italy, given the practice of multiple loans, a unique bad bank would have allowed the joint management of all the exposures to the same firm by all banks having credits towards it (see Barucci and Milani, 2016). A joint management of exposures could also have helped ailing firms to restore their payment capacity, which would have benefited both the banks and the economy. This was a proposal (the one agreed by the government with European Commission) for the creation of many bad banks from the troubled banks.It was questionable why the state should intervene as the proposed arrangement is similar to leaving each bank looking for its own problems by using market instruments. There is no reason why the banks burdened with non-performing loans could not have followed this path themselves without waiting for the guarantee of the state. Indeed, as Boda (2016) observes, they could have issued ABS, asked for a rating and bought a credit default swap (CDS).

It is no surprise that the plan did not work. A true unique bad bank in which all non-performing loans could be transferred and managed had been established in Spain and Ireland in previous crises, but this solution was precluded by the new BRRD, the directive on bank resolution approved in 2014 and converted into Italian legislation at the end of 2015. In the new legal context, the bad bank solution would have required the involvement of shareholders, bondholders and depositors in the losses, according to the hierarchy of claims set up in the directive.

At this point, one wonders why the Italian authorities, the government, the Bank of Italy and the Italian Banking Association were all unconditionally in favour of the new resolution directive given that the original purpose to mutualize bank losses at the European level and to institute a common deposit guarantee had not been realized. The Banking Union's plan in the modalities up to the moment of writing would surely have increased the costs of dealing with the big banking crisis that was shortly to occur in Italy. However, the Italian authorities seemed not to care about it.

So the banks, with the exception of some of the large ones that succeeded in selling stocks of loans in the world markets, kept the non-performing loans on their balance books. In between the credit crunch and the missing payments for the provision of public services, increased arrears among firms decreased their rating and made it even more difficult for them to receive credit. Firms therefore could not pay their debts because they were not receiving payments from either their customers or the sellers of intermediate products.

The first thing to do would have been to pay immediately the firms claiming credits to the public administrations and to provide relief to the firms struggling under the credit crunch to make even payments to providers and workers.[8] The increase in the number of bankruptcies was certainly due to the fall in aggregate demand, but the liquidity problems did not ease the situation even for firms whose demand had not fallen very much.

A turn in the stalling situation was given by the worsening of the conditions of one of the major banks, Monte dei Paschi di Siena. The bank started having problems after the purchase in 2007 of another bank, Antonveneta, from Santander at a price much higher than its value. The bank bought at such a high price carried with itself a load of debts that were added to those of Monte dei Paschi. The same year started the financial crisis in the US and there was a general fall in stock exchanges all over the world. In order to hide some losses on a participation in another bank's shares, that would have required new capital, the bank became involved in complex derivatives dealings with two leading world investment banks, Nomura and Deutsche Bank, and changed the contracts various times in order to conceal new losses. In particular, there was an exchange between fixed interest and a variable one that became very expensive to serve with low interest rates. In 2013, the derivatives contracts that had been concealed became public knowledge and the bank's management was prosecuted. The management was replaced by a new one that succeeded in bringing it to a very modest positive result and in closing at high costs all derivatives contracts still in operation. Meanwhile, the new European supervision and the new regulatory framework that used the microeconomic tools contained in the changed Basel III agreement were implemented. The stress tests conducted in 2014 and 2016 according to these new rules found that Monte dei Paschi was one of the major undercapitalized banks in Europe. The tests do test for solvency but not for liquidity, so the French, German and other core countries' banks that sit on a mountain of derivative contracts all due to each other were not considered as lacking capital in the worst stress test scenario. Only some banks from southern Europe and other peripheral countries were found to have capital shortfalls (Vestergaard and Retana, 2014) because of their high share of loans over total assets, the impossibility of using mitigation tools to reduce the amount of capital required (securitization is not practised widely) and the increase in non-performing loans due to bad macroeconomic conditions. Both in the 2014 and 2016 stress tests, Monte dei Paschi performed very badly and was compelled to increase its capital to avoid that, under the conditions quite unlikely of the worst scenario (a repetition of the 2011 crisis in a period in which the European Central Bank (ECB) was flooding the banks with liquidity), it would be insolvent. Meanwhile, its share price was falling in value and its cost of capital increasing.

Non-performing loans were on the rise, too, as in all the other banks. This time, the government realized that it should intervene because the bank is one of Italy's largest banks, but in between the BRRD had been approved in 2014 and translated into Italian law at the end of 2015. So, in case of a bank's insolvency, the state could not intervene without activating the participation of shareholders, bondholders and even uninsured depositors according to the Cyprus template.

The government hesitated to continue with the resolution procedure and preferred to start a new market recapitalization, launched by JPMorgan and other banks. At this point and through the summer of 2016, the conditions for the bank worsened because a real deposit run was occurring. The bank lost €11 billion in deposits, but the government claimed that the situation was under control in order to avoid repercussions on the forthcoming referendum. After the referendum, when the market recapitalization failed, the government decided to intervene with a decree that approved the raising of new debt for €20 billion in order to refinance the ailing banks.

A few days after the decree had been approved, the European supervision sent a letter to the government which declared that the capital shortfall had changed from €6 billion to €8.8 without giving any explanation for the change as no new stress test had been carried out after July 2016. The intervention by the state was approved by the European Commission as a precautionary recapitalization without triggering the resolution procedure.

This intervention, however, will certainly increase the public debt and thus cause problems with the fiscal ratios to be maintained in compliance with the fiscal compact. If the required primary surplus has to be maintained or even increased to comply with the planned reduction of public debt, then the state will have to increase taxes for a corresponding amount to maintain the current primary surplus, causing another recession and another round of increase in non-performing loans, which now seem to be stabilized, although at a high level. Besides that, in order to accomplish obligations already taken in the past as conditions for fiscal flexibility, the government should raise the value added tax from an already high level (22 per cent).

Moreover, the entrance of the state into the capital of the banks should be strictly limited in time and the banks should quickly be resold to private entities according to the new European law on resolution. This means that the citizens should bear the burden of new taxes in order to rescue banks and then sell the same banks at presumably fire-sale prices to private and most likely foreign entities. The latter, if the current recession continues, will profit more from liquidating all the assets and seizing guarantees from the debtors, both families and firms, than from continuing business. Eventually, they could sell them for a profit, close them or merge them with bigger foreign banks already owned by them.

If the foreign buyers were European Union members, the most likely pattern is that core countries' banks would become the owners of peripheral countries' ones. Core countries' banks enjoy a better macroeconomic environment and are privileged by the way that stress tests are conducted given their lower levels of risk-weighted assets to total exposure at default than peripheral countries' banks. Besides that, they have been supported with state aid without risking any bail in centred resolution procedure and thus a run on deposits. A template for that process is the Greek banking system that has been recapitalized by the state (that has borrowed from the European Stability Mechanism to do that) and now is owned mostly by foreign entities.

It is desolating to contrast this way for resolving crises with the way followed in Italy in the 1930s after the 1929 crisis, in which universal banking caused big losses to banks. In the crisis of the 1920s, the state saved the banks and their claims on the firms were transformed into participations that created the bulk of the Istituto per la Ricostruzione Industriale (IRI), which was a conglomerate of firms owned by the state that represented the claims of the banks over the firms that were not able to fulfil their promise of payments. The IRI was at the centre of the industrial development of Italy in the period after the Second World War.

That solution would be the only one to preserve both banks and firms if accompanied by a macroeconomic reflation policy. However, the European rules that the Italian government has underwritten prohibit this type of intervention, requiring that all the solutions must be based on the market. Even in the United States, there was a state recapitalization first, then the non-performing assets that burdened the banks' balance sheets, which were not loans but securities backed by the loans, were bought by two public entities, Fannie Mae and Freddie Mac, both of which were government-sponsored enterprises. In the US, the banks, free of all bad assets and after having been recapitalized, resumed their lending to an economy that came out of the recession. In Europe, too, Germany, the Netherlands and Great Britain have all recapitalized their banks by using state funds without resorting to false market solutions.

A conversion of the banks' claims to firms to allow state participation in those same firms, a sort of new IRI, where all these participations could be collocated, would help to revive the economy if the state also became the starter of investment projects using the new institution. Germany, for example, after having supported its banks with state funds, has now excluded most of its savings banks from the common resolution and supervision by agreeing to a threshold for the common resolution and supervision that allowed most of its banks lending to small and medium enterprises to be supervised only by the German supervisory authority (BAFIN).

Unwisely, Italian authorities, although aware of the problems of their banks and the constraints imposed by tough fiscal policy rules at the European Union level, have approved an incomplete banking union in which losses are not mutualized and which does not foresee any common deposit protection.

The combination of all these features risks shaking the trust of people in depository institutions, make bank runs revive after centuries and jeopardize the payments system.

Conclusions

Italy's banking crisis is different from those that previously occurred in the European Union. Its origins lie in the faulty macroeconomic policy response to the so-called sovereign debt crisis that caused a slump in aggregated demand, industrial production and employment. Despite the prevalence of macroeconomic explanations, changes in the bank–enterprise relationship at the microeconomic level also contributed to its unfolding. Understanding them requires a historical journey in the Italian banking system from the end of the nineteenth century up to the present time. The return to universal banking in Italy, required by the new European Union regulation, has occurred in a way that has increased the average dimension of banks. While the tradition of German mixed banking has not been

D'Aurizio, L. and Depalo, D. (2016) An evaluation of the policies on repayment of government's trade debt in Italy, Temi di discussione (Economic working papers) 1061, Bank of Italy, Economic Research and International Relations Area. Available at: https://ideas.repec.org/p/bdi/wptemi/td_1061_16.html

de Cecco, M. and Ferri, G. (1996) *Le banche d'affari in Italia*. Bologna: Il Mulino.

Demma, C. (2015) Localismo bancario e crisi finanziaria. Bank of Italy, Occasional Paper No. 264.

Ferri, G. and Rotondi, Z. (2016) Misure del rischio di credito nel finanziamento delle imprese e incidenza dei prestiti in default: un'analisi comparata per le banche europee. MOFIR Working Paper No. 122.

Gambacorta, L. and Mistrulli, E. (2011) Bank heterogeneity and interest rate setting: What lessons have we learned since Lehman Brothers? Bank of Italy, Temi di discussione, No. 829.

Kattel, R., Kregel, J. and Tonveronachi, M. (eds) (2015) *Financial Regulation in the European Union*. London and New York: Routledge.

Masera, R. (2013) US Basel III, Final rule on banks' capital requirements: A different-size-fits-all approach, *PSL Quarterly Review*, 66(267): 387–402.

Minsky, H.P. (1994) Financial instability and the decline (?) of banking: Public policy implications. Hyman P. Minsky Archive. Paper 88. Available at: http://digitalcommons.bard.edu/hm_archive/88

Notarpietro, A. and Rodano, L. (2016) The evolution of bad debt in Italy during the global financial crisis and the sovereign debt crisis: a counterfactual analysis. Bank of Italy, Occasional Paper No. 350. Available at: www.bancaditalia.it (accessed 20 February 2017).

Piluso, G. (2010) From the universal banking to the universal banking: A reappraisal. *Journal of Modern Italian Studies*, 15(1): 84–103.

Rapacciuolo, C. (2013) Credit crunch & recessione: Il circolo vizioso si spezza solo con una politica economica che rilancia la crescita. CSC Nota dal Centro Studi Confindustria, No. 2013–2. Available at: www.confindustria.it/studiric.nsf/e5e343e6b316e614412565c5004180c2/0f425c531ebcfe88c1257b2b0039cbc0/$FILE/Nota%20CSC%20credito%20bancario.pdf (accessed 3 April 2017).

Treaty on Stability, Coordination and Governance in the Economic and Monetary Union, 2 March 2012. Available at: www.eurozone.europa.eu

Tropeano, D. and Vercelli, A. (2016) Debt deflation theory and the Great Recession. In N. Levy-Ohrlik and E. Ortiz (eds) *The Financialization Response to Economic Disequilibria*. Cheltenham, UK and Northampton, MA: Edward Elgar, pp. 47–67.

Tutino, F., Brugnoni, G.C. and Siena, M.G. (2015) Italian banks facing Basel 3 higher capital requirements: Which strategies are actually feasible? In B. Beccalli and F. Poli (eds) *Bank Risk, Governance and Regulation*. Houndmills: Palgrave Macmillan, pp. 206–31.

Vestergaard, J. and Retana, M. (2014) At the brink of insolvency: Shallow recapitalization exercise fails to bolster Europe's ailing banks. In C. Goodhart, D. Gabor, J. Vestergaard and I. Erturk (eds) *Central Banking at a Crossroads: Europe and Beyond*. London and New York: Anthem Press, pp. 75–95.

Whelan, K. (2015) The ECB and financial assistance programmes: Has ECB acted beyond its mandate? In The ECB's role in the design and implementation of (financial) measures in crisis-hit countries. Monetary Dialogue Compilation of Notes, European Parliament Directorate General for internal Policies, IP/A/ECON/NT/2015-07, p. 37.

Index

Page numbers in *italic* denote figures and tables.
Added to a page number 'n' denotes a note.